Sovereign Rules and the Politics of International Economic Law

How ought scholars and students to approach the rapidly expanding and highly multidisciplinary study of international economic law? Academics in the field of international political economy (IPE) used to take for granted that they worked with the overarching concepts of rules and governance, while legal scholars analyzed treaties and doctrines. However, over the past twenty years formerly disparate fields of study have converged in a complex terrain, where academic researchers and governmental policy analysts use a pluralistic set of theoretical and methodological tools to study the ongoing development of international economic law.

This volume argues that the extensive development of international economic law makes it impossible to discuss international political economy and international law as if they were mutually exclusive processes, or even as if they were separate and mutually reinforcing. Rather, we must think of them as a deeply interconnected set of rapidly evolving activities. This is a paradigm shift in which we cease to think about an international system in which politics and law interact, and begin to think about an international system in which politics take place in a legal frame. Froese terms this a shift from politics and law, to the politics of international economic law.

This book does for political economy what others have already done for law—introduces political scientists, economists, and other practitioners of IPE, to the potential of engaging with legal theory and method; it will be of great interest to scholars in a range of areas including IPE, global governance, international relations, and international law.

Marc D. Froese is Professor of Political Science and Founding Director, International Studies Program at Burman University, Canada.

Global Institutions

Edited by Thomas G. Weiss
The CUNY Graduate Center, New York, USA
and Rorden Wilkinson
University of Sussex, Brighton, UK

About the series

The "Global Institutions Series" provides cutting-edge books about many aspects of what we know as "global governance." It emerges from our shared frustrations with the state of available knowledge—electronic and print-wise, for research and teaching—in the area. The series is designed as a resource for those interested in exploring issues of international organization and global governance. And since the first volumes appeared in 2005, we have taken significant strides toward filling conceptual gaps.

The series consists of three related "streams" distinguished by their blue, red, and green covers. The blue volumes, comprising the majority of the books in the series, provide user-friendly and short (usually no more than 50,000 words) but authoritative guides to major global and regional organizations, as well as key issues in the global governance of security, the environment, human rights, poverty, and humanitarian action among others. The books with red covers are designed to present original research and serve as extended and more specialized treatments of issues pertinent for advancing understanding about global governance. And the volumes with green covers—the most recent departure in the series—are comprehensive and accessible accounts of the major theoretical approaches to global governance and international organization.

The books in each of the streams are written by experts in the field, ranging from the most senior and respected authors to first-rate scholars at the beginning of their careers. In combination, the three components of the series—blue, red, and green—serve as key resources for faculty, students, and practitioners alike. The works in the blue and green streams have value as core and complementary readings in courses on, among other things, international organization, global governance, international law, international relations, and international political economy; the red volumes allow further reflection and investigation in these and related areas.

The books in the series also provide a segue to the foundation volume that offers the most comprehensive textbook treatment available dealing with all the major issues, approaches, institutions, and actors in contemporary global governance—our edited work *International Organization and Global Governance* (2014)—a volume to which many of the authors in the series have contributed essays.

Understanding global governance—past, present, and future—is far from a finished journey. The books in this series nonetheless represent significant steps toward a better way of conceiving contemporary problems and issues as well as, hopefully, doing something to improve world order. We value the feedback from our readers and their role in helping shape the on-going development of the series.

A complete list of titles can be viewed online here: https://www.routledge.com/Global-Institutions/book-series/GI.

The UN Military Staff Committee (2018)
by Alexandra Novosseloff

The Use of Force in UN Peacekeeping (2018)
edited by Peter Nadin

Human Rights and Conflict Resolution (2018)
edited by Claudia Fuentes Julio and Paula Drumond

Global Trends and Transitions in Security Expertise (2018)
by James G. McGann

UNHCR as a Surrogate State (2018)
by Sarah Deardorff Miller

The British Media and the Rwandan Genocide (2018)
by John Nathaniel Clarke

The League of Nations (2018)
by M. Patrick Cottrell

Global Governance and China (2018)
edited by Scott Kennedy

Sovereign Rules and the Politics of International Economic Law

Marc D. Froese

LONDON AND NEW YORK

First published 2018
by Routledge
2 Park Square, Milton Park, Abingdon, Oxon OX14 4RN

and by Routledge
711 Third Avenue, New York, NY 10017

Routledge is an imprint of the Taylor & Francis Group, an informa business

© 2018 Marc D. Froese

The right of Marc D. Froese to be identified as author of this work has been asserted by him in accordance with sections 77 and 78 of the Copyright, Designs and Patents Act 1988.

All rights reserved. No part of this book may be reprinted or reproduced or utilised in any form or by any electronic, mechanical, or other means, now known or hereafter invented, including photocopying and recording, or in any information storage or retrieval system, without permission in writing from the publishers.

Trademark notice: Product or corporate names may be trademarks or registered trademarks, and are used only for identification and explanation without intent to infringe.

British Library Cataloguing in Publication Data
A catalogue record for this book is available from the British Library

Library of Congress Cataloging in Publication Data
A catalog record for this book has been requested

ISBN: 9780815361756 (hbk)
ISBN: 9781351115582 (ebk)

Typeset in Times New Roman
by Taylor & Francis Books

For Gina and Arabel

Contents

List of illustrations	x
Acknowledgements	xii
Abbreviations	xiv

1	Introduction: Sovereign rules	1
2	The politics of international economic law	18
3	Legal theory as analytic lens	37
4	Legal development at the WTO	63
5	Regionalism and the centralization of trade governance	88
6	Legal development without multilateral coordination	121
7	Creating international economic law beyond the state	148
8	Conclusion: Political futures and the changing terrain of international economic law	185

Index	214

List of illustrations

Figures

3.1 Cross-fertilization: international economic law and international political economy	46
4.1 Shifting equilibria in the world trading system, 1940–2015	70
5.1 Dispute settlement arrangements in regional trade agreements	101
5.2 The development of RTAs, 1947–2013	102
5.3 Excluded clauses in RTA dispute settlement	104
5.4 Special provisions in RTAs	105
6.1 The proliferation of international investment agreements, 1959–2015	133
6.2 Clauses relating to standards of treatment, 1959–2015	134
6.3 Dispute settlement clauses, 1959–2015	135
6.4 Legal language affirming state regulatory space, 1959–2015	135
7.1 Cases cited, all completed panels, sorted by year	161
7.2 WTO cases cited, sorted by year	162
7.3 WTO cases cited, Appellate Body reports, sorted by year	162
7.4 WTO cases cited, all other arbitration, sorted by year	163
7.5 GATT cases cited, sorted by year	164
7.6 Case citation averages broken down by respondent	167
7.7 Case citation averages broken down by complainant	168
7.8 Legitimacy and authority in the postwar legal order	173
7.9 A Grotian moment in IEL?	178
8.1 Panels with amicus curiae briefs, by year	204

Tables

4.1 Substantive decisions and future agenda, WTO ministerial conferences, 1996–2015	77

List of illustrations xi

5.1 Legal clauses in RTAs — 103
5.2 Exclusions and special provisions in RTAs, sorted by region — 106
7.1 The citation of selected prominent early cases — 165
8.1 The submission of amicus curiae briefs — 205

Acknowledgements

As with any scholarly project that takes years to complete, there are many people to thank, from the senior scholars who provided much needed intellectual support, to the kindnesses offered by generous colleagues, friends and family. J.P. Singh and Rorden Wilkinson commented on critical portions of the text. In fact the entire tone and style of the book turned upon a small comment made by Professor Wilkinson at the International Studies Association annual meeting several years ago. The project began its germination process more than five years ago during a brief conversation with Pierre Lizée about the relationship between legal functionalism and international political economy.

In the political economy of trade, public policy, and globalization, so many of my colleagues are emerging intellectual lights. Their work guides my own in large and small ways. Erin Hannah, Silke Trommer, James Scott, Gabriel Siles-Brügge, Laura Mahrenbach, and many others have provided stimulating panels on which to present my research, not to mention excellent dinner conversation, wherever we find ourselves.

This project would not have been possible without Burman University's generous institutional research funding and sabbatical time. Our small university is full of tremendously kind colleagues and friends. Noble Donkor has provided incredible research leadership. John McDowell has been unfailingly encouraging of all my research endeavors. Glen Graham's interests in peace, justice, and the public interest closely mirror my own; and our many conversations have been a crucial part of the intellectual scaffolding of academic life.

In practical terms, the hagiographic writing of 12th-century Anglo-Norman cloistered women is far removed from the politics of 21st-century international economic law. Yet my partner Gina LoCicero-Froese's subtle understanding of the rhythms of medieval political discourse

Acknowledgements xiii

continues to sharpen my own study of the many twists and turns, inversions and ellipses in contemporary global political economic debate. Her skepticism about the conventional wisdom consistently reminds me to never take the world at face value. And of course Arabel, who wants to grow up to be both a scientist and an artist, has shown me that in childhood, as in political economy, the biggest challenges can usually be explored with helpful reference to the Greek myths.

Abbreviations

AB	Appellate Body
BIT	bilateral investment treaty
BRICS	Brazil, Russia, India, China and South Africa
CERDS	Charter of the Economic Rights and Duties of States
CETA	Comprehensive Economic and Trade Agreement
DSB	Dispute Settlement Body
DSM	dispute settlement mechanism
DSU	Dispute Settlement Understanding
EC	European Communities
EEC	European Economic Community
EFTA	European Free Trade Agreement
EU	European Union
FCN	Friendship, Commerce and Navigation
FDI	foreign direct investment
FTA	free trade agreement
G8/G20	Group of Eight/20
GATS	General Agreement on Trade in Services
GATT	General Agreement on Tariffs and Trade
GSP	Generalized System of Preferences
HST	hegemonic stability theory
ICSID	International Centre for the Settlement of Investment Disputes
IEL	international economic law
IIA	international investment agreement
IL	international law
IO	international organization
IP	intellectual property
IPE	international political economy/global political economy
IR	international relations

ISDS	investor-state dispute settlement
ITO	International Trade Organization
LDC	least developed countries
MAI	Multilateral Agreement on Investment
MFN	Most-Favored Nation
NAFTA	North American Free Trade Agreement
NATO	North Atlantic Treaty Organization
NGO	nongovernmental organization
NIEO	New International Economic Order
NT	national treatment
OECD	Organisation for Economic Co-operation and Development
OEP	open economy politics
PIEL	politics of international economic law
PTA	preferential trade agreement
RTA	regional trade agreement
SPS	sanitary and phytosanitary standards
TBT	technical barriers to trade
TPP	Trans-Pacific Partnership
TRIPS	Agreement on Trade-Related Aspects of Intellectual Property Rights
TTIP	Transatlantic Trade and Investment Partnership
UN	United Nations
UNCTAD	United Nations Conference on Trade and Development
WTO	World Trade Organization

1 Introduction

Sovereign rules

- **Divergence and convergence**
- **Defining our terms**
- **Structure of the argument**

A financial crisis rocked the global economy ten years ago. Since the collapse of Lehmann Brothers bank in 2008, national leaders, global publics and academics have focused intensely upon the architecture of the global economy, searching for signs of further systemic instability. Such post-traumatic stress-induced vigilance is not without good reason. After all, the mortgage bubble in the United States, and the financial tsunami it caused, followed hard on years of coordination failures in the global political system. It is not an exaggeration to say that ever since that fateful day in September 2001, the world economy has tried and failed to regain the sunny outlook that epitomized the 1990s.

The Doha Round of trade negotiations at the World Trade Organization (WTO) crawls forward at a glacial pace. The G8/G20 have arisen to fill a leadership gap that seems too large for the Bretton Woods institutions to take on alone; but even here the political payoff of multilateral cooperation seems inadequate to the challenges at hand.[1] On the credit side of the ledger, hundreds of regional trade agreements and thousands of international investment agreements have proliferated—pretenders to the throne perhaps, and none with the scope or vision to act as a template for future multilateral endeavor. On the debit side, we may add the worrisome rise of populist nationalism that has fueled Britain's exit negotiations with the European Union, not to mention the increasingly inflammatory and xenophobic rhetoric in other countries in North America and Europe.

Scholars of global political economy are particularly engaged with the narrative of systemic weakness because prior warnings of economic

2   Introduction

instability now bear the halo of prophecy. The pessimism of the dismal science has been proven to be prescient. Dan Drezner attempted to buck this trend by writing a recent book in which he argued that the system worked, by which he meant that our existing financial architecture kept the financial crisis from running away unchecked and wrecking the entire global economy.[2] This is indeed true as far as the argument holds. I would like to make a more pointed argument that speaks to both the questions of governance effectiveness and systemic stability. I will argue that whether or not the system performed to expectation, the institutional order of global economic regulation is bigger than it has ever been in the history of human attempts at economic control, and this scope and scale bring risks and rewards. Secondarily, political scientists who study political economy are missing a lot of this growth because it takes place in the realm of law, an area of study that is still relatively neglected despite a sustained focus on global governance in the post-Cold War era.

This book has two goals. First, it attempts to chart the growth of international economic law (IEL) and analyze its tremendous importance to the study of trade and investment. Second, it shows how the insights of legal scholars may enrich the study of global governance. I suggest that because politics increasingly takes place in a legal frame, we are now studying the politics of international economic law rather than political economy simply stated. The big idea here is that we as political scientists, economists and assorted social scientists have not integrated legal insight into our way of understanding the world to the degree that we ought to. Yet when we do take legal insights on board, they subtly transform our perspectives and allow us to view the world of global economic governance with greater clarity.

There is much debate about the place of law in a globalized terrain of politics and economics. It is clear to everyone, from legal practitioners to policy analysts and citizen activists, that law and politics are deeply interconnected in the space beyond the state. For the most part, how one thinks about that connection is a function of where one stands. Legal scholars, concerned with the creation and application of law, view politics as a force that needs to be tamed through legislative and juridical action. Politics happens when law fails. Policy analysts view rules as a means to political ends, both in terms of a policy agenda, as well as in terms of political compromise. Law is necessary for political success, but it is not always the first step towards an orderly international system. Citizen activists also view politics as a means to an end as they attempt to change rules and practices that they consider harmful to the public good. For all of these actors,

Introduction 3

politics and law are a means for social progress and reform, but it is not always clear how politics and law fit together.

Politics and law are discrete realms of study with ontological and epistemological distinctions, but they are now closer than ever before because governments are creating global institutional and juridical arenas and thereby shaping the logic of political agency that orders the new world of international economic law. Much like we see in the domestic context, international legal environments are becoming the sites at which governments and private entities wage political battles over process and outcome. Political scientists and scholars of international law have been noting the convergence of their disciplines for a couple decades, at least. However, the linkages between these silos of scholarly activity are still quite often tenuous.

It is generally believed that legal scholars have been more heavily influenced by international relations (IR) research than the other way around.[3] My own experience suggests that this is indeed the case, if only for two reasons. First, legal research adds a third dialect of academic language that political economists must learn in addition to the language of economics and political science. Second, law faculties exist as professional schools outside of the faculties that provide a home for the social sciences in most universities, and their practitioners often have at least one foot in professional debates that do not always overlap with the debates in other fields. These academic worlds are just far enough apart that up until recently, lawyers and political economists have not found themselves at the same water cooler.

By examining the politics of international economic law I aim to bring together several threads of research that I think will give a sense of where the political and legal processes underway are likely to lead. The new questions that we need to ask are: How do we think about this new world of legalized governance? What are its strengths and weaknesses? Who rules this brave new future and what are the implications?

Divergence and convergence

Over the past several decades, the politics/law divide has narrowed, even as it remains a persistent feature of global governance research. But it wasn't always like this.[4] In the late 19th century, the growth of international law went hand in hand with political economy, and both fields of study were broadly considered to have developed through the march of empire, strategic political compromise, and an emerging consensus about the benefits of commerce for growth and industrial

4 *Introduction*

development.[5] Scholars in both law and political economy (which later became the disciplines of political science and economics) were discussing similar issues and using similar research methods. For the most part both drew method and inspiration from history, philosophy, the diplomatic arts, and the inductive reasoning that was the hallmark of post-Enlightenment public discourse.[6]

The rise of political realism following the First World War put political science and the emerging field of international relations on a different trajectory. Realist theorists, such as E.H. Carr, argued that law, as a force for good, mattered less in international relations than did the eternal struggle over wealth and power, which other scholars would term the balance of power.[7] Law, realists argued, had failed to stop the senseless tragedy of the First World War. If law was incapable of maintaining peace, where ought scholars to search for this undiscovered country? The answer was found in history. From the Peloponnesian War of Ancient Greece to the Concert of Europe that structured European relations following the Napoleonic Wars, peace was found in the forces that keep war at bay. Where law fails, a careful counterbalancing of interests and material capability maintains an absence of war, which became a rough and ready definition that contains a certain, positivistic, ring of truth.

Building upon key concepts such as state sovereignty, anarchy, and the Westphalian system, political scientists constructed a compelling realist argument about the weakness of law and the primacy of national interests in the creation of a world in which war has not been eliminated, but it has been controlled and shaped for rational ends. To make matters worse, legal scholars saw international law's crowning achievement, the League of Nations, stillborn, and rather than directly challenge the peace-as-absence-of-war thesis, they turned inward in the interwar period, looking for the theoretical and diplomatic insights that would allow the fragile order a greater chance at success.[8]

Following the Second World War, the intellectual divergence continued as political scientists looked to state power to maintain global stability. Law schools began to develop the academic and technical experts who built the global economy, but spent less time thinking theoretically about the place of law in a global political environment. Political scientists and legal scholars spoke to each other less and their scholarly paths, which used to converge to a certain extent around research methods, began to diverge. Political science embraced the positivist turn that was also favored by economics departments. Then in the late 1980s, with the fall of the Berlin Wall, some legal scholars began to engage with political science, particularly with international

Introduction 5

relations theory.[9] At the same time other legal scholars became engaged with economic theory, and the neorealism of political science and the rationalism of economics met in a flowering of legal scholarship that brought empiricism and political realism into the study of law.[10]

Slaughter charted the beginnings of a renewed relationship between law and political science by suggesting that Kenneth Abbott's 1989 article urging international law scholars to consider regime theory was the beginning of the cross-fertilization of international relations and international law.[11] For law, international relations offers parsimonious causal theories that bring a much-needed empirical dimension to legal research. For international relations, law offers rational explanations for why states cooperate that go beyond the realist paradigm and thicken the analysis of institutional behavior that was relatively new when Slaughter wrote. She suggested a joint discipline that would attempt to explain state behavior after the institutional turn in international relations.

Nearly two decades on, this has not occurred in any sort of sustained way, but law's interest in political science and economics was reciprocated. Particularly in political science, where a new and growing body of literature has developed with the aim of showing what international relations research can offer the study of law.[12] Interestingly, global political economy, which is becoming one of the foremost subfields in IR has been less engaged with law than have scholars of security, humanitarianism, and development. By this I mean that even though legal scholars have incorporated many insights from political science and economics, we don't have much going in the other direction; we have relatively few books and articles that attempt to show what international law scholarship adds to the study of global political economy. Even so, as legal ideas filter through international relations, global political economy has begun to pay attention. In this corner of the social sciences, interest in the relationship between politics, economics, and law has begun to pay dividends in a slowly emerging political economy of law.[13]

Defining our terms

In a study that crosses disciplinary boundaries and draws extensively upon a multidisciplinary approach to theory and method, it is perhaps wise to define some basic concepts. I will begin with a very brief overview of the definitions that I draw from international political economy and international economic law. Then I will say a few words about two significant concepts that underpin this study—the politics of law and sovereign rules.

6   *Introduction*

International political economy

International political economy (IPE) is a discipline that defies easy definition. Lake has called it a "maturing interdiscipline," because since the 1970s it has predominantly combined the study of economics and political science.[14] Other scholars unwilling to narrow the scholarly world in this way, suggest that international political economy belongs to a long-standing and ecumenical social scientific tradition that attempts to come to grips, both theoretically and methodologically, with the connection between state and market.[15] Seen in this light, global political economy encompasses a broad number of traditions, including law, sociology, and even literary studies.

Even so, a brief and contextual definition is required. Economics studies the way that humans satisfy wants and needs. Political science examines the way that humans organize their governance. Political economy studies the intersection of economic activity and governmental organization, or to problematize the field in broad terms, the intersection between wealth and power. The field is popularly known as international political economy because by the 1970s scholars had begun to understand that they could not examine the political economy of state evolution and development without studying political economy beyond the state—patterns of trade, financial flows, the workings of multinational corporations and the development of patterns of organization that allowed for an interconnected global political economy. Today, we recognize that these forces are not only international (between states), but are truly global, involving states and non-state actors. We have begun to refer to the field as global political economy because we recognize so many actors beyond the state, but in shorthand, we still use the acronym IPE.

As a field of study IPE has never been shy about adopting any and all concepts and traditions that can shed light on the relationship between wealth and power. Certainly in this context, the incorporation of legal insights in general terms is not new. Even before he met Karl Marx, Friedrich Engels had written a short book called *The Condition of the Working Class in England*, in which he noted that juridical and economic forces worked together to move peasants off the land and into cities.[16] Famously, Marx referred to the state as a handmaiden of the bourgeoisie, by which he meant that the state uses its power, including legal power, to aid the capitalist class in its accumulation of wealth.[17]

In the modern era, much work has been written examining the role of law in the development of state power, the creation of markets, and the crafting of strategic and profitable relations between state and market.[18] All of this is to say that law plays an inescapably large role in most discussions of the relationship between state and market, but even here law remains an intervening variable, one of the factors in the equation, but not a subject of political economic analysis on its own, with certain exceptions of course.[19] With a small and ironic genuflection, we may even suggest that the political economy of law is a (somewhat) new terrain of inquiry.[20] At the very least, treating it as a new terrain allows us to approach it with a new combination of conceptual tools.

In the chapters that follow, our approach to the study of global political economy will be both historical and institutional.[21] There is a rich history in IPE of tackling problems in the present by presenting their historical genealogy. Irwin's history of free trade and Beckert's recent history of North Atlantic capitalism (contextualized as a history of cotton production) are excellent examples of big-picture historical thinking in global political economy.[22] Rather than confine ourselves to the larger view, we will also use the excellent analytical tools available through the study of historical institutionalism. Historical institutionalism is the study of how institutions grow and develop, and how their origins and subsequent trajectory of growth lay a pattern for future development.[23] In paying attention to the way that the past influences the future, we will be better able to think analytically about the many factors that structure relationships between governments, international organizations, nongovernmental organizations and law.[24]

International economic law

Like global political economy, IEL is a broad terrain of inquiry. The legal development of the General Agreement on Tariffs and Trade (GATT)/WTO mirrors and has acted as a spur to the larger project of legal development across the terrain of international economic law. In traditional terms, IEL often refers primarily to trade law, but in its more modern iteration we tend to mean the law governing the movement of goods, services, people and money for the purposes of cross-border commerce. IEL includes the regulation of many areas of international economic activity beyond the reach of the WTO, such as development, trade, aid, monetary policy, investment, and even labor and migration.[25] For our purposes we will be dealing with IEL related to trade and investment.

IEL usually takes pride in its de-politicization. Broude, Busch and Porges note that discussing the political dimension of rulemaking is sometimes controversial, and I argue that the same may be said of the

8 *Introduction*

legal dimension of politics.[26] We do not like to think that politics constrains lawmaking, or that, conversely, the law constrains political action, although law does shape political agency in many ways. When legal scholars think about the relationship between politics and economic law, they tend to look at ways that politics creates a context for legal frames. Koskenniemi describes how the fight for international law is often seen as a fight to constrain politics.[27] From our multidisciplinary perspective, we will look at the other side of this coin, how legal systems frame, discipline, and provide incentives for political actors.

More than 20 years ago Jackson suggested that 90 percent of all work done by lawyers in international law takes place in international economic law.[28] Today that percentage is likely even higher. For Jackson, the problem that requires greater multidisciplinary exploration is the regulation of international economic behavior. This involves the basic problems of sovereignty, interdependence and equity. Jackson refers to his position as "normative realism," which has much in common with the ideas contained in functionalist legal scholarship and liberal institutional approaches to political economy. Jackson's normative realism will serve as a useful starting point for our entry into the world of international economic law.

Legal scholars use the concept of realism a little differently from scholars in IPE. In global political economy, global governance may be understood in realist terms that refer to power, the state, national interest, and the Westphalian international system. We can see this in power-based approaches for understanding trade and the institutional origins of the Bretton Woods institutions.[29] However, when legal scholars speak of realism, they tend to mean a pragmatic, and empirically informed approach to understanding law. This is a meaning like what political economists mean by realism, but less weighed down by long-standing attempts to quantify national interest or qualify the rationality of states.

The politics of law

Legal scholars occasionally refer to the politics of law, by which they mean that the creation and application of law are not always a straightforward process of applying reason to create rules. We must also take many factors into consideration, from the values and beliefs of decision-makers, to the context of the decision-making process. When political economists study the politics of law, they recognize that the formation of law always takes place in a political arena in which

Introduction 9

ideas and interests are heavily contested. In this way the politics of law speaks to a larger phenomenon, which has been explored in many of its theoretical variations across international relations and international law.[30] In fact, in IR, positions have been staked across the terrain of theory. For realist thinkers power politics renders law impotent, while scholars of the liberal tradition argue that the economic fact of interdependence makes rule-making a rational endeavor.

Law may be defined as a set of rules that govern relations between members of a society. Law has a basis in obligation and contains enforcement measures and a process for determining violation.[31] When scholars speak of the politics of law, it is usually in the context of a critique from the left of the role of ideology in legal processes, and certainly that is a part of what we discuss below.[32] Conversely, Rochester thinks that the purpose of law is to improve politics, and he is right as well, as far as that argument goes. I would move one more step forward and suggest that politics is just as necessary for law as law is for politics because politics provides a crucial early basis for compromise that is necessary for law to develop and evolve.

The politics of law may be defined as political contention over the way that rules are made and applied. It also refers, somewhat implicitly, to the developing institutional frame in which politics takes place beyond the state. We are now talking about politics in the context of law—a movement from politics and law, to a politics of law. That there is indeed a politics of international economic law is a somewhat counterintuitive argument to make for two reasons. First, because the place of law in the study of global politics has always been a little bit ambiguous, as I discussed above. Second, and as a corollary to the first point, because much attention has been focused on two intellectual countermovements in global politics that have attempted to show the basic contradictions in the conception of the rule of law beyond the state.

There are some scholars who argue that international affairs are governed by a global social compact, and that "international society" is organized by legal frames to some degree.[33] Others argue that international law is a tool of state power, and therefore ought to be considered as an approach to politics and diplomacy that governments use when it suits them.[34] Interestingly, in both of these positions politics is often framed as action that is external to law.[35] It is the sorts of things that actors do to strategize before they enter the legal arena, or the sorts of things that bracket the legal process itself.

In this sense, we may speak of politics as a wide terrain of activity, while the law remains a bounded arena where the rules of politics are contested. However, I think that politics is not external to law. Almost

10 *Introduction*

every action an individual (or business, or a government) undertakes today is regulated to some degree. However, this is a somewhat controversial proposition if we are extending it to the international system. Even so, whether we are talking about the law as a frame for global society, or the realist strategies pursued by governments in the name of national interest, global politics is ruled as much (or more) by the "rule of lawyers," as by the ethos of diplomats, to paraphrase a well-worn maxim.[36]

Sovereign rules

Sovereignty is an early modern concept that emerged from the Thirty Years War of the 17th century. It was originally part of a philosophical attempt to articulate the territorial authority of monarchs who could no longer trace their authority through the medieval concept of the great chain of being, wherein kings ruled as part of a hierarchy that included God and the Church. Sovereignty, as the right to govern a territory without outside interference, was then, and is today, a contested concept. In the modern period this antique Westphalian understanding of territorial integrity has come under stress from multiple sides. Political scientists have noted that it is increasingly unsuited to describing the world we live in today.[37] Beginning in the 1990s we began to hear about the end of sovereignty. Krasner went so far as to call it "organized hypocrisy," although he also believed that it was the best hope for the growth of an orderly international system.[38] At present, sovereignty remains a frayed yet workable concept to describe the basic truism that there is no formal governmental system that approximates the rule of territorial states at the global level.

Legal scholars like to talk about law in a way that stresses a more complex relationship between subject and law. For legal scholars, law is not just an order backed up by a threat. Beyond a set of written rules, law is a way of thinking and acting that has been internalized by the subject of the law.[39] Political scientists think about law a little differently. They tend to refer to "the rules of the game" more often than they talk about law for two reasons. First, because the international system tends to fall short of the standard by which we judge domestic legal systems in terms of the legitimacy and enforceability of law. Economic rules are frequently contested and prior to 1995 there were few enforcement mechanisms. Therefore, both legal scholars and political economists sometimes refer to some international treaties as soft law. They rely on the political will of states for enforcement.

Second, diplomats and the bureaucrats who populate intergovernmental economic governance institutions have been, until very recently,

Introduction 11

reluctant to refer to the evolving system of rules as law. Marceau argues that in its early years the GATT displayed "a Janus-faced approach to law ... a suspicion of formal legalism on the one hand, but a deep commitment to rules and rules-based conduct on the other."[40] Even when the GATT began to slowly create a body of law, the secretariat required that lawyers maintain a low profile. An Anglo-American understanding of law as a fundamental organizational rubric was not allowed to overshadow the institutional processes and political compromises of multilateralism. Even in the modern WTO, there is some care taken to avoid the impression of overt juridical and legal development. Dispute settlement reports are often said to not create precedent in the way that courts do in the domestic context.[41] And only now, 20 years after the creation of the WTO, do we have sustained scholarly discussion of the importance of law and lawyers to the development of the trading system.[42]

Therefore because of the unfinished nature of the legal development process and the reluctance of the people working in global economic governance to call their work what it really is, legal development, IPE scholars have tended to talk about rules rather than law. Further, because many US-trained IPE scholars have emphasized a positivist approach to studying the global political economy they tend to view law in a rational and functional manner that makes it more amenable to the application of empirical methods.

There is one more reason to talk about law as rules. The great analytic philosopher of law, H.L.A. Hart developed a conceptual frame wherein law may be defined as a set of primary and secondary rules. Primary rules are generally expressed as "thou shalt not," while secondary rules are expressed as "you ought to." "Rules of the first type impose duties; rules of the second type confer powers, both public and private."[43] Primary rules are the most basic type of law, sometimes rooted in custom or generalized practice. Secondary rules build upon the first set and "provide for operations which lead not merely to physical movement or change, but to the creation or variation of duties or obligations."[44] So secondary rules can create, change, or negate primary rules in certain circumstances. This basic conception of law as primary and secondary rules has heavily influenced legal theory. Particularly in international law, with its division between customary international law and treaty, it provides a useful starting point for our discussion of the politics of international economic law.

Any discussion of the sovereignty of rules contains contradictions because states are sovereign and rules are only a useful heuristic to the extent that states agree to follow them. However, in that context we

12   *Introduction*

must remember that sovereignty and international anarchy are themselves social constructions. We do not yet know whether IEL will gain legitimacy and enforceability on par with a domestic body of law. If it ever does, it will be the result of many subtle changes in the way we understand sovereignty and global order. Nevertheless, in the current drive to create better and more effective rules for international conduct, IEL is the burning end of the spear because stable markets require institutional and legal frames to operate effectively, as Polanyi has shown.[45] It is this fact, that rules of conduct are not only nice to have but are fundamentally necessary for any effective operation of markets, that gives IEL its potentially transformative power.

If states wish to reap the rewards of interdependence, they must not only cede some sovereignty to the multilateral system, but also treat global rules with the same respect they reserve for domestic law. This is what I call the sovereignty of rules. In the ancient world, it was possible to facilitate economic growth through imperial forms of wealth transfer. Up through the 19th century metropolis/hinterland relations and gunboat diplomacy accomplished similar ends. Today, stability in markets is maintained through membership in intergovernmental organizations, binding dispute settlement and bilateral deal-making. The growing necessity of the rule of law means that the sovereign state must cede a great deal of authority to the laws and organizations that stabilize the system.

Since 1945 we have seen the rapid growth and thickening of economic, legal and social ties. Political ideas, economic forces, and new technology that increases the speed and decreases the cost of transportation and communication have driven this globalization process. In a world of rapidly intensifying economic and social interdependence, rules for economic conduct have become very necessary. Are rules sovereign in the way that we think of state sovereignty? Certainly not, but in practical terms we have begun to think of international economic law as not just a good idea, but rather a capstone that holds up the rest of the global order.

Rules may not be sovereign in a formalistic, or literal, sense but we are building a system of rules that limits certain aspects of state sovereignty in the collective interest, while simultaneously developing mechanisms to provide incentives and sanctions for states that accede to the international legal system.[46] Today government lawyers and diplomats are more likely to work through institutions than work around them when attempting to solve issues relating to international economic interdependence. This book, then, is a way to chart a cognitive shift that is now occurring in certain corners of the international

Introduction 13

relations and international law literature, which has significant implications for those scholars who study political economy, global governance, and the politics of law.

Structure of the argument

Some research is shaped by theories, some by engagement with particular methods. Still other research engages with certain modes of reasoning and argumentation. This book is shaped by an engagement with a multidisciplinary approach to political economy. As such, it has four basic purposes. First, I aim to make an original argument about the increasing centrality of formal legal mechanisms to the processes and outcomes in the global political economy. Second, I will provide an overview of this changing political terrain, particularly as it relates to the institutionalization processes underway in the realm of international economic law. Third, this book will bring together disparate literatures in IPE and in law around the theme of global governance, so that fourth, we may contextualize and explore the multidisciplinary possibilities that grow out of these literatures.

Most scholars understand the reciprocal relationship between global politics and international law. I want to go a little further and explore how that relationship is evolving in an era of contentious power politics, technological globalization and extensive levels of economic integration. My argument follows the basic pattern of inductive reasoning in the social sciences, offering hypotheses for further investigation. Through the pattern of these hypothetical offerings I intend to offer a larger argument about the development of international economic law and the changing context of global politics.

Chapter 2 examines the issue of disciplinarity and the study of IEL. One of the hallmarks of the study of IPE has been a self-conscious attempt to deliver upon the benefits of an interdisciplinary approach. Likewise, the study of IEL is increasingly benefitting from research that bridges disciplinary divides. Scholars must move beyond the law/politics divide to examine the link between political legitimacy and legal authority that is necessary for the maintenance of global economic order.

Chapter 3 surveys legal approaches to the study of IEL, with the goal of highlighting the potential for cross-fertilization with global political economy. I begin to tighten the warp and weft of multidisciplinary endeavor by suggesting quantitative and qualitative avenues of potentially fruitful multidisciplinary research.

Using case studies, I offer four hypotheses about this emerging global legal frame for politics. First, I hypothesize that systematized

14 *Introduction*

institutional dynamics are driving legal development at the WTO. Second, I suggest that regional trade agreements extend the use-value of the WTO's centralized dispute settlement system. Third, I hypothesize that some market-oriented intergovernmental mechanisms further the development of law even when formal multilateral frames are absent. Finally, I argue that international judicial processes create international law using arbitral precedent even though state support for such institutional autonomy is slow to materialize. I explore each of these hypotheses through an inductive process in which I provide empirical studies of a set of politico-legal relations to lay the analytic foundation for the future testing of theoretical propositions around the development of international economic law.

Chapter 4 shows how the WTO's use of regular ministerial meetings has created a dynamic of shifting institutional equilibria with which to maintain forward momentum of trade law issues. Chapter 5 examines the second hypothesis, that regional trade agreements may make multilateral judicial mechanisms even more important than they already are. Academics have paid a lot of attention to the proliferation of trade and investment agreements, suggesting that legal proliferation has a fragmenting effect on global governance. I disagree, arguing that far from fragmenting international law, treaty proliferation creates more law that abuts the WTO system, essentially developing and extending that system in new directions—particularly as it relates to dispute settlement.

Chapter 6 analyzes a growing market for law, by which I mean that law is increasingly created at the point where demand for regulation meets supply within a marketplace where buyers and sellers attempt to reach agreement on price. Using this law market hypothesis, we can see how investment law evolves in the absence of formal multilateral coordination.[47] Chapter 7 presents the final hypothesis about this new legal environment—that there is a rapidly growing capacity on the part of international organizations themselves to create rules for state and market interaction. The use of precedent in investment and trade dispute settlement suggests that the international legal system is becoming less dependent upon the formal support of states to uphold the expanding umbrella of international economic law.

These four studies take a thematic approach. Each uses an organizational schema that has been designed to highlight both topical issues and problems relating to the development of theory and method. The first section of each chapter contains a brief history of the political, legal and institutional questions relating to our study, and then provides a context-oriented and analytical overview of the literature. The

Introduction 15

second section develops an empirical basis for our discussion of the politics of international economic law. Using time series, process tracing, and other social scientific methods that attempt to track change over time, I examine the impact of institutional and legal development on the global political economy. The third section considers emerging political issues and current legal problems in order to ground our empirical study in the evolving relationships between market and intergovernmental law and policy. In each conclusion, we consider possible research trajectories, highlighting areas where new scholarship may help elucidate the relationship between law and politics in the global economy.

Notes

1 Nicholas Bayne and Stephen Woolcock, eds., *The New Economic Diplomacy: Decision-Making and Negotiation in International Economic Relations*, 3rd edn (Farnham: Ashgate, 2011).
2 Daniel W. Drezner, *The System Worked: How the World Stopped Another Great Depression* (Oxford: Oxford University Press, 2014).
3 Anne-Marie Slaughter, Andrew S. Tulumello, and Stepan Wood, "International Law and International Relations Theory: A New Generation of Interdisciplinary Scholarship," *American Journal of International Law* 92, no. 3 (1998): 367–397.
4 J. Martin Rochester, *Between Peril and Promise: The Politics of International Law* (Washington, DC: CQ Press, 2006), 130.
5 Mark Mazower, *Governing the World: The History of an Idea* (New York: The Penguin Press, 2012).
6 Jürgen Habermas, *The Structural Transformation of the Public Sphere: An Inquiry into a Category of Bourgeois Society* (Cambridge: Polity Press, 1989).
7 David Goldfischer, "E. H. Carr: A 'Historical Realist' Approach for the Globalization Era," *Review of International Studies* 28, no. 4 (2002): 697–717.
8 Jeffrey L. Dunoff and Mark A. Pollack, "International Law and International Relations: Introducing an Interdisciplinary Dialogue," in *Interdisciplinary Perspectives on International Law and International Relations: The State of the Art*, ed. Jeffrey L. Dunoff and Mark A. Pollack (Cambridge: Cambridge University Press, 2013), 6.
9 Slaughter et al., "International Law and International Relations Theory."
10 Jack L. Goldsmith and Eric A. Posner, *The Limits of International Law* (New York: Oxford University Press, 2005).
11 Kenneth W. Abbott, "Modern International Relations Theory: A Prospectus for International Lawyers," *Yale Journal of International Law* 14, no. 2 (1989): 335–411.
12 Jeffrey L. Dunoff and Mark A. Pollack, eds., *Interdisciplinary Perspectives on International Law and International Relations: The State of the Art* (Cambridge: Cambridge University Press, 2013).
13 David Kennedy, "Law and the Political Economy of the World," *Leiden Journal of International Law* 26 (2013): 7–48.

16   *Introduction*

14 David Lake, "International Political Economy: A Maturing Interdiscipline," in *The Oxford Handbook of Political Economy*, ed. Donald A. Wittman and Barry R. Weingast (Oxford: Oxford University Press, 2008).

15 Geoffrey R.D. Underhill, "State, Market, and Global Political Economy: Genealogy of an (Inter-?) Discipline," *International Affairs* 76, no. 4 (2000): 805–824.

16 Friedrich Engels, *The Condition of the Working Class in England* (New York: Penguin, 1987).

17 Michael Evans, *Karl Marx* (London: George Allen and Unwin Limited, 1976), 167.

18 Richard Rosecrance, *The Rise of the Trading State: Commerce and Conquest in the Modern World* (New York: Basic Books, 1986); Hendrik Spruyt, *The Sovereign State and Its Competitors: An Analysis of Systems Change* (Princeton NJ: Princeton University Press, 1996); Istvan Hont, *Jealousy of Trade: International Competition and the Nation-State in Historical Perspective* (Cambridge: Belknap Press, 2010).

19 China Mieville, *Between Equal Rights: A Marxist Theory of International Law* (Leiden: Brill, 2005).

20 Ugo Mattei and John Haskell, eds., *Research Handbook on Political Economy and Law* (Cheltenham: Edward Elgar, 2016).

21 Benjamin J. Cohen, *International Political Economy: An Intellectual History* (Princeton, NJ: Princeton University Press, 2008).

22 Douglas A. Irwin, *Against the Tide: An Intellectual History of Free Trade* (Princeton, N.J.: Princeton University Press, 1996); Sven Beckert, *Empire of Cotton: A Global History* (New York: Knopf, 2015). The fact that both scholars self-identify as historians makes little difference to political economists who claim as kindred most of the research that overlaps with the terrain of political economy.

23 John Zysman, "How Institutions Create Historically Rooted Trajectories of Growth," *Industrial and Corporate Change* 3, no. 1 (1994): 243–283.

24 Rorden Wilkinson, *What's Wrong with the WTO and How to Fix It* (London: Polity Press, 2014). See also Mark Blyth, *Great Transformations: Economic Ideas and Institutional Change in the Twentieth Century* (Cambridge: Cambridge University Press, 2002).

25 Tomer Broude, Marc L. Busch, and Amelia Porges, eds., *The Politics of International Economic Law* (Cambridge: Cambridge University Press, 2011); Tomer Broude, "At the End of the Yellow Brick Road: International Economic Law Research in Times of Uncertainty," in *International Economic Law: The State and Future of the Discipline*, ed. Colin B. Picker, Isabella D. Bunn, and Douglas W. Arner (Oxford: Hart Publishing, 2008).

26 Tomer Broude, Marc L. Busch, and Amelia Porges, "Introduction: Some Observations on the Politics of International Economic Law," in *The Politics of International Economic Law*, ed. Tomer Broude, Marc L. Busch, and Amelia Porges (Cambridge: Cambridge University Press, 2011), 6.

27 Martti Koskenniemi, "The Politics of International Law," *European Journal of International Law* 1, no. 1 (1990): 4–32.

28 John H. Jackson, "Interdisciplinary Approaches to International Economic Law: Reflections on the 'Boilerroom' of International Relations," *American University Journal of International Law and Policy* 10 (1994): 595–603.

29 Rochester, *Between Peril and Promise*, 125.

Introduction 17

30 Christian Reus-Smit, ed., *The Politics of International Law* (Cambridge: Cambridge University Press, 2004).
31 Rochester, *Between Peril and Promise*, 34–35.
32 David Kairys, ed., *The Politics of Law: A Progressive Critique* (New York: Basic Books, 1998).
33 Daniel M. Green, "Introduction to the English School in International Studies," in *Guide to the English School in International Studies*, ed. Cornelia Navari and Daniel M. Green (Oxford: Wiley Blackwell, 2014), 1.
34 Goldsmith and Posner, *The Limits of International Law*.
35 Jens David Ohlin, *The Assault on International Law* (Oxford: Oxford University Press, 2015), 87.
36 J.H.H. Weiler, "The Rule of Lawyers and the Ethos of Diplomats: Reflections on the Internal and External Legitimacy of WTO Dispute Settlement," in *The Jean Monnet Seminar and Workshop on the European Union, NAFTA, and the WTO: Advanced Issues in Law and Policy* (Cambridge, Mass.: Harvard Law School, 2000).
37 Christian Kreuder-Sonnen and Bernhard Zangl, "Which post-Westphalia? International Organizations Between Constitutionalism and Authoritarianism," *European Journal of International Relations* 21, no. 3 (2015): 568–594.
38 Stephen D. Krasner, *Sovereignty: Organized Hypocrisy* (Princeton, N.J.: Princeton University Press, 1999).
39 H.L.A. Hart, *The Concept of Law* (Oxford: Oxford University Press, 1961).
40 Gabrielle Marceau, ed., *A History of Law and Lawyers in the GATT/WTO: The Development of the Rule of Law in the Multilateral Trading System* (Cambridge: Cambridge University Press, 2015), 7.
41 John H. Jackson, *Sovereignty, the WTO and Changing Fundamentals of International Law* (Cambridge: Cambridge University Press, 2006).
42 Peter Williams, "Law and Lawyers in the Multilateral Trading System: Back to the Future," in *A History of Law and Lawyers in the GATT/WTO: The Development of the Rule of Law in the Multilateral Trading System*, ed. Gabrielle Marceau (Cambridge: Cambridge University Press, 2015), 85–108.
43 Hart, *The Concept of Law*, 79.
44 Hart, *The Concept of Law*, 79.
45 Karl Polanyi, *The Great Transformation: The Political and Economic Origins of Our Time* (Boston, Mass.: Beacon Press, 2001).
46 Karen J. Alter, *The New Terrain of International Law: Courts, Politics, Rights* (Princeton, N.J.: Princeton University Press, 2014).
47 Erin A. O'Hara and Larry Ribstein, *The Law Market* (Oxford: Oxford University Press, 2009).

2 The politics of international economic law

- Disciplinarity and international economic law
- Interdisciplinarity and global political economy
- Interdisciplinarity in IEL
- Beyond interdisciplinary approaches
- Conclusion

The study of international economic law is a multidisciplinary endeavor. Political science, economics, and law are natural partners in this project. Other disciplines such as sociology and anthropology have also begun to consider IEL an increasingly important lens through which to examine international order. In order to highlight the possibilities in this brave new world of multidisciplinary effort I will draw upon literatures ranging across political science, global political economy, economics, sociology, and law. I offer a cross-disciplinary overview of interdisciplinary approaches within law and IPE in order to show how tools in both fields are mutually beneficial for our purposes. I conclude the chapter with a brief overview of the five most significant strengths of a multidisciplinary approach. The development of IEL is not unlike that of IPE. Just as economists and political scientists came together to study the growth of global markets, so political economists and legal scholars are creating a new terrain of engagement around the law that governs global markets.

Disciplinarity and international economic law

In some ways, talking about disciplinarity in 21st-century social science is a contradiction in terms. So much of the human world studied by social scientists does not fall into neat scholarly boxes. Each of the disciplines, from political science, through economics and law, has a modern claim to some level of disciplinarity. And yet they began their

The politics of international economic law 19

intellectual lives in the early 20th century as hybrid forms of intellectual engagement. Driven by political need and the vagaries of history, they rose in prominence and became, through the necessities of university life, distinct fields of study rooted in literature that may reasonably claim to speak today to disciplinary specialists. Now these fields of study in the human sciences continue to spread and branch out, meeting new needs and producing new forms of knowledge, and they also continue to transgress the silos of scholarship we create to give form to an amorphous intellectual project.[1]

Now that I have just made the argument for a lack of disciplinarity in the social sciences, I need to back up and suggest that even though at a certain level much of what happens in the social sciences creates knock-on effects that reverberate beyond the silo of discipline, there is a case to be made for discipline-specific research. The fields of global political economy and international economic law are large, and it is only reasonable that the many thousands of scholars who work in each will have more to say to each other than they will to scholars outside their specializations. And perhaps this is the way that we can imagine the practical significance of the concept of disciplinarity—it organizes a global conversation about goals and ends, theories and methods, that provides coherence to huge bodies of knowledge.

This chapter examines the way that disciplinarity may give rise to interdisciplinary research, which may, in its turn, give rise to multidisciplinary approaches to social scientific problem-solving. I will discuss the interdisciplinary connections between international relations and international law, and then discuss the place of multidisciplinary research in global political economy and international economic law. In IPE, the concept of interdisciplinarity has a settled meaning and a well-defined set of theoretical questions and research methodologies. In international economic law literature the concept of interdisciplinarity is less well-developed, but consensus has begun to coalesce around the interplay between law, political economy and economics. I will give a few examples so that I can elucidate a point that has only been made implicitly in the literature—that the fields of political economy and law as they relate to the global economy are better conceptualized as a larger multidisciplinary field of research. Interdisciplinarity imagines a pollination process by which two disciplines combine genetic material with the end goal being the creation of a new body of knowledge. Multidisciplinarity imagines that same process, with cross-pollination occurring between three or more disciplines. In our case creating a new body of knowledge requires input from (at least) the three disciplines present in its nomenclature—international relations/IPE, economics, and law.

20   *The politics of international economic law*

Turning first to a recent example of cross-fertilization, we will examine the interdisciplinary relationship between international relations (IR) and international law (IL). In a recent volume of essays Dunoff and Pollack show the possibilities for collaboration. They note that in the 1990s much of the creative fertilization between politics and law ran in one direction. In the United States, international law scholars looked to international relations for methodological novelty and began to apply the theories and methods of political science to the study of international law. The publication of a special issue of *International Organization*, a preeminent journal of political economy, in the early 2000s marked the rediscovery of international law by political scientists.[2] By this point larger changes within the study of both law and politics aided the interdisciplinary project. Scholars in both disciplines had begun to move beyond internal debates over method and towards research that is more problem driven—a shift towards what at least some political scientists have termed "eclectic theorizing."[3]

The interdisciplinary linkages between IR and international law underscore the possibility of dialogue between disciplinary traditions. Although, it is necessary to note that the relationship between IR and IL is not necessarily a marriage of easy compatibility. IR theories are more likely to stress the problem of cooperation under anarchy, highlight the role of state power in the problem of compliance, and question the effectiveness of institutions. IL theories are more likely to pay attention to the question of legal process, examine the interpretive methodologies used by judges and dispute settlement panelists, examine the normative underpinnings of institutions, and examine the consequences of IL.[4] In short, international relations frequently concerns itself with the theoretical and empirical dimensions of power and political disequilibrium, while international law looks at procedural factors related to the legal process.

Dunoff and Pollack further note that in broad terms, political science (including IR research) is largely positivist with a focus on experience and testing, while IL is more oriented towards textual interpretation and an "authority paradigm" in which legal study happens from inside legal sources.[5] They refer to this as a dialogue between positivism and internalism, or externalism and internalism. Furthermore, IL and IR have different understandings of what law is. For political science, law is the rules created and maintained by purposive political actors; this is law as the rules of the game. For IL scholars, it is more difficult to quantify the features of law. Law is not only rules, but also contains a normative space—what we frequently refer to as the spirit of the law—and they would assert that it is impossible to quantify its impact on behavior.[6]

The politics of international economic law 21

Yet, what appears on the surface to be an uneasy relationship has become one of the more fruitful interdisciplinary collaborations of the early 21st century. IR's emphasis on positive hypothesis testing and the rules of the game offers law an empirical dimension that is often lacking. Law's subtle understanding of the comparative, historical and cognitive dimensions of governance elevates IR discourse beyond a materialist understanding of the "rules of the game." A deeper understanding of the place of law in the human sciences offers thick description and robust theoretical insights for future research on sovereignty, interdependence, cooperation, and the growth of institutions of global governance. With this basic example of interdisciplinary cooperation as our backdrop, let us turn now to the place of interdisciplinarity within IPE and IEL.

Interdisciplinarity and global political economy

So we can see that when we talk about interdisciplinarity across IR and law there is already a fruitful example of how the relationship might work. Now we ought to turn to the question of what we mean when we speak about interdisciplinarity within international political economy. Rather than offer a genealogy of interdisciplinary development in IPE, I will show, through a number of snapshots of both classic and recent literature, the cross-disciplinary potential of the political economy approach.

Kindleberger is one of the earliest and most successful proponents of an interdisciplinary approach in IPE. He is also one of the few economists-by-training to fully engage in an interdisciplinary dialogue with political science. As early as 1974 Kindleberger was stressing the importance of political and sociological factors in the analysis of economics. In one of his best-known articles, he suggested that in order to understand the rise of free trade in Western Europe in the middle of the 19th century, scholars must pay attention to the world of ideas and diplomacy. "Free trade in Europe in the period from 1820 to 1873 had many different causes." Not least of which was a movement to free trade for "ideological or perhaps better doctrinal reasons ... [the] Manchester [School] and the English political economists persuaded Britain which persuaded Europe, by precept and example."[7] Kindleberger explains that British industrialization provided a powerful incentive to copy British methods and by necessity pay attention to British ideas about the place of trade in industrial development.

This makes European market access less the result of a virtuous circle of increasing economic efficiency and more the result of political decisions that accompany industrial development in the shadow of the

22 *The politics of international economic law*

British Empire. The Manchester School was convincing not entirely because of the logic of its argument, but also because of where it came from and the interests it represented. For Kindleberger, as one of the earliest and most influential members of the American school of IPE, political economy is economics analyzed through the lenses of political power and the power of ideas. As such, his thought sits at the intersection between institutionalism, constructivism and, read in a certain light, critical political approaches as well.

By the early 1980s Kindleberger was fully engaged in an interdisciplinary dialogue with political science, publishing early articles on collective goods and noting in his presidential address to the 98th meeting of the American Economics Association that his intention was to "conduct a conversation with a new, impressive, and growing breed of political scientists working on international economic questions."[8] Kindleberger's conversation with political science left a deep mark on the nascent field of political economy. His belief that the international order for trade and finance requires a single powerful state willing to shoulder the burden of stabilizing the system animated late 20th-century IPE. As a scholar, Kindleberger was skeptical about the mathematical turn in the economics profession and believed that economics was abdicating its role in defining and developing the debates that would animate political economy well into the 21st century.

Modern American political economists are developers of quantitative hypotheses. Many are positivists, oriented towards the refinement of parsimonious theory. But in the larger tradition, much of the historical, normative, and constructivist research carried out in American, Canadian, British, Australian and Japanese IPE programs owes a large debt to Kindleberger and his path-breaking work in the economic history of trade and finance. As Cohen notes in his recent intellectual history of IPE, Keohane may legitimately claim to have first articulated hegemonic stability theory, the first big theory of IPE, but it is Kindleberger's work that gave it narrative form and animated the many normative questions that informed the debate.[9]

As one of the American scholars who was present at the creation of North American IPE, Robert Keohane's research has had a formative impact on almost every IPE doctoral candidate since the early 1970s. In a recent retrospective, he notes that at the time, political economy was out of favor in political science because it did not concern itself with the hard-power politics of force and statecraft that shaped the international system during the Cold War.[10] In economics it bore the stigma of being overly political, and in that way related to the old world of 19th-century political economy. In response to the dominance of political

The politics of international economic law 23

realism, he and Nye sketched out a liberal conception of world order that they termed complex interdependence.[11] It built upon Kindleberger's understanding of the role of hegemonic states in securing stability, as well as his understanding of that stability as a collective good.

This was a robust interpretation of history and liberal political and economic theories that emphasized the common good of open markets and the centrality of transnational economic actors and global regimes for economic governance in its conception of world order. As such, it drew extensively from literature on the development of the multi-national corporation, economic theories such as comparative advantage, and the liberal political philosophy of 19th-century reformers from Mill to Cobden and even Marx, who argued that global order would come about through the self-interest of economic actors rather than the ambitions of powerful political leaders.

Keohane's work evolved, moving from conceiving power in terms of hegemonic actors towards a view of IPE that blended rationalist and constructivist understandings of agency to focus on new ways to conceptualize structural power.[12] He remains ambivalent about the rise of a strongly rationalist and materialist IPE, led by the Open Economy Politics (OEP) approach championed by Lake and others.[13] In stronger terms, Kirshner identifies a hyper-rationalist, individualist and materialist turn in IPE as a second crisis, the first being the challenge of its formation in the 1970s when political analysis was verboten in economics.[14] History, sociology and narrative-driven economic analysis take a back seat to econometric modeling in this new IPE. This is IPE far removed from the robust, multidisciplinary interests of Kindleberger, Hirschman, and Strange, where big-picture historical research stood side by side with close analytic description and robust, empirically informed processes of inductive reasoning.[15]

Could it be that in certain corners, IPE is becoming less interdisciplinary? I would suggest that if we mean interdisciplinary in the sense of scholarship that seeks out disciplinary limits and then crosses them, then indeed American IPE may be building its own silo in academia. It seems to be becoming more disciplinary, in that it seeks to define its parameters and create a more structured culture, at least in terms of ontological assumptions and research methods.[16] Yet even as the OEP school becomes increasingly dominant in American IPE, the older tradition of eclectic theorizing remains a force to be reckoned with. Furthermore, there is also an increasingly important constructivist strain of IPE that emphasizes the importance of ideas, the significance of culture and language, and the centrality of changing norms to understanding the global political economy.[17]

24   *The politics of international economic law*

Campbell argues that sociologists approach the terrain of IPE differently from scholars trained in political science and economics. Sociologists emphasize the role of norms and ideas, rather than material interests, in shaping the agency of actors. They have put this approach to work examining norm diffusion, which is the way that "normative principles and practices diffuse across nation-states in ways that lead to isomorphic—that is, homogenous—outcomes."[18] IPE scholars tend to believe that norm diffusion takes place through a process of carrots and sticks, with some norms being spread through coercive practices, and others taken up because it is in the interest of states to do so. Sociologists have shown that this is not the entire story. Campbell adds: "the practices of nation-states are enactments of broad-based cultural prescriptions operating on a global level."[19]

Neoliberal beliefs about the importance of low taxes, open markets, and smaller safety nets spread not through hegemonic dictate, but through the movement of elites through American universities and into positions of prominence back in their home country, to use the case of Mexico.[20] Of course the best-known sociological research in IPE is that of Immanuel Wallerstein, who argues, following the work on Dependency Theory in the 1970s, that there exists a global division of labor in which the global economic system is organized into a series of political units in order to more efficiently channel the profits of capitalism north.[21] This is, on a basic level, the notion of a value chain applied to the world system.[22]

Oliver turns the concept of "new IPE" on its head, arguing that the new IPE is not the consensus-driven open economy politics of leading IPE programs in the United States.[23] That "neoliberal IPE," as he terms it, has been around for many years. The really new IPE focuses on concepts such as world order, social movements, social forces, and an approach to political economy that emphasizes the global over the international. On one level this debate over what is properly "new" in IPE shows that IPE scholars are not always in agreement on the major trends in intellectual development. But on another, it suggests that both positivist and critical IPE scholars have legitimate claims to both tradition and novelty in the field. He goes on to argue that the key ingredient in this new political economy is economic history, by which he means an appreciation for, and analytic focus upon, the ways that markets, political actors, and broad social forces structure the global political economy over time.[24]

The emphasis on the historicity of political economy is not new. Hegel and Marx were the first to emphasize in structural terms the importance of social change over time.[25] But Oliver is correct in his

The politics of international economic law 25

assessment that a focus on historical change tends to be the binding factor within and between much of the research that takes as its starting point the eclectic theorizing of Kindleberger, Strange, Cox, and company. It also tends to be conspicuously absent from much of what Keohane calls the "new IPE"—the positivist turn in American academia.

Germain's recent work is important because it goes back to the roots of IPE and in so doing draws together many of the themes discussed above, including early realism, critical structuralism and a deep appreciation of history.[26] Germain examines the work of Susan Strange, who Cohen has called one of the foremost intellectual entrepreneurs in IPE, alongside the realist IR theory of E.H. Carr.[27] Carr was the godfather of 20th-century political realism, and later in a counterintuitive twist that is less ironic than it appears at first glance, a Marxist political theorist. In resituating Strange, Germain weaves together a number of theoretical strands that represent the past and future of IPE. Most importantly, he takes Strange's concept of structural power, which is a state's ability to set the rules of the game, and places it alongside Carr's historical realism.

Carr's work on historical interpretation of fact adds to Strange's counterintuitive understanding of American economic power.[28] Further, as Germain notes, both have complementary views "on the importance of domestic authority relations within great powers for IPE."[29] In short, power radiates outward from domestic authority along channels that are determined by the relations of power within a state, and how we as social scientists interpret the formation and application of those power relations depends on where we stand. As we can see from this rearticulation of classical ideas, before it was an "interdiscipline," IPE was an approach—represented by a skeptical cast of mind, a penchant for big-picture analysis and a flair for inductive theory building, which begins with a set of data points and then builds theory using the tools of history, social and political theory, and economics.

IPE of the future may carry on this tradition of messy, open-ended questioning, but only if scholars continue to value the benefits of interdisciplinary and multidisciplinary research. Next we turn to the use of interdisciplinary approaches in the study of international economic law. Scholars are increasingly concerned with the questions of how to merge the study of law with other disciplines and how to do so in a way that elucidates the most important questions facing the field; how does economic law emerge in the space beyond the state, and what is the place of law in a system that is often described as governance without government?[30]

26 *The politics of international economic law*

Interdisciplinarity in IEL

International economic law is like early IPE in that it has not coalesced into a discipline per se, but remains a broad field of study, rooted in law, but expansive in reach. This breadth has strengths and weaknesses, as we saw in IPE above. In terms of its strength, it remains open to many different approaches and draws broadly from several different disciplines. However, it has yet to decide which approaches are most valuable, nor is there consensus on which avenues of research are most important to pursue. Looking at the example of IPE, this may not be a weakness at all, but there is a line to walk between coherence and creativity. IPE in the United States seems to be trending towards the former, while the latter would seem to be the terrain of most fruitful endeavor. Of course the question of whether any one set of scholars ought to define that line for the rest of us is another issue entirely.

Professor John Jackson, the foremost scholar of international trade regulation in the United States, called for "interdisciplinary approaches to IEL" more than 20 years ago.[31] He argues that there are four main characteristics of IEL research. First, IEL cannot be compartmentalized from public international law. Economic law is part of the larger world of international law. Second, scholars cannot compartmentalize this body of international law from national law because there are too many substantive links between domestic and international law. Third, IEL research cannot draw a firm line between disciplinary and interdisciplinary approaches. Good research requires both disciplinary approaches and the perspective of experts from outside the study of law. Finally, the resulting scholarship will not be able to draw a firm line between theory- and policy-oriented approaches. This insight is echoed by Trachtman, who refers to IEL as a "policy science."[32] I ought to note here the difference between private versus public international law. Public international law refers to rules applied by states in their international relations. Private law refers to rules used by individuals in commercial transactions.[33] A blurring of these boundaries is made possible by the growth of IEL.

Following Jackson, Abbott and Snidal emphasize the separation and interconnection between law and politics.[34] They focus primarily on the IR/IL interface, but their work has resonance for those scholars of IEL working on trade issues. They lay out three research agendas where much interdisciplinary work remains. First, they suggest that much work remains to be done in the area of legalization– that is, what accounts for the growth of the legal system in different areas? Why, for example, do we see a significant growth in areas of international economic law, but less comparatively speaking in international security?

The politics of international economic law 27

Or why significant legalization of the trading system, but comparatively less in the monetary system? These are questions that the study of law, by itself, cannot answer.

Second, how may we account for international legal design? Do norms or interests bear greater responsibility? In a critical context, what role for structural power? Do dominant states create the rules of the game? What about the arena in which the game is played? Third, in the areas of implementation and compliance, much work remains. What role for norms in the state compliance with WTO panel decisions? What about the impact of national law and politics on compliance? Do countries with a strong common law tradition comply more or less with decisions taken at the international level? Perhaps what Abbott and Snidal offer that is most important, is a perspective in which these questions are posed in a way that highlights the intangible elements of law.[35] For example, compliance is about more than obeying rules. It is about how governments and international actors think about these rules, how norms both in national and international environments support or undermine the rules, and it is about the way that actors internalize ideas about legitimacy, fairness, self-interest, and the notion of the collective good beyond the bounds of the state.

Lang applies the sociological approach discussed above to the institutions of the global trading system.[36] Following Kindleberger's 1975 argument that ideas play a significant role in the spread of free trade, he asks if the trade regime has played a role in generating and disseminating the ideas that underpin trade policy after 1945. He then goes on to show how this sociological approach opens a dialogue with law around questions of how institutions spread ideas and how these ideas may work for or against the legalization process underway in the global trading system. He suggests that this idea of norms diffusing out from international organizations has three implications for lawyers. First, students of IEL need to think critically about "the processes by which WTO Members become persuaded that these legal disciplines—and liberal trade policies generally—are in their interest."[37] Second, lawyers ought to be aware that the machinery of governance such as dispute settlement can work against the socializing pressures that have created the trading system.

Lang is suggesting that if aspects of the trading system were to work against the material interests of members while simultaneously maintaining the socialization narrative, the resulting cognitive dissonance may undermine the WTO's legitimacy. Third, Lang argues that we cannot "conceptualize law and legal practice as separate from, or independent of, the normative and cognitive processes at work in the

28   *The politics of international economic law*

trade regime."[38] Put simply, law does not exist separately from the other cognitive practices that make up the trading system. On the one hand, this suggests that law plays an important socialization role—a point that few jurists would disagree with. But on the other, it means that law does not exist above or beyond the rest of the processes at play. The rule of law, therefore, is not an ideal, but a set of practices with real world implications that reverberate through the global trading system, often on a case-by-case basis.

Legal scholars have begun to stress the political elements of international law. Koskenniemi emphasizes that law is not only about rules and institutions; it is also a political project. As such, the politics of law loom large in his thinking about the future of the global legal system.[39] In the context of IEL, Wang argues that scholars must produce research that lies at the nexus of international law, international economics and international relations. For him, law is one of three equal partners in the analysis of market and juridical activity beyond the state.[40] Kennedy agrees, noting that the "interpenetration of global and political economic life has changed the context of international scholarly inquiry."[41] However, he also suggests that in certain important ways, law devoted to the international system has a hard time dealing with questions related to global political economy.[42]

This is the case because law takes its political economic environment as given, and works within this environment to civilize it, which ultimately means that law is more concerned with maintaining the basic congruency between institutions and their external forces, than with a critical examination of that relationship. As a result, international lawyers need to "grasp the depth of injustice in the world today, the urgency of change and the significance of their professional routines in the reproduction of political incapacity."[43] Legal scholars need to engage with new political and economic ideas, become part of the conversation about the system, rather than actors who remain inside its legal and institutional parameters.

A recent edited volume by international legal scholars Broude, Busch and Porges provides one of the best attempts to think critically and creatively about the politics of IEL. They argue that governments are under constant pressure to both enforce and resist international economic law. Politics and law constantly interact, and the relationship between politics and law cannot be reduced to a basic set of principles.[44] Another way to say this is the line between law and politics is frequently unclear. Law is political and global politics nearly always operates within (or at the very least adjacent to) legal frames, from the rules of war to the decisions handed down by the WTO's Appellate Body.

The politics of international economic law   29

The primary question animating Broude et al. is, "why is the law as it is?" by which they mean, how has politics shaped the creation and evolution of international economic law?[45] The scholars in the Broude volume use a distinctly legal sensibility, which means that while they are somewhat sensitive to sociological and other political economic answers, they prefer to look for interaction within and between systems of law, offering answers that are in many ways nuanced, but less interested in the larger dynamics of international economic relations. Importantly, Broude et al. conclude that more empirical work is required. Not only empirical research into the working of the international economic legal system, but also into the way that global political interaction takes place within and through legal arenas.[46]

We may sum up interdisciplinarity in IPE and IEL by suggesting that these two fields are already hybrid sites of engagement that recognize the importance of bringing together at least two disciplinary perspectives when thinking about the problems of global governance. As I noted above, the benefit of the interdisciplinary approach in IPE is that we have a long history of bringing together theory and method across disciplinary divides to tackle the real-world problems that transcend academic boundaries. Even so, interdisciplinarity in IPE is somewhat settled. We know what we mean, we know the strengths and weaknesses of crossing boundaries, and we have developed transdisciplinary approaches that are becoming somewhat disciplinary in their turn. In IEL, interdisciplinarity is less settled. Like the interdisciplinarity of early IPE, it is driven more by the needs of the research than by the dictates of career building in academic departments. The next step is to self-consciously approach the potential for combining political science, economics and law in a multidisciplinary approach to organizing our study of the legal dimensions of the global political economy. This is the project of the chapters that follow.

Beyond interdisciplinary approaches

Multidisciplinarity has become a buzzword in the social sciences in the past decade, with many scholars and university administrators looking for new ways to blend the insights of different disciplines, not to mention the money of the public and private sectors, to solve the problems of the 21st century. However, genuinely multidisciplinary research is often difficult to come by for a variety of reasons having to do with not just the intellectual silos of academic training, but also the practical challenges of learning how to translate insights in one discipline into workable hypotheses in another, or even how to properly state one's

30   *The politics of international economic law*

assumptions so that team members (or other researchers) may begin their research on the same page. This general idea that multi-disciplinarity is a bigger basket of approaches than is interdisciplinary research tends to be the accepted definitional difference between the terms in the academic literature, and we will start here.

Multidisciplinary research is problem-oriented and takes insights from several disciplines. Everybody knows multidisciplinary research when they see it, but measuring its impact on knowledge development is difficult. Co-authorship where at least one author is affiliated with a different discipline is usually the way that we measure whether research is multidisciplinary. Finding instances of this basic approach is not very difficult. After all, the production of knowledge in the natural and social sciences is increasingly a team effort. Wuchty, Jones and Uzzi studied 19.9 million papers in the Web of Science database covering the natural sciences and engineering, the social sciences, and the arts and humanities, and also patent data from US patents recorded since 1975. They found that research is done in teams across nearly all fields. The most highly cited research is done by teams, and while the popular image of the solitary genius resists, nevertheless "the mantle of extraordinarily cited work has passed to teams by 2000."[47]

Yet despite the dominance of teams, truly multidisciplinary research is still somewhat difficult to come by. Barthel and Seidl examine inter-disciplinary collaboration between the natural sciences and the social sciences, using groundwater research as a case study. They examined journal articles in the field of water research that were written by mul-tiple authors from different disciplines. Looking at research published between 1990 and 2014, they found that multidisciplinary publications accounted for a low-single-digit percentage of all publishing in the area, and they saw only a slightly increasing trend towards more multidisciplinarity over the time period.[48]

Bendersky and McGinn study the barriers to the production of multidisciplinary knowledge and conclude that bringing together researchers from different backgrounds in the same physical space is a great way to begin, but it is not nearly the entire story when it comes to producing multidisciplinary knowledge.[49] They argue that incom-patible assumptions on the part of team members are perhaps the big-gest barriers to knowledge creation. Researchers have to be on the same page in terms of what they take for granted, and what questions they wish to ask, in order to build knowledge together. Osterloh and Frost also examine this idea of interpersonal assumption within multi-disciplinary groups and argue that starting from the wrong assumption may occur when one discipline dominates the others, as sometimes

The politics of international economic law 31

happens when economic assumptions come to dominate in multi-disciplinary research environments. They propose a method for researchers to use when bringing their ideas together that they call multidisciplinary mapping.[50] These maps are designed to lay out the ideas and assumptions that build knowledge in each discipline at the table in plain language to bridge disciplinary approaches by making explicit the intellectual starting points of each researcher.

Such an approach would be particularly useful when approaching team research that involves professional practitioners, for whom disciplinary assumptions are usually implicitly held. Venzke argues that a multidisciplinary approach is required when studying practice-oriented fields such as law because by viewing international law as a practice we are able to see how legal professionals make law and the law makes legal professionals.[51] We will further discuss this idea about how the social world of legal professionals helps to develop certain basic ideas in international law in Chapter 7. Here, however, it is suffice to say that Venzke's idea of multidisciplinarity as an approach undertaken by a single scholar using multi-perspectival tools in a quest to understand a complex set of phenomena, best approximates what I am attempting to do in this study.

Even today, much of the social scientific and legal literature uses the terms interdisciplinary and multidisciplinary somewhat interchangeably to describe any research that does not fall into the neat boxes of disciplinary publication. There is a basic logic to this interchangeability because interdisciplinary can mean "between more than one discipline" and multidisciplinary means "between more than two disciplines." Both terms can refer to research that crosses the boundaries of three or more disciplines. In this research, I use the term interdisciplinary to refer to political economy research that brings together insights and/or methods from political science and economics, and international economic law research that brings together law and economics. I use the term multidisciplinary to refer to research that brings together the interdisciplinary work of political economy with legal research, so that when I refer to the multidisciplinarity of the politics of international economic law, I am referring to a mix of politics, economics and law.

There are at least five strengths of a multidisciplinary approach that blends these three fields of study and practice. First, multidisciplinarity places more emphasis on problem-solving than theory-making. This is an obvious point in IPE, with its emphasis on the importance of the practical over the theoretical. Political economists always argue (sometimes convincingly) that they are studying the "real world" of

32 The politics of international economic law

power, ideas, interests and interconnection. The same goes for international economic law, and one can hear echoes of this argument in Jackson's argument for greater interdisciplinarity in IEL.

Second, with at least three disciplines we are less concerned with the capture of one discipline by another, as is arguably taking place with the open economy politics in American IPE, and we are free to pick and choose among theoretical insights. A multidisciplinary approach allows scholars to make more strategic decisions about the best way to combine theory and method. In a larger terrain of scholarship we may simultaneously gain flexibility and insight while preserving what is distinct about each theoretical approach because the focus of method is not synthesis, but rather plurality.

Third, with at least three methodological traditions, it becomes more and more obvious that new methods are needed, rather than merging existing methods or colonizing one with the ideas of another. For example, law offers an intriguing approach to the study of agency, interests and normative claims that is often lacking in political economy. We are often trapped in realist, liberal and constructivist boxes, whereas law offers an entirely different perspective on rationality, consensus building and the creation of social meaning. With new perspectives comes the possibility of new ways to think about methods.

Fourth, the development of a multidisciplinary approach offers an opportunity to think about global problems using theory and method that is more ecumenical and less freighted with the concerns of certain countries. Anglo-American schools of thought dominate the global teaching and research in political science, political economy and international economics. And while it is certainly true that the common law tradition of legal scholarship dominates most research in international law, and Anglo-American interests shape the study of IEL to a great extent, the legal perspective, as a perch outside IPE, offers a new way to think about normativity, equity, rights, and interests outside the mainstream. To put it bluntly, IPE sometimes suffers from a tyranny of the majority. At the very least, inequitable outcomes that undermine legal legitimacy are a major problem in legal studies, a perspective that offers new insights on how and why institutions change, and new ways to consider the cause of pluralism within and beyond the academy.

Finally, future challenges to global order require simultaneously more expertise to resolve as well as a multi-perspectival approach. Looking at a problem from more angles is always better. Perhaps the biggest gift of a multi-perspectival approach is that it is just that, an approach. Disciplines tend to organize their thinking around theories, while multidisciplinary fields of study organize their thinking around

The politics of international economic law 33

approaches. An approach draws upon theory across disciplines to create a relational, yet tightly organized method with which to study a large body of (sometimes heterogeneous) knowledge. Therefore an approach highlights what might be important among many data points, and allows for relational connections to be made between points that may appear to have little in common. In this way theory and method are used not to maintain disciplinary rigor, but rather to build lookouts from which to survey an evolving intellectual terrain.

Conclusion

We have surveyed the possibilities of interdisciplinary and multi-disciplinary collaboration, and I have shown how both IPE and IEL understand this potential. Now we need to turn to the particular insights offered by IEL that inform our study. In the next chapter I lay out the three theoretical approaches based in legal theory (functionalism, constitutionalism, and socio-legal approaches), to show how legal theory may have a complementary, cross-pollinating effect on IPE and on other future multidisciplinary endeavors to study global economic governance.

Notes

1 Chen-Yu Wang, "Different Scholarships, the Same World: Interdisciplinary Research on IEL," in *International Economic Law: The State and Future of the Discipline*, ed. Colin B. Picker, Isabella D. Bunn and Douglas W. Arner (Oxford: Hart Publishing, 2008).
2 Jeffrey L. Dunoff and Mark A. Pollack, "International Law and International Relations: Introducing an Interdisciplinary Dialogue," in *Interdisciplinary Perspectives on International Law and International Relations: The State of the Art*, ed. Jeffrey L. Dunoff and Mark A. Pollack (Cambridge: Cambridge University Press, 2013), 10–12.
3 Peter J. Katzenstein and Rudra Sil, "Eclectic Theorizing in the Study and Practice of International Relations," in *The Oxford Handbook of International Relations*, ed. Christian Reus-Smit and Duncan Snidal (Oxford: Oxford University Press, 2008).
4 Dunoff and Pollack, "International Law and International Relations," 14–15.
5 Dunoff and Pollack, "International Law and International Relations," 15.
6 Dunoff and Pollack, "International Law and International Relations," 18–19; H.L.A. Hart, *The Concept of Law* (Oxford: Oxford University Press, 1961).
7 Charles P. Kindleberger, "The Rise of Free Trade in Western Europe, 1820–1875," *Journal of Economic History* 35, no. 1 (1975): 49–51.
8 Charles P. Kindleberger, "Standards as Public, Collective and Private Goods," *Kyklos* 36, no. 3 (1983): 377–396; Charles P. Kindleberger,

34   *The politics of international economic law*

"International Public Goods without International Government," in *Comparative Political Economy: A Retrospective*, ed. Charles P. Kindleberger (Cambridge, Mass.: MIT Press, 2000), 441–442.

9   Benjamin J. Cohen, *International Political Economy: An Intellectual History* (Princeton, N.J.: Princeton University Press, 2008), 68–72.

10 Robert O. Keohane, "The Old IPE and the New," *Review of International Political Economy* 16, no. 1 (2009): 34–46.

11 Robert O. Keohane and Joseph S. Nye, *Power and Interdependence: World Politics in Transition* (Boston, Mass.: Little Brown, 1977).

12 Robert O. Keohane, "The Old IPE and the New."

13 Robert H. Bates, *Open-Economy Politics: The Political Economy of the World Coffee Trade* (Princeton, N.J.: Princeton University Press, 1999).

14 Jonathan Kirshner, "The Second Crisis in IPE Theory," in *International Political Economy: Debating the Past, Present and Future*, ed. Nicola Phillips and Catherine E. Weaver (New York: Routledge, 2011), 203.

15 Albert O. Hirschman, *National Power and the Structure of Foreign Trade* (Los Angeles: University of California Press, 1945); Susan Strange, *Sterling and British Policy: A Political Study of an International Currency in Decline* (Oxford: Oxford University Press, 1971).

16 Kathleen McNamara, "Of Intellectual Monocultures and the Study of IPE," in *International Political Economy: Debating the Past, Present and Future*, ed. Nicola Phillips and Catherine E. Weaver (New York: Routledge, 2011).

17 Rawi Abdelal, Mark Blyth, and Craig Parsons, eds., *Constructing the International Economy*, ed. Peter J. Katzenstein, Cornell Studies in Political Economy (Ithaca, NY: Cornell University Press, 2010).

18 John L. Campbell, "What Do Sociologists Bring to International Political Economy?" in *Routledge Handbook of International Political Economy (IPE): IPE as a Global Conversation*, ed. Mark Blyth (New York: Routledge, 2009), 266–267.

19 Campbell, "What Do Sociologists Bring to International Political Economy?" 267.

20 Campbell, "What Do Sociologists Bring to International Political Economy?" 270.

21 Samir Amin, *Unequal Development: An Essay on the Social Formations of Peripheral Capitalism* (New York: Monthly Review Press, 1976).

22 Immanuel Wallerstein, ed., *The Essential Wallerstein* (New York: The New Press, 2000); Benjamin D. Brewer, "Global Commodity Chains and World Income Inequalities: The Missing Link of Inequality and the 'Upgrading' Paradox," *Journal of World Systems Research* XVII, no. 2 (2011): 308–327.

23 Michael J. Oliver, "Economic History and International Political Economy," in *Routledge Handbook of International Political Economy (IPE): IPE as a Global Conversation*, ed. Mark Blyth (New York: Routledge, 2009).

24 Oliver, "Economic History and International Political Economy," 281–282.

25 Robert Gilpin, *The Political Economy of International Relations* (Princeton, N.J.: Princeton University Press, 1987).

26 Randall Germain, ed., *Susan Strange and the Future of Global Political Economy: Power, Control and Transformation*, RIPE Series in Global Political Economy (New York: Routledge, 2016).

27 Cohen, *International Political Economy*, 8.

28 E.H. Carr, *What is History?* (London: Macmillan, 1961).

The politics of international economic law 35

29 Randall Germain, "Susan Strange and the Future of IPE," in *Susan Strange and the Future of Global Political Economy: Power, Control and Transformation*, ed. Randall Germain (New York: Routledge, 2016), 6.

30 James N. Rosenau and Ernst-Otto Czempiel, eds., *Governance without Government: Order and Change in World Politics* (Cambridge: Cambridge University Press, 1992).

31 John H. Jackson, "Interdisciplinary Approaches to International Economic Law: Reflections on the 'Boilerroom' of International Relations," *American University Journal of International Law and Policy* 10 (1994): 595–603.

32 Joel Trachtman, "International Economic Law Research: A Taxonomy," in *International Economic Law: The State and Future of the Discipline*, ed. Colin B. Picker, Isabella D. Bunn, and Douglas W. Arner (Oxford: Hart Publishing, 2008), 43.

33 Martin J. Rochester, *Between Peril and Promise: The Politics of International Law* (Washington, DC: CQ Press, 2006), 123.

34 Frederick M. Abbott and Duncan Snidal, "Law, Legalization, and Politics: An Agenda for the Next Generation of IL/IR Scholars," in *Interdisciplinary Perspectives on International Law and International Relations: The State of the Art*, ed. Jeffrey L. Dunoff and Mark A. Pollack (New York: Cambridge University Press, 2013).

35 Abbott and Snidal, "Law, Legalization, and Politics."

36 Andrew T.F. Lang, "Some Sociological Perspectives on International Institutions and the Trading System," in *International Economic Law: The State and Future of the Discipline*, ed. Colin B. Picker, Isabella D. Bunn, and Douglas W. Arner (Oxford: Hart Publishing, 2008).

37 Lang, "Some Sociological Perspectives on International Institutions and the Trading System," 84.

38 Lang, "Some Sociological Perspectives on International Institutions and the Trading System," 85.

39 Martti Koskenniemi, *The Politics of International Law* (Oxford: Hart Publishing, 2011), 331.

40 Chen-Yu Wang, "Different Scholarships, the Same World: Interdisciplinary Research on IEL," in *International Economic Law: The State and Future of the Discipline*, ed. Colin B. Picker, Isabella D. Bunn, and Douglas W. Arner (Oxford: Hart Publishing, 2008), 122.

41 David Kennedy, "Law and the Political Economy of the World," *Leiden Journal of International Law* 26 (2013): 7.

42 Kennedy, "Law and the Political Economy of the World," 31.

43 Kennedy, "Law and the Political Economy of the World," 48.

44 Tomer Broude, Marc L. Busch, and Amelia Porges, "Introduction: Some Observations on the Politics of International Economic Law," in *The Politics of International Economic Law*, ed. Tomer Broude, Marc L. Busch, and Amelia Porges (Cambridge: Cambridge University Press, 2011), 4.

45 Broude et al., "Introduction: Some Observations on the Politics of International Economic Law," 4.

46 Broude et al., "Introduction: Some Observations on the Politics of International Economic Law," 15.

47 Stefan Wuchty, Benjamin F. Jones, and Brian Uzzi, "The Increasing Dominance of Teams in Production of Knowledge," *Science* 316 (2007): 1038.

36 *The politics of international economic law*

48 Roland Barthel and Roman Seidl, "Interdisciplinary Collaboration Between Natural and Social Sciences—Status and Trends Exemplified in Groundwater Research." *PLOS One* 12, no. 1 (2017).

49 Corinne Bendersky and Kathleen McGinn, *Incompatible Assumptions: Barriers to Producing Multidisciplinary Knowledge in Communities of Scholarship* (2007). http://dx.doi.org/10.2139/ssrn.1077673.

50 Margarit Osterloh and Jetta Frost, "Bad for Practice—Good for Practice: From Economic Imperialism to Multidisciplinary Mapping," First IESE Conference on Humanizing the Firm and the Management Profession (Barcelona, 2008).

51 Ingo Venzke, *Multidisciplinary Reflections on the Relationship between Professionals and The(ir) International Law.* http://dx.doi.org/10.2139/ssrn. 2363630 (2013).

3 Legal theory as analytic lens

- **Functionalism**
- **Constitutionalism**
- **Socio-legal approaches**
- **Towards multidisciplinarity: new approaches to international economic law**
- **International economic law as policy science**
- **New legal realism: the politics of international economic law**
- **Conclusion**

The previous chapter discussed interdisciplinarity as it relates to the study of international political economy and international economic law with an eye to mutual compatibility. I argued for a multidisciplinary approach that brings political economy and law together in the study of international economic law. In this chapter I argue that much of the study of international economic law is rooted in the methods and theory of legal scholarship, and these offer several promising additions to a multidisciplinary scholarship. Functionalism, constitutionalism, and socio-legal approaches complement several tools used in political economy. In the second half of the chapter I will offer two research approaches that are evolving across these scholarly contexts. International economic law as policy science and legal realism, or what I term the politics of international economic law, have distinct trajectories and they represent the frontiers of IEL research, suggesting a remarkable depth and breadth of possibility for future multidisciplinary approaches.

Functionalism

Functionalist legal theory as it relates to international law and global governance has two sides. The first is the idea that the practical needs

38   *Legal theory as analytic lens*

of governance ought to shape law, and legal research ought to be rooted in political and economic context.[1] The other side of that coin is the idea that the shape of law is the result of an evolutionary process that has produced current forms of governance.[2] This is the idea that the system looks the way it does because that is the most useful shape. In some ways functionalism can be considered a very conservative approach to theorizing because it owes a debt to political philosophy that emphasizes the organic nature of social change, and casts a skeptical eye on more normative theories that emphasize the desirability and/or necessity of faster change. But on the other side, functionalism is one of the most practical approaches to thinking about the development of law beyond the state.[3] Without any overarching political authority, the only way for legal development to proceed is through piecemeal progress—small steps bolster the legitimacy of what has come before while laying the foundation for the future.

This practicality has driven the popularity of functionalist theory because within evolutionary change lies a way forward for thinking about possible future iterations of international law. Trachtman provides one of the best examples of how functionalism may be a forward-looking and change-oriented approach to thinking about international law. In a recent book on the future of international law, he suggests that there is increasing demand for international regulation in a number of areas, from human rights, to the laws of war and international economic law. A corresponding demand for more and better law creates a density of international law that arises organically, rather than through an overarching plan for legal improvement.[4]

Legal density gives rise to "natural and created relationships between different areas of international law," creating an expanding network of interlinking bodies of regulation.[5] The logical outcome of a growing net of law and an organic increase in its density is demand for enforcement mechanisms that improve the reliability of regulation. Ultimately, Trachtman predicts that "these institutions of legislation, adjudication, and enforcement, as they develop organically—functionally—will seem increasingly governmental."[6] The functional development of international law, he maintains, will eventually lead to something resembling a global government, if only because increasingly wide and deep bodies of governance require increasingly robust institutional and legal support.

Tractman's prediction is bold, yet shows very well how functional theory can offer a robust and forward-looking approach to analyzing the current dynamics of development in international law. Even so, there are a number of weaknesses and strengths of a functional approach. When done badly it can be an attempt to defend systemic inadequacies.

Legal theory as analytic lens 39

Scholars in the critical tradition point out that assuming the functional importance of current arrangements of global governance places at a disadvantage normative approaches that highlight the way that governance institutions lock in unequal outcomes. They might say that functionalism is a theoretical tool designed to maintain current relationships as they are, because it privileges practical approaches to theory that tinker around the edges of current configurations of power.[7]

In defense of functionalism, I would argue that such an approach challenges theorists to take legal form and institutional function on their own terms, accounting for current contours by looking for the historical, political and economic factors that created their form. None of this is to say that scholars ought not to critique the shape of the current system, but rather that they ought to fully understand the logic behind its form, which may then suggest places for possible improvement. Furthermore, functionalism pairs well with institutional and constructivist political economy because this perspective offers a new layer of analytic depth to institutionalism and is itself deepened by constructivist thought. Functionalism brings together rich historical description with an empirical focus on explaining the factors that lead to institutional success or failure. Its hypothetical, inductive method offers a strongly rational approach to mapping change and analyzing not only causes but potential consequences of legal development over time. Its key weakness is that it relies heavily upon rationalist explanations of institutional change, and we understand that there are often other, less obvious factors in play, from changing ideas about the rules of the game, to socio-legal dynamics of power, that we will discuss below.

Functionalism is a useful adjutant to institutionalism. Institutional modes of analysis are primarily concerned with the development of international organization, frequently using historical or rationalist frames for argumentation. Institutionalism is a broad array of theoretical approaches, hypothetical inferences and methodological strategies aimed at understanding the way that politics creates order in the international space beyond the state. In the historical context a functional approach to law that foregrounds the basic use-value of current regimes may offer a number of counterintuitive insights that show how historically rooted trajectories of development may evolve based not only on prior institutional trajectories but also on the changing needs of members and other political agents. For example, accounting for the development trajectory of the International Monetary Fund using only an historical institutional perspective leaves a great deal to be desired, but when the narrative is problematized in a functional legal context, a political economic account of system evolution becomes much richer.

40 *Legal theory as analytic lens*

Secondarily, functionalism may be informed by the insights of constructivism. The concept of norm diffusion (norms of behavior move across time and space, creating social expectations that in turn influence the development prospects for global governance) offers functionalism a lens through which to problematize change in the functional parameters of legal governance over time. Despite, or perhaps because of, functionalism's roots in legal practicality and an organic approach to institutional change, it offers robust collaborative potential. Not only can it broaden and deepen the thick description required for historical institutional analysis, but it can also be improved by exchange with constructivist thought where norm diffusion offers a way to think about the mechanisms by which organic change takes place.

Constitutionalism

The constitutionalist position argues that the ongoing institutional and legal development of international economic order is laying the groundwork for future legal development. While the current institutions are not a template for future growth per se, their contours will shape legal development in the future, much like constitutional law creates the parameters of legal development at the national level. In political economy, constitutional theory crosses the ideological spectrum, from those who see the WTO as an ideal template for future development, to those who worry that its narrow promotion of economic interests threatens the future stability of economic governance. Predictably, constitutionalism is also of interest to a broad swath of legal academia, from the American constitutional law scholars McGinnis and Movsesian who argue that the WTO is a Madisonian constitution for world trade, to the work of European scholars of international law such as Cass, and Jeorges and Petersmann, who attempt to draw out the multiple meanings of constitutionalism.[8]

International legal constitutionalism is a bit of a soft concept. Without an overarching form of legitimate political authority, the basic foundations required for the crafting of constitutional law remain incomplete beyond the state, to say the least. But constitutionalism works well as a metaphorical lens through which to examine the potential implications of current institutional and legal development. In IEL, the WTO is often theorized as having a constitutional role in the global economic legal order. Cass suggests that the WTO is not a constitution in any literal meaning of the term, but suggests that there are three basic conceptions of constitutionalization that currently animate this field of research.

Legal theory as analytic lens 41

The first views the WTO to be a tool of institutional management that provides for ordered relations (both in terms of competition and conflict) between states. The second views the WTO as creating a system of rights, which empower economic actors and extend the notion of economic liberty beyond the state. The third considers the "judicialized rulemaking" at the WTO to be the basis for a constitutional analytic approach.[9] All three of these approaches share one thing in common—they see the current dynamic of legal intensification continuing into the future where it provides a replicable basis for subsequent legal development. Political scientists might suggest that this is a big assumption. Many political events may intervene between the present and hypothetical future. But nevertheless, the approach challenges political economists to engage with the processes of international rulemaking as a basic shaper of current (and future) economic relations beyond the state.

Paulus considers both the United Nations system and the system of international economic law and contends that while neither meets the traditional definition of a constitution, one way beyond the limitations of our current impasse (law without a constitutional basis) may be a "constitutional reading of the constitutive instruments of international organizations."[10] By this he means that the principles that underlie international mechanisms ought to be read as an organizational template. Such an approach may protect the boundaries between public and private, as well as the lines between domestic and international by limiting the powers of international organization in such a way that "might get us nearer to the rule of law in international affairs."[11] Likewise, Pauwelyn understands the current search for constitutional order to be somewhat limited. He looks for forms of international regulation that do not correspond with the state-as-subject of enforceable economic law model of regulation currently embodied by the WTO. He looks to root the foundational understanding of international law in "softer forms of regulation and norms or standards created by, and for, non-state actors."[12] Taken together these readings of international law broaden and deepen the search for the sources of global order, and does so in such a way as to not inordinately privilege a state-centric (and therefore power-based) reading of the legal foundations of global order.

Trachtman develops an economic argument for the necessity and inevitability of international constitutional development. He argues that the demand by political and economic actors for liberalized markets has created a corresponding demand for an international law of liberalization. The growth of international economic law, in turn, has

42 *Legal theory as analytic lens*

created a double movement. On the one hand, there is a growing demand for a constitution that enables the growth and reach of economic law. On the other, we see growing demand for "constraining constitutionalization" to protect the public interest beyond the state.[13] Ultimately, Trachtman argues that the development of international constitutional law will be governed by an economics of constitutionalism, in which the costs of helping and harming citizens are weighed in the context of the politics of international economic law.

The main strength of the constitutional literature is a trend towards the use of big-picture thinking to define the boundaries of current legal scholarship. This literature takes a macro-scale approach to analyzing the developing contours of international law. Constitutionalism is further advanced in IEL than in other areas precisely because the development of the WTO put into place mechanisms for the enforcement of law that brought the legal system beyond the realm of soft law, or to use Petersmann's terms, brought the system beyond rule by law, and into the rule of law.[14] The main weakness of this literature is that there is no such thing as a global constitution because contracting states cannot agree on what such a document would even look like, let alone how it would interact with constitutional authority of territorial states. The international trading order was developed in an explicitly political, diplomatic way that left very little room for an explicitly legal approach to trade multilateralism. This was done because the idea of foundational law (or even the basic rule of law beyond the state) flew in the face of postwar conventional wisdom about the role of international governance vis-à-vis the state.

Constitutionalism has its uses for our study of international economic law. We can see that international legal theories of constitution building are broadly applicable to research in a variety of theoretical approaches across the spectrum of IPE. Institutionalism is pretty good at answering the question of how institutions grow and change. But constitutionalism provides an overarching rationale to answer the question of why certain institutions have developed in the way they do. In the absence of a foundational legal order for institutional development, institutions themselves have had to generate that order, working partly from a normative belief in the importance of foundational law, and partly from a practical understanding that rules require a base in a shared understanding of the goals of the game.

Constitutionalism is aided in its attempt to extrapolate possibilities for the institution of foundational law by constructivist IPE theory. Constructivism examines the politics of perception, the importance of ideas, and the diffusion of concepts, norms and social values across national borders and through formal and informal international institutions. Constitutional legal theory can make much of an approach that attempts to understand how incremental legal development may seek to create a coherent and consistent set of legal precepts. Further, constructivism can offer constitutionalism the tools with which to explain the process by which complex ideas and formative hypothetical assumptions are conveyed and become the norm, just as we discussed with functional theory above.

In a twist that is either ironic or perfectly logical, depending on your perspective, constitutionalism, as the legal theory that looks for the foundational legitimacy in the international institutional order, has grabbed the attention of critical political economists precisely because they too are looking for the legal foundations of order. But in the critical perspective, the creation of foundational law is less about legal development, and more about locking in the relations of production that have created a global capitalist world order. Critical constitutionalism in IPE takes as its foundational hypothesis Lenin's assertion that empire is the highest mode of capitalist social relations.[15] They see globalization not as a network of complex interdependence among sovereign states, but as an "empire of capital" in which state power and capitalist interests work in tandem to organize a hierarchy of global production.[16]

The glue holding this precarious pyramid of inequality together is the legal system that structures inequality by linking together many neoliberal market disciplines through the WTO's single undertaking for membership, binding dispute settlement and other forms of economic regulation that present no alternative to current systems of governance that are weighted in the favor of highly developed states. Where legal constitutional scholars see greater possibility for legal legitimacy, critical IPE constitutionalists see the seeds of system failure as it becomes increasingly clear to global publics that trade governance benefits the few at great cost to the majority. The critical constitutional perspective shares with socio-legal theory this concern with the justice of market relations and the morality of current approaches to international economic law.

Socio-legal approaches

Socio-legal approaches to IEL begin with the idea that law is not value-neutral. It reflects the values and interests of those who create it and this reflection of certain values matters a great deal for the legitimacy of law. Practitioners go beyond the text to consider its context

44 *Legal theory as analytic lens*

and subtext.[17] They argue that the time is ripe for legal analysis that blends sociological inquiry because law has been "travelling on an interdisciplinary path for some time now," and international economic law draws theoretical and practical insights from economics and political science.[18] Alongside the rise in interdisciplinarity there is also a political struggle over the terrain of legal development. The socio-legal perspective understands this political struggle in a way that reflects a basis in practical functionalism—whoever makes the rules stands to benefit from them.

Socio-legal approaches share a normative perspective with the politics of law literature. Kairys argues that there is no one right legal method for reaching the correct conclusion in legal argumentation. This is partly the function of language and interpretation. "The law provides a wide and conflicting variety of stylized rationalizations from which courts choose" when determining correct facts and methods.[19] If law is not a neutral function of fact and logic, but is rather a product of interests, ideas, ideologies and institutional imperatives, then a government that styles itself as governing according to the law is often governing by lawyers.[20] Critical legal studies concerns itself with the way in which this basic insight about the political nature of law reframes questions of equity, freedom and democracy.[21]

Extending the politics of law debate into socio-legal theory, Yearwood and Davis examine the debate around the place of WTO law in the larger context of public international law.[22] They lay out three basic positions in the literature—the WTO as an open system in which public international law may be used by a respondent to defend national trade policy,[23] the WTO as a closed system that may not allow recourse to other forms of law,[24] and third the WTO as a system that overrides other forms of law in certain circumstances.[25] To this Yearwood and Davis add a fourth, socio-legal perspective they call constrained openness.[26] They argue that the WTO's openness is constrained by the fact that every system is limited in its ability to comprehend new perspectives by the original institutional and intellectual frames in which they were created. "Systems can comprehend new data, but to do so they draw on existing data, or frameworks of thought to make practical use of the new data ... our assessments proceed from our particular (internal) point of view."[27] The WTO exhibits a set of cultural constraints rooted in institutional logics that limit its ability to relate to the larger world of public international law.

In showing the cognitive and normative basis of the WTO's systemic legal limitations, Yearwood and Davis highlight the benefit of the socio-legal perspective that attempts to look at bodies of law as social

Legal theory as analytic lens 45

constructions and normative frames rather than as the aggregation of political fact and received wisdom. Halliday and Block-Lieb argue that socio-legal theory represents a return to the legal text by viewing it not as a given, but as a sociological problem. This can create new research opportunities in both law and sociology because "both are drawn inside the framework of the recursivity of law."[28] This recursion is not only a replication, but also a reframing of the politics of the text within a "systemic theory of globalization, and law, and transnational legal orders."[29] In so doing, the politics of law informs larger debates about the substance and process of globalization. So, we can see that socio-legal theory allows us to travel outward from the political debates that inform the creation of law towards larger debates about the creation of global legal order, and inward through the legal-order debates towards the political compromises at the heart of the legal text.

The strength of the socio-legal perspective is its normative approach that critically engages with the subtext of law, or what IPE scholars might call the political foundations of legal order. Its ability to place law in social context and thereby highlight aspects of the legal system that undercut its legitimacy with certain stakeholders is also a noted strength. Finally, its ability to maintain a normative focus on creating a more equitable and therefore more durable international system is significant. Like many critical approaches, it focuses more on critique and less on practical steps for improvement. And while it may not always appreciate the organic, incremental nature of international legal development, it maintains a keen appreciation for the ways that political agents may use the system, and its organic modes of operational change, for their own ends.

As I show below, the socio-legal perspective is useful to this study partly because it provides a counterpoint to, and critique of, rationalist modes of thought, and partly because it informs historical and institutional modes of analysis with a much needed normative dimension. Further, the socio-legal perspectives suggest that law is never politically neutral, and ideas are never value-neutral. In this critique of the values and ideas that underpin economic regulation, the question of which norms travel across national and institutional boundaries, and how these norms gain traction, become questions about the reproduction of legal inequality. Not surprisingly, socio-legal theory also meshes well with other critical political perspectives because this normative ethic maintains a larger goal of progress towards a system of greater transparency and substantive legal equality (see Figure 3.1).

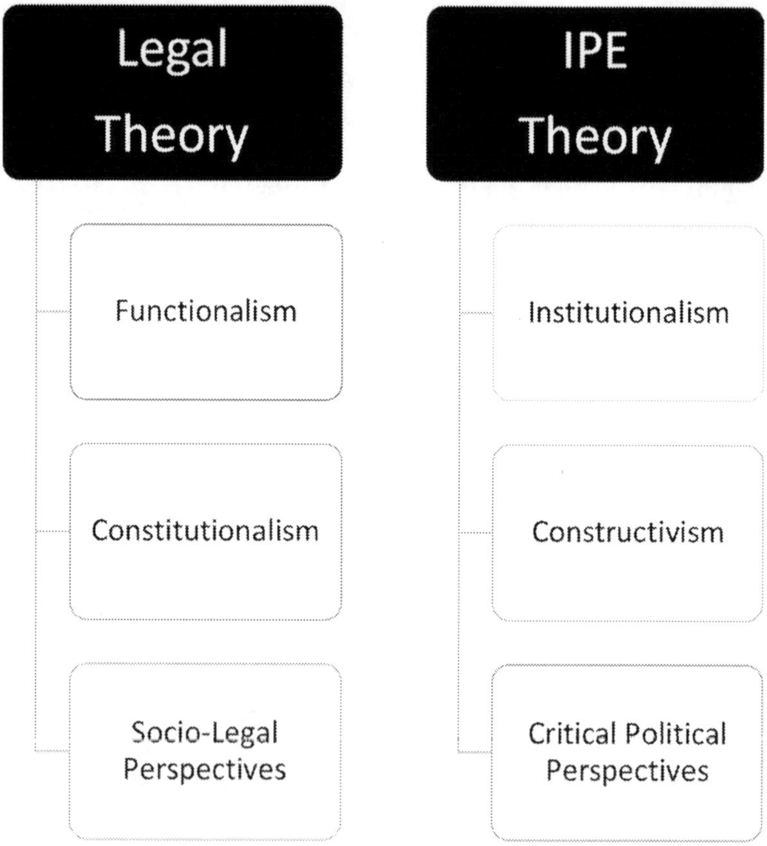

46 *Legal theory as analytic lens*

Legal Theory	IPE Theory
Functionalism	Institutionalism
Constitutionalism	Constructivism
Socio-Legal Perspectives	Critical Political Perspectives

Figure 3.1 Cross-fertilization: international economic law and international political economy

Surce: Author's own creation.

Towards multidisciplinarity: new approaches to international economic law

The first half of this chapter considered a number of legal theoretical positions, and I suggested that legal theory may improve research in political economy, and vice versa. A great deal may be gained from an approach that blends legal theory with IPE. The second half explores two main multidisciplinary approaches to the study of IEL. First, I examine international economic law as a policy science, arguing that rational choice institutionalism and other approaches rooted in the ontological assumptions of neoclassical economic theory may benefit from functional understandings of international economic law.

Legal theory as analytic lens 47

Second, I argue that the new legal realism has much to offer constructivist and critical analytic approaches to IEL. I also suggest that the critical political economy tradition is enriched by the inclusion of socio-legal perspectives on the role of law in global governance. Legal realism's attempt to build bridges between "the world and legal institutions without reducing one to the other" offers an important new dimension to methodologically pluralistic IPE.[30] Nothing here will be of surprise to scholars who work in these areas, but my aim is not to break new ground at the moment, but rather to show how a self-consciously multidisciplinary approach to political economy and law may open new avenues of research for the future.

International economic law as policy science

Now that we have looked at some of the potential links between international law scholarship and research in IPE, we can turn to ways we may approach the politics/law nexus, in order to think more clearly about how both lawyers and social scientists may conceptualize the politics of international economic law. The economic approach to social science that privileges parsimonious theory and a rationalist understanding of agency has reigned supreme in American social science for almost 40 years. Law came late to positivism, but over the past decade a rationalist approach to legal analysis has become increasingly popular. There are two main positivist approaches to the study of international law. The first is a rationalist critique of the concept of law beyond the state by Goldsmith and Posner that culminates in a defense of political realism.[31] The second is a rationalist defense of international law and a call by Trachtman to develop IEL as a policy science.[32]

We begin with Goldsmith and Posner's critique of public international law, in which they argue that we cannot assume that states obey international law. Rather, "the best explanation for when and why states comply with international law is not that states have internalized international law, or have a habit of complying with it, or are drawn by its moral pull, but simply that states act out of self-interest."[33] Their rationalist rebuttal of the conventional wisdom that has shaped postwar thinking about international law came at a time when American political elites had begun to question the efficacy of multilateral cooperation during the Second Gulf War. We can read the Goldsmith/Posner thesis as a conservative indictment of American engagement with international law, and there is certainly that message in the literature. But read in a different way, we can also see it as an attempt to reconsider classical international relations in the context of American

48 *Legal theory as analytic lens*

legal theory and foreign policy action—a nuance to the rationalist approach, which lends it a greater sense of political significance.

Guzman and Trachtman each responded to this broadside by using an economic approach to argue for the rationality of international law.[34] Perhaps the most interesting response, however, came in a recent volume by Ohlin in which he documents a decade-long attempt by a few American scholars, including Goldsmith and Posner, to apply the principles of realism to the analysis of law.[35] Ohlin reads Posner and Goldsmith's argument that in the absence of a sovereign authority, legal authority cannot exist, as the basis for arguments made by Bush Administration officials during the Second Gulf War. Ohlin provides a rationalist defense of international law that takes seriously the point made by realists about divergence between interest and obligation, and that is his most significant contribution. He argues that the tension between self-interest and obligation is a bit of a false dichotomy. Accepting limits on state behavior imposed by international law is rational. "States accept constraints on their behaviour as part of a strategy of constrained maximization."[36] Further, in cases where a state's interest clearly diverges from international law it is still rational to act out of obligation because compliance with international law is part of a state's long-term interest. To throw over international law in one instance is to undercut its utility in future instances where cooperation is more directly in line with a state's national interest.

The rational choice approach is well situated to theorize the development of international law. Trachtman develops a social scientific analysis of international law that begins where economics begins, with the individual as basic unit of analysis. Trachtman believes that methodological and normative individualism, the ontological assumptions that individuals seek to maximize their own preferences and that only individuals are bearers of values, have much to offer law. He chooses a social scientific method because it represents a dual approach to the study of law that both attempts to describe in empirical terms how human institutions affect behavior and in normative terms how changes in institutions might change behavior. So, an economic approach to law is useful because it offers "useful methods for analyzing the actual or potential consequences of particular legal rules."[37]

Importantly, Trachtman sees normative individualism as particularly central to the study of law not only because the idea of the individual as the bearer of an ethical understanding of the world is the basis for a liberal philosophy of modern government and the marketplace, but also because a commitment to normative individualism forces the scholar to consider analytical scholarship and advocacy work as

Legal theory as analytic lens　49

separate modes of endeavor. He believes that too much international law scholarship is given over to advocating for certain policies, rather than delineating and analyzing different policy options. To the question of what is good research, Trachtman replies, "good research illuminates the consequences of policy choices and therefore allows people to make better policy choices."[38] This process of theorizing and testing that requires an empirical and consequentialist approach to learning is at the heart of the economic approach. Trachtman calls international economic law a policy science because he understands the primary goal of the legal scholar to be the clarification of causal relationships.[39]

We may relate a functional and rational approach to international law to the emergent open economy politics approach in IPE. As the most forceful proponent of rationalist approaches in IPE, Lake defines OEP as a step forward from the interdisciplinarity of first-generation IPE towards a new paradigm that improves upon the connection between political science and economics in a way that creates cumulative knowledge such as we see in the natural sciences, hence the use of the paradigm metaphor.[40] In this context OEP is the study of how institutions regulate economic behavior.[41] Lake gives a bit of background to the shift towards an institutional approach to organizing research on international governance, suggesting that IPE emerged as an interdisciplinary field in the 1970s out of the postwar international economic order managed by the Bretton Woods institutions on the one hand, and the end of the dollar's convertibility into gold, which effectively launched a global system of floating exchange rates.[42]

In this era three main theoretical approaches to IPE took shape. These were dependency theory, with its emphasis on unequal outcomes of interdependence; hegemonic stability theory, which extended the historical experiences of Great Britain in the 19th century and the United States in the 20th century to attempt to generalize about the role of major states in underwriting international economic stability; and a branch of IPE, mainly rooted in American schools, that focused on the role of domestic interests in shaping national policy preferences. Lake argues that open economy politics is a direct descendant of the interest group or rational choice approach to framing policy preferences, although in the larger context I think that as much of the work that we may generally group around OEP also originated in hegemonic stability theory (HST). But given the fact that HST devolved into a number of approaches, including political constructivism, Lake is concerned to protect the neoclassical economic base of his paradigm, so he maintains its links to the branch of IPE that most closely corresponds to economic theory.

50 *Legal theory as analytic lens*

Open economy politics moves from individuals (or individual sectors, or factors of production), theorizing domestic governance institutions as aggregators of domestic interests, then suggests that domestic institutions "structure the bargaining of competing societal groups" at both the domestic level as well as at the international level where they constrain the bargaining positions of states.[43] So OEP attempts to create a rational and unbroken chain of causation from the interests of economic actors, through the aggregation of those interests at the national level, to the role of states in creating international institutions to bargain with other states in order to further economic interests at the international level. "International institutions, in turn, condition how this bargaining takes place and what outcomes are reached."[44] In this way we may explain outcomes in the world economy as derived from "interests, institutions, and international bargaining" in linear ways that offer a clear and parsimonious set of falsifiable hypotheses.

Is OEP really a paradigm? Probably not, for two simple reasons. First it is entirely rooted in an understanding of politics and a set of methodological approaches that are tuned perfectly to the American political system. It is not clear to what extent the insights of OEP map on to different democratic systems. This goes double for non-democratic political systems, a weakness that even Lake acknowledges.[45] Second, it is a curious paradigm that emerges even as we see a massive explosion of theories, approaches, and objects of study in IPE. Perhaps the true test of the OEP paradigm will be if it outlives Professor Lake's attempt to classify it as such. Even so, what is important in Lake's work is his attempt to synthesize much of what has become an econometric approach to IPE, and in so doing describe its most important strengths and weaknesses. The OEP focus on material interests as building blocks of international economic outcomes works well alongside a functional approach to law because it provides a material basis upon which to theorize the structure of international economic law. Functionalist research may build on the gains of OEP by examining how evolutionary changes in material interests at the domestic level and subsequent shifts in bargaining positions at the international level guide the subsequent evolution of international law.

Further, as Lake notes, there are a few lacunae in the reasoning that underpins this literature. For example, the relationship between politics and material interest is not well-theorized. It is usually assumed that material interests are exogenous to politics, or to put it better, the egg of interest comes before the chicken of politics. Lake leaves open the possibility that interests are endogenous to politics, that material interests are "products of political strategies or manipulations."[46]

Legal theory as analytic lens 51

Ultimately Lake concludes that "if international institutions really matter, they will alter the interests and possibly institutions within states as well."[47] Leaving aside the distinctly constructivist tone of these suggestions that interests are not straightforward reflections of material configurations and international institutions may change the basis of domestic rationality, this opening suggests a place for law as an intervening variable that may also reorganize the calculation of material interest.

The rationalist approach to mapping the relationship between interests, political outcomes and law offers several places where legal scholarship and IPE scholarship may complement one another. Jupille, Mattli and Snidal provide one of the best examples of a rational choice institutional approach that attempts to develop the tools to answer questions about legal and institutional change over time.[48] They conclude that a bounded rationality approach to institutionalism that emphasizes the importance of sequencing, power, and the cognitive limitations of actors is the best approach to questions of when and why states use certain legal fora, select between competing legal mechanisms, change existing rules or create new arrangements. The main strength of Jupille et al. is the use of a social scientific approach that respects the limits of parsimonious theory in a world of great complexity. It is important to note that I have not substantially critiqued the economic foundations of rationalism because holding one approach to IEL as superior to another is not my primary goal. However, this study does privilege one approach to the politics of law over others from time to time, and this may be read as an inferential critique, although even here my goal is to make a strategic rather than normative choice to privilege inductive over deductive reasoning.

New legal realism: the politics of international economic law

For political scientists, realism has two variants. The first is an historiographical approach to theorizing conflict that began with Thucydides' Melian Dialogue where the Athenians laid out a logic of security in which might makes right because security is of a higher value than is justice (or at the very least security cannot be separated from justice in the larger calculus). The second closely related strain is a 20th-century study of security in which political economic instability creates a logic of security seeking that undercuts collective security. The neorealist developments during the Cold War added a rationalist foundation in which human nature, the rational pursuit of state goals, and global conflict may be theorized through the lens of national interest.[49] Both

52 *Legal theory as analytic lens*

of these realisms (the historiographical and the rationalist) share an understanding of the human condition in which the tendency of individuals and states to continuously seek security leads to a paradox in which greater security undercuts the security of neighbors and increases the insecurity of all.

When legal scholars speak of realism, they mean an approach to theory that is more contextual, an approach to legal insight that takes seriously the sociological and political world in which the law operates. Legal realism as it arose in the 1930s took as one of its philosophical touchstones the idea that the study of law must begin with the world as it is. It stood in contrast to an approach to legal theorizing that began with doctrine and was highly influential with scholars and judges in the United States at that time. The new legal realism builds upon the premise of the old and has become increasingly popular in recent years. The depth and breadth of its implications are explored in two recent papers by Shaffer in which he argues for an analytical endeavor informed by empirical methods that "stresses the importance of empirically informed analyses of the contexts in which law is made and operates."[50]

Shaffer calls for a method that examines institutions as they operate in the real world, and urges scholars to stay away from "normative prescriptions based on abstract principles," by which he means the principles that undergird neoclassical economic theory.[51] I should note that Trachtman argues that there are three heirs to the American legal realist movement—"critical legal studies, public choice, and empirical consequentialism."[52] He imagines his own work to fall into the consequentialist tradition, but basically paints legal realism as the fount of both approaches to IEL I am discussing here. Nevertheless, following Shaffer I narrow the scope of legal realism for our discussion to delineate these two theoretical traditions—the first which takes as its starting point the rational individual, and the second which takes as its starting point the community as a political collective.

The new legal realism is a response to an economic rationalism that Nourse and Shaffer call the new formalism. They argue that legal scholars are showing much interest in the new legal realism, an approach to scholarship that questions the rationality of markets and the "inevitable failure of politics."[53] In response to a formalistic approach to law that removes the political dimension, legal realism aims to show how "law cycles recursively over time between the world and legal institutions."[54] To this end they develop the principle of spontaneity, by which they mean that "law, politics, and society, not to mention markets and governments, cannot be reduced one to another

Legal theory as analytic lens 53

because they interact simultaneously."[55] The old legal realists, they suggest, were motivated by socio-political conflict and the struggles around the implementation of the American New Deal in the 1930s. They believed that formalist legal reasoning masked a certain set of political choices, which at that time would have been choices that privileged capitalist interests over labor. New realism believes that rationalism is insufficient to "explain law's reach and aspirations."[56] Legal realism both old and new stands in contrast to doctrinal approaches to research that separate law and legal theory from the political processes that create, sustain, and change the law.

Nourse and Shaffer describe the new realist legal scholarship as "empirical, multidisciplinary, [and] multi-method."[57] It resists ontological assumptions about the individual and the state because it considers an assumption of rationality to be highly normative in that it is oriented towards a status quo vision of law that leaves little room to theorize the relationship between politics and law. The basic challenge, then, for legal realism lies in overcoming the law/politics divide to begin to create a "theory of the mediation between law and politics."[58] Such a theory would avoid the trap of dichotomies, recognizing that law and politics are in constant interaction, work in parallel, and are continuously operating alongside each other.

How does the new legal realism work with what I call the politics of IEL, or PIEL? In some ways, the new legal realism, like much of the research in political economy, eschews the rational, yet sterile world of rational choice that sacrifices much of the complexity of real-world politics in the service of parsimonious theory building. Rationalism begins with two assumptions—that the individual is a rational actor, and that states are unitary actors, that is, they act with singularity of purpose to achieve identifiable goals.[59] This approach tends to imagine that the preferences of states are relatively stable over time, and emerge in a rational way from the preferences of individual citizens.

Legal realism, in its attempt to account for the way things are, remains sensitive to the fact that the way things are now does not necessarily account for the way things will always be. It is important to understand at this point in our argument the connection between realism and critical approaches to IPE. Realism has been conceptualized, especially in the neorealist variations in IR theory, as both an empirical approach to analyzing security, as well as a normative approach to advocating for system stability. But realism has not always been conceptualized as status quo-oriented—and legal realism reaches back to this earlier period of realist scholarship. Early critiques of capitalism offered a strongly realist understanding of the relationship between

54   *Legal theory as analytic lens*

wealth and power, and in fact one does not have to travel very far to see in Marx's own writing an early iteration of what realist scholars would call the paradox of security, by which states seeking security tend to destabilize the status quo, and thereby leave the state in greater insecurity. Furthermore, the realist inclination to describe the world in terms of power, the counterbalancing of forces and the clash of interests lines up quite nicely with critical ideas around the power of ideas, the institutionalization of inequality and the creation of unsustainable systems of global governance. Indeed, it is no surprise that the godfather of modern realist thought, E.H. Carr, evolved into a critical materialist IR theorist, and admirer of Soviet-style social progress.[60]

Turning to the different modes of PIEL research, we can see at least three themes emerging in the literature—a theme of socio-legal and political critique of the current modes of global order, a theme that seeks to address the thorny issue of institutional reform, and finally a thematic approach to thinking about changing contours of governance. The basic outline of the socio-legal critique has been discussed above. To this we may add the critical constitutionalism of Stephen Gill.[61] Realists are not the only ones to be skeptical about the direction of the development of international law. Critical constitutionalists argue that international law formalizes global relations of social inequality.[62] On the face of it, this argument seems to be about the hegemonic nature of rules, but underneath it runs an argument about the illegitimacy of rulemaking, not because it is an unconstitutional constraint on executive power as Goldsmith and Posner suggest, but because it is an unjust imposition on global publics.

Both positions consider international law to impose new disciplines upon democratic law and traditions, in the first instance as an illegitimate externality impinging upon domestic law and institutions, and in the second case as a strategy pursued by states and intergovernmental organizations to undercut grassroots democratic reform. The politics of IEL shares with legal realism a skepticism about the durability of law if it were removed from present relations of power (see also the economic sociology of Frerichs,[63] and the postcolonial international legal scholarship of Pahuja[64]). The socio-legal and political critics provide important correctives to the conventional wisdom of the post-Cold War years, that economic homogenization was inevitable, the American century would extend far into the 21st century, and the political and economic theory of the Anglo-American world effectively ended debates about alternatives.[65] They are in many ways a normatively oriented answer to the provocative question posed by Fukuyama about the end of history.[66] In answering the question the way they do, both

Legal theory as analytic lens 55

rationalists and radicals anticipate the question of what comes next, or as Sylvia Ostry asked, who rules the future?[67]

Straddling the distance between critique and institutional reform we have Hannah, Scott and Trommer, whose recent work takes stock of the role of expert knowledge in global trade, examining the linguistics of economic knowledge production, and the place of law, power and political agency in the creation of knowledge about global trade.[68] Squarely situated in the theme of institutional improvement and reform, Wilkinson's diagnosis of *What's Wrong with the WTO*, examines a number of concrete approaches to improving an international legal system in which a number of socio-legal and political inequities threaten to destabilize an institution that in many ways reflects an outdated 20th-century approach to multilateral trade regulation.[69] Drahos attaches a significant importance to the power asymmetries in international bargaining, arguing that when the weak bargain with the strong the resulting agreements benefit the dominant and stronger partner in many large and small ways.[70]

The third theme examines the changing contours of global governance. It focuses on how changing balances of power, changing ways of thinking about order, and changing ways of locating authority, have begun to shift our understanding of global governance. This research includes much of the political economy scholarship that seeks to examine the development of law beyond the state.[71] This research shares with legal realism the belief that the status quo, while apparently monolithic today, may not be so tomorrow. It also understands the usefulness of constructivist accounts of trade governance when paired with legal realist understanding of the place of law in a social context.[72]

The rational choice approach to the study of IEL described above rests upon an ontological assumption that individuals, states and international organizations act in a rational manner by organizing their resources in such a way as to maximize their benefit and thereby achieve their goals, which are usually defined as a maximization of material benefit or a minimization of material harm. In epistemological terms, a method that privileges the rational individual and a normative basis in liberal individualism underpins this approach. An approach coming out of legal realism and a political understanding of IEL (what we might term PIEL) is rooted in an ontological assumption of the group as primary unit of analysis, with a secondary assumption of political conflict—over scarce resources, access to material and non-material goods, the relative superiority of ideas, not to mention class, status, and control over organization and hierarchy. Its epistemology privileges methodological pluralism with an emphasis

56 *Legal theory as analytic lens*

on critical analytic, constructivist, and historical modes of analysis, from historical materialism to historical institutionalism.[73]

Methodological pluralism maintains an overarching consistency of focus by rooting itself in normative communitarianism. The normative individualism of rational choice theory draws upon a liberal political theory that posits peaceful competition as the highest form of cooperation. In contradistinction, normative communitarianism is also usually expressed in liberal political terms, but maintains a focus on social cohesion, pluralism, justice and inclusion. It also draws much theoretical energy from an examination of the limits of liberalism and possibilities for fairness in a power-based system. The methodological pluralism and normative communitarianism of PIEL come out of medieval European concepts of the collective, Enlightenment critiques of the means and ends of political stability, 19th-century social justice movements, and 20th-century engagement with the concepts of hegemony, stability, and the politics of change, from state transformation to global governance.

It is important to note that the PIEL approach ought not be considered in opposition to the rationalist policy science described above. Rather it is useful to consider these as two schools of theory and method that share similar goals of explanation and normative improvement. They are, like the deductive and inductive methods of reasoning in which they are rooted, two sides of the same coin.[74] The major difference is that while the hypothetical deductive rationalist approach leaves its normative aims to be inferred from its appeal to universality, the PIEL approach makes its normative aims more explicit, partly because methodological pluralism is not a unifying device from which a mode or model of the ideal may be drawn.

Therefore, methodological pluralism is frequently a companion of explicitly normative theorizing that draws upon historical and theoretical narratives of social change.[75] Where right methods lead to correct analysis and thereby better governance in the rationalist school, in the pluralist school many methods sharpen the contest over ideas and when guided by a normative understanding of fairness and justice, produce outcomes through which the concept of the good is always tempered by language, context, and the constraints of compromise.

Conclusion

This chapter and Chapter 2 have attempted to analyze, in a number of dimensions, the benefit of a multidisciplinary approach to the study of the politics of international economic law. The first section discussed

Legal theory as analytic lens 57

the place of interdisciplinary scholarship in the development of IEL. I began with interdisciplinary connections between international law and international relations in order to introduce the concept of cross-fertilization between disciplines. We then moved to a discussion of interdisciplinary research in IPE and suggested that IEL similarly benefits from openness to theoretical and methodological innovation. I argued that with the rising importance of legal analysis of global affairs we need to start referring to research in this area as multidisciplinary because so much of it self-consciously brings together political science, economics, law, sociology, and critical social and even literary theory.

Then, to show the potential in multidisciplinarity I discussed three broad schools of legal theory that may inform IPE. Functionalism, constitutionalism and socio-legal approaches offer several insights that improve IPE research and point it in new directions. Functionalism offers institutional and constructivist research a way to consider the process of legal change over time. Functionalism is becoming a necessary complement to literature on institutional change and is itself informed by a constructivist understanding of how the ideas that inform legal development move through time and space.

Constitutionalism—the idea that current legal development is laying the foundation for future legal development—also offers insights for institutional, constructivist and critical political economy. In particular, constitutional legal theory offers a way to organize legal ideas and it goes some way towards explaining how they may play a foundational role in legal development—in short, constitutionalism offers a way to order the ideas examined by constructivists. Importantly, constitutionalism has also deeply informed critical IPE which has attempted to discover the mechanisms by which legal processes are used to legitimate international order and structure current relations of inequality in the global political economy. Socio-legal approaches bring a sociological approach to the study of IEL. As such, these pluralistic approaches to the sociology of international law offer a normative critique of law that both influences critical political economy and offers an important counterpoint to institutional and functional ideas on how and why systems of economic regulation develop and change.

I tied together our discussion of multidisciplinary potential with our discussion of the insights offered by legal theory in order to offer two potential multidisciplinary approaches to the study of IEL. International economic law as policy science offers a way to bring together rationalist and functional modes of explanation to strengthen institutional and economic ideas around legal development. The legal realist,

58 *Legal theory as analytic lens*

or politics of IEL, approach engages with historical and empirical research that brings together literature on the relationship between politics and law to create inductive hypotheses with the goal of theorizing in the middle range. This political approach draws from critical analytic approaches to IEL in order to bring together constructivist, critical political economy, and socio-legal perspectives in order to develop theoretically informed critique of the overarching trajectory of IEL.

The politics of IEL approach provides the tools for a reflexive treatment of the normative and intellectual foundations of IEL as well as policy-oriented analysis of current approaches to making and reforming international law. The realist aspect of this literature engages with critical modes of analysis while maintaining a policy orientation that speaks to the political context of functional legal change. Legal realism is skeptical of strongly rationalist modes of argumentation. The resulting politics of IEL blends the functional and institutional focus on stability and incremental change with critical enquiry into the norms and values that influence legal development beyond the state.

The following chapters will draw from this politics of IEL approach while simultaneously engaging with the theoretical and policy-oriented aspects of the policy science perspective. A number of guiding principles will orient our study in the upcoming chapters. First, and most obviously, the research emphasizes multidisciplinarity. Second, it attempts to create a reasonable balance by focusing on both structure and agency in our discussion of institutional and legal change. Institutions have historically rooted trajectories of growth, but they also change according to changing ideas and interests. Third, I will attempt to recognize the normative elements of social scientific endeavor. Knowledge is always incomplete, interpretation is mediated by language, research always embodies inequalities, and the foundations of order are always contested. Fourth, we must also bear in mind that change is usually incremental, to a greater or lesser extent, barring exogenous shock. Fifth, the global system as we understand it is rooted in a complex ideational field that also evolves over time. With these basic concepts in mind, we move into a discussion of legal transformation at the WTO.

Notes

1 Hans J. Morgenthau, "Positivism, Functionalism and International Law," *American Journal of International Law* 34, no. 2 (1940): 260–284.
2 Kerry Rittich, "Functionalism and Formalism: Their Latest Incarnations in Contemporary Development and Governance Debates," *The University of Toronto Law Journal* 55, no. 3 (2005): 853–868.

Legal theory as analytic lens 59

3 Ralf Michaels, "The Functional Method of Comparative Law," in *The Oxford Handbook of Comparative Law*, ed. Mathias Reimann and Reinhard Zimmermann (Oxford: Oxford University Press, 2006).

4 Joel P. Trachtman, *The Future of International Law: Global Government* (Cambridge: Cambridge University Press, 2013), 287.

5 Trachtman, *The Future of International Law*, 288.

6 Trachtman, *The Future of International Law*, 289.

7 Christopher May, *The Rule of Law: The Common Sense of Global Politics* (Cheltenham: Edward Elgar, 2014).

8 John O. McGinnis and Mark L. Movsesian, "The World Trade Constitution," *Harvard Law Review* 114, no. 2 (December 2000): 511–605; Deborah Z. Cass, *The Constitutionalization of the World Trade Organization: Legitimacy, Democracy and Community in the International Trading System* (Oxford: Oxford University Press, 2005); Christian Jeorges and Ernst-Ulrich Petersmann, eds., *Constitutionalism, Multilevel Governance and International Economic Law* (Oxford: Hart Publishing, 2011).

9 Cass, *The Constitutionalization of the World Trade Organization*, 3.

10 Andreas L. Paulus, "The International Legal System as a Constitution," in *Ruling the World? Constitutionalism, International Law, and Global Governance*, ed. Jeffrey L. Dunoff and Joel Trachtman (Cambridge: Cambridge University Press, 2009), 108.

11 Paulus, "The International Legal System as a Constitution," 108.

12 Joost Pauwelyn, "Non-Traditional Patterns of Global Regulation: Is the WTO 'Missing the Boat'?" in *Constitutionalism, Multilevel Trade Governance and International Economic Law*, ed. Christian Jeorges and Ernst-Ulrich Petersmann (Oxford: Hart Publishing, 2011), 226–227.

13 Trachtman, *The Future of International Law*, 277.

14 Ernst-Ulrich Petersmann, "The Establishment of the GATT Office of Legal Affairs and the Limits of 'Public Reason' in the GATT/WTO Dispute Settlement System," in *A History of Law and Lawyers in the GATT/WTO: The Development of the Rule of Law in the Multilateral Trading System*, ed. Gabrielle Marceau (Cambridge: Cambridge University Press, 2015).

15 Vladimir Lenin, *Imperialism: The Highest Stage of Capitalism* (New York: Penguin, 2010/1917); Michael Hardt and Antonio Negri, *Empire* (Cambridge, Mass.: Harvard University Press, 2001).

16 Ellen Meiksins Wood, *Empire of Capital* (London: Verso, 2005); Immanuel Wallerstein, *Historical Capitalism* (London: Verso, 2011).

17 Amanda Perry-Kessaris, ed., *Socio-Legal Approaches to International Economic Law: Text, Context, Subtext* (New York: Routledge, 2013).

18 Amanda Perry-Kessaris, "What Does it Mean to Take a Socio-Legal Approach to International Economic Law?" in *Socio-Legal Approaches to International Economic Law: Text, Context, Subtext*, ed. Amanda Perry-Kessaris (New York: Routledge, 2013), 5.

19 David Kairys, "Introduction," in *The Politics of Law: A Progressive Critique*, ed. David Kairys (New York: Basic Books, 1998), 5.

20 Kairys, "Introduction," 5–6.

21 Kairys, "Introduction," 13.

22 Ronnie R.F. Yearwood and Ross C. Davis, "How World Trade Organization Law Makes Itself Possible: 'Every Time I Describe a City, I am Saying

60 *Legal theory as analytic lens*

Something About Venice'," in *Socio-Legal Approaches to International Economic Law,* ed. Amanda Perry-Kessaris (New York: Routledge, 2013).

23 Joost Pauwelyn, "The Limits of Litigation: 'Americanization' and Negotiation in the Settlement of WTO Disputes," *Ohio State Journal on Dispute Resolution* 19 (2003): 121–140.

24 Joel Trachtman, "The Domain of WTO Dispute Resolution," *Harvard International Law Journal* 40 (1999): 333–377.

25 Lorand Bartels, "Applicable Law in WTO Dispute Settlement Proceedings," *Journal of World Trade* 35 (2001): 499–519.

26 Yearwood and Davis, "How World Trade Organization Law Makes Itself Possible," 54.

27 Yearwood and Davis, "How World Trade Organization Law Makes Itself Possible," 55.

28 Terence C. Halliday and Susan Block-Lieb, "Global Duelists: The Recursive Politics of the Text in International Trade Law," in *Socio-Legal Approaches to International Economic Law: Text, Context, Subtext,* ed. Amanda Perry-Kessaris (New York: Routledge, 2013), 95.

29 Halliday and Block-Lieb, "Global Duelists," 95.

30 Victoria Nourse and Gregory C. Shaffer, "Varieties of the New Legal Realism: Can a New World Order Prompt a New Legal Theory?" *Cornell Law Review* 95, no. 61 (2009): 63.

31 Jack L. Goldsmith and Eric A. Posner, *The Limits of International Law* (New York: Oxford University Press, 2005).

32 Joel Trachtman, "International Economic Law Research: A Taxonomy," in *International Economic Law: The State and Future of the Discipline,* ed. Colin B. Picker, Isabella D. Bunn and Douglas W. Arner (Oxford: Hart Publishing, 2008), 43.

33 Goldsmith and Posner, *The Limits of International Law,* 225.

34 Andrew Guzman, *How International Law Works: A Rational Choice Theory* (Oxford: Oxford University Press, 2008); Joel Trachtman, *The Economic Structure of International Law* (Cambridge, Mass.: Harvard University Press, 2008).

35 Jens David Ohlin, *The Assault on International Law* (Oxford: Oxford University Press, 2015).

36 Ohlin, *The Assault on International Law,* 228.

37 Trachtman, *The Economic Structure of International Law,* 2.

38 Trachtman, *The Economic Structure of International Law,* 51.

39 Trachtman, *The Economic Structure of International Law,* 49.

40 David Lake, "Open Economy Politics: A Critical Review," *Review of International Organization* 4 (2009): 220.

41 Lake, "Open Economy Politics: A Critical Review," 221.

42 Lake, "Open Economy Politics: A Critical Review," 222.

43 Lake, "Open Economy Politics: A Critical Review," 225; Joseph Jupille, Walter Mattli, and Duncan Snidal, *Institutional Choice and Global Commerce* (Cambridge: Cambridge University Press, 2013).

44 Lake, "Open Economy Politics: A Critical Review," 228.

45 Lake, "Open Economy Politics: A Critical Review," 227.

46 Lake, "Open Economy Politics: A Critical Review," 233.

47 Lake, "Open Economy Politics: A Critical Review," 237.

48 Jupille et al., *Institutional Choice and Global Commerce.*

Legal theory as analytic lens 61

49 Kenneth Waltz, *Man, the State and War: A Theoretical Analysis* (New York: Columbia University Press, 1959).

50 Nourse and Shaffer, "Varieties of the New Legal Realism"; Gregory C. Shaffer, "A New Legal Realism: Method in International Economic Law Scholarship," in *International Economic Law: The State and Future of the Discipline*, ed. Colin B. Picker, Isabella D. Bunn, and Douglas W. Arner (Oxford: Hart Publishing, 2008), 38.

51 Shaffer, "A New Legal Realism," 29.

52 Trachtman, "International Economic Law Research: A Taxonomy," 48.

53 Nourse and Shaffer, "Varieties of the New Legal Realism," 61.

54 Nourse and Shaffer, "Varieties of the New Legal Realism," 61.

55 Nourse and Shaffer, "Varieties of the New Legal Realism," 62.

56 Nourse and Shaffer, "Varieties of the New Legal Realism," 95.

57 Nourse and Shaffer, "Varieties of the New Legal Realism," 101.

58 Nourse and Shaffer, "Varieties of the New Legal Realism," 122.

59 Niels Petersen, "Review Essay: How Rational Is International Law?" *Max Planck Institute for Research on Collective Goods* (2009). www.coll.mpg.de.

60 E.H. Carr, *What Is History?* (London: Macmillan, 1961).

61 Stephen Gill, "Constitutionalizing Inequality and the Clash of Globalizations," *Millennium* 23, no. 3 (1995): 399–423; Stephen Gill, "New Constitutionalism, Democratization and Global Political Economy," *Pacifica Review* 10, no. 1 (1998): 23–38.

62 Stephen Gill and A. Clair Cutler, eds., *New Constitutionalism and World Order* (Cambridge: Cambridge University Press, 2014).

63 Sabine Frerichs, "Law, Economy and Society in the Global Age: A Study Guide," in *Socio-Legal Approaches to International Economic Law: Text, Context, Subtext*, ed. Amanda Perry-Kessaris (New York: Routledge, 2013).

64 Sundhya Pahuja, *Decolonizing International Law: Development, Economic Growth, and the Politics of Universality* (Cambridge: Cambridge University Press, 2011).

65 Daniel Drache and Marc D. Froese, "Globalization, World Trade and the Cultural Commons: Identity, Citizenship and Pluralism," *New Political Economy* 11, no. 3 (2006): 359–380.

66 Francis Fukuyama, *The End of History and the Last Man* (New York: Free Press, 1992).

67 Sylvia Ostry, "Who Rules the Future? The Crisis of Governance and Prospects for Global Civil Society," presented at the New Geographies of Dissent: Global Counter-Publics and Spheres of Power, Robarts Centre for Canadian Studies, York University (2006); Sylvia Ostry, *The Post-Cold War Trading System: Who's on First?* (Chicago, Ill.: University of Chicago Press, 1997).

68 Erin Hannah, James Scott, and Silke Trommer, eds., *Expert Knowledge in Global Trade* (New York: Routledge, 2015).

69 Rorden Wilkinson, *What's Wrong with the WTO and How to Fix It* (London: Polity Press, 2014).

70 Peter Drahos, "When the Weak Bargain with the Strong: Negotiations in the World Trade Organization," *International Negotiation* 8 (2003): 79–109. See also Daniel Drache and Leslie A. Jacobs, eds., *Linking Global Trade and Human Rights: New Policy Space in Hard Economic Times*

62   *Legal theory as analytic lens*

(Cambridge: Cambridge University Press, 2014); and Ferdi De Ville and Gabriel Siles-Brugge, *TTIP: The Truth About the Transatlantic Trade and Investment Partnership* (Cambridge: Polity Press, 2015).

71 Marc D. Froese, *Canada at the WTO: Trade Litigation and the Future of Public Policy* (Toronto: University of Toronto Press, 2010).

72 Francesco Duina, *The Social Construction of Free Trade: The European Union, NAFTA and Mercosur* (Princeton, N.J.: Princeton University Press, 2007); Rawi Abdelal, Mark Blyth, and Craig Parsons, eds., *Constructing the International Economy* (Ithaca, NY: Cornell University Press, 2010).

73 Peter A. Hall and David Soskice, eds., *Varieties of Capitalism: The Institutional Foundations of Comparative Advantage* (New York: Oxford University Press, 2001).

74 David Blagden, "Induction and Deduction in International Relations: Squaring the Circle between Theory and Evidence," *International Studies Review* 18 (2016): 195–213.

75 Karen J. Alter, *The New Terrain of International Law: Courts, Politics, Rights* (Princeton, N.J.: Princeton University Press, 2014), xix.

4 Legal development at the WTO

- **Shifting equilibria and the GATT/WTO**
- **Legal development at the GATT/WTO**
- **Critical junctures**
- **The space between**
- **Shifting equilibria in the larger context**
- **Conclusion**

Much political economy research studies the institutional development, power politics, multilateral negotiations and dispute processes of the World Trade Organization. In emphasizing the role of powerful states, we still frequently conceptualize the trading system as a diplomacy-driven institution rooted in postwar power politics. This chapter examines the issue of how to think about institutional change in the context of legal development, using the WTO as a primary case study. I begin with a set of legal insights and aim to show how, in institutional terms, politics and law interact to create an international legal system.

This first case study brings together historical institutional approaches in political science with research on the legal development of the trading system to reorient our consideration of the GATT/WTO from one that emphasizes a set of treaties maintained by the political will of powerful states, to one that reflects its present and possible future as the hub of trade regulation and a major source of international economic law. To that end, there are two ways of thinking about change in the legal environment at the WTO. The first considers the WTO as an institution to maintain a steady state of operation in which change comes from shocks that affect the larger international system, such as wars, recessions or financial crises. The second considers change to come from internal factors. Without discounting the importance of global politics, this position considers change to come from the needs

64   *Legal development at the WTO*

of the actors in the institution as much as it does from exogenous shock.[1] While most research emphasizes one or the other, I attempt in this chapter to develop a method that examines external and internal drivers of change together, through a process that I term shifting equilibria.

I organize this chapter with the conceptual frames of punctuated change, shifting equilibria, and positive feedback to begin to explain the two-dimensional process by which institutional development at the WTO occurs. Legal and institutional development takes place through periods of political bargaining and periods of housekeeping, which are the day-to-day institutional processes that occur in Geneva and are quite separate from activities associated with biennial ministerial conferences. Legal development is the result of both political action on the part of member states and the increasing legal complexity of the issues dealt with by institutional actors in the secretariat.[2] Following Howse, I argue for an approach to understanding legal evolution in which political moments of change alternate with periods of internally driven growth, giving a Kuznets wave shape to legal development at the WTO.[3] In many ways this is a hybrid historical institutional and legal functionalist argument in which change happens through the shifting of the institution's equilibria, whereby problems that are intractable at one point of contact, may be resolved at another.

The first section examines key literature around the concept of punctuated equilibrium, which is the closest that political economy research has come to thinking about the process of change happening through shifts in the locus of institutional momentum. I use the work of Howse as a starting point for making a case for an alternating equilibria pattern of legal development in the global trading system. The second section updates his observations by tracking the progress of shifting equilibria across 29 data points representing moments of multilateral political movement in the development of the trading system. The goal is to show an empirical pattern that we may explore in greater detail, both in terms of critical political junctures, as well as the subtler developmental processes underway between these points.

The third section examines the implications of a shifting equilibria pattern of institutional development for the legal evolution of the WTO. Here I answer two questions. First, how do shifting equilibria drive legal development? Concomitantly, what does this empirical pattern say about the ways that politics and law work together? The chapter concludes with a brief discussion of research trajectories, suggesting that a multidisciplinary approach is particularly well-suited to research projects related to the place of the WTO in international

Legal development at the WTO 65

economic law, the conceptual relationship between multilateralism and legal development, and other studies drawing upon the literatures examining economic convergence and the development of law.

Shifting equilibria and the GATT/WTO

In an influential article that tackled the conceptual basis of the treatment of non-tariff barriers to trade, Howse argued that the main problem facing the WTO was one of reconciling the goals of economic growth and macroeconomic stability with diverse national approaches to achieving this objective.[4] He described a pattern of sequential eras of problem-solving in which the postwar objective of open markets and full employment were engaged at the GATT/WTO through two modes of development that he termed the political (by which he meant domestic and multilateral strategies for solving the problems of governance coordination), and the technocratic (by which he meant institutional strategies for developing the organizational tools necessary for successful trade governance).

In the two decades following the Second World War, a "messy, multifaceted legal solution" was crafted.[5] This solution to postwar coordination challenges consisted of three pillars. The first was global governance, a deeply contested idea and perhaps the least successful aspect of the legal solution. The second was the non-violation, nullification and impairment clause of GATT that allowed members to make a claim against other members for compensation even where there was no specific violation of GATT provisions. This was a way of protecting the spirit of the GATT. The third pillar was the norm of non-discrimination, which Howse calls "a highly useful default rule, a tentative sorting of domestic policies."[6] This approach worked because of a shared commitment to embedded liberalism on the part of the early signers of the GATT. Embedded liberalism was a commitment to open markets, the welfare state, and a pluralistic respect for diverse approaches to solving the postwar challenge of full employment.[7]

The success of the "embedded liberalism bargain" led to forgetfulness about its nature as a "specific and contingent bargain about the interaction between freer trade and the welfare state."[8] Professionalization of the GATT proceeded apace as embedded liberalism began to be recast in the Anglo-American context as a deterministic brand of economic theory with a strong preference for open markets. In this way embedded liberalism may be considered a victim of its own success. Trade policy professionals lost sight of the basic principles of redistributive justice because those had always been the domain of the

66 *Legal development at the WTO*

welfare state. Ideological shifts at the national level began to shift the goal posts of national commitment to embedded liberalism throughout the late 1980s and 1990s as governments began to focus on the aggregate gains from market openness, rather than the careful balance between markets and social protection. The primary result was a new professional consensus on the centrality of open markets to global growth, and a basic forgetfulness about the importance of embedded mechanisms of social protection. The renewal of political debates over the usefulness of trade to the maintenance of the compromise embodied by embedded liberalism was a secondary result—in short, a return to politics, hence the title of his article, "From Politics to Technocracy—and Back Again."

Political scientists think a lot about how to theorize, track, and predict institutional change. There are a number of ways to think about change. We can imagine change as driven by internal or external factors, as happening slowly or in faster bursts of agency, and as happening incrementally or in a more wholesale fashion. Historical institutional approaches problematize the timing and sequencing of change. The argument about the pace and sequence of change in the global system of trade law begins with the assumption that the apparatus of trade governance is engaged, or its course corrected, by political events. These political events are often theorized as causal mechanisms that influence institutional change and legal development.

In the world of punditry and foreign affairs this is a basic truism, but is a little more challenging for social scientists to accept because it is difficult to draw a direct causal link between political event and subsequent institutional change. It is easier to draw links between micro-level causal mechanisms and institutional change.[9] For example, the actions of individuals can be traced quite easily to subsequent changes in political and economic processes if those individuals are in a decision-making role. But it is almost impossible to draw direct causal links between political events and institutional change. Probably the only truly effective way to do so would be through the lens of history and with the use of punctuated equilibrium theories that examine certain variables before and after the event.

Punctuated equilibrium was first developed in the life sciences as a way to theorize the process of evolutionary change in biological and ecological systems. Scientists understood that sometimes change happens slowly and steadily, and sometimes is occurs very suddenly. For example, dramatic shifts in environmental factors may require organic life to adapt in abrupt ways. This concept of punctuated change migrated to the social sciences over the past 25 years. Gersick

Legal development at the WTO 67

examined punctuated equilibrium theories in a number of scientific fields in order to hypothesize that punctuated equilibrium ought to be considered a paradigmatic hypothetical with a wide range of applications across the physical and social sciences.[10]

Roe examined the classic evolutionary model of change, looking for ways to adapt it for use in the social sciences. He argued that chaos theory, path dependence and punctuated equilibrium were unique, yet potentially interrelated approaches to thinking about organizational change.[11] Subsequently, scholars of a rational choice approach to understanding social change began to use punctuated equilibrium to explain path dependence. If institutions evolve according to set trajectories, how do causes change? Their answer was exogenous shock. This basic understanding of punctuated change as exogenous shock was further fleshed out by Levinthal, who examined punctuation in the context of technological change.[12] He showed that the critical event, or causal mechanism, is not a change in technology, but rather the application of existing technology to a new domain of application. While he does not undermine the basic understanding of the role of exogenous factors in institutional change, this speciation approach, to borrow a term from the biological sciences, has implications for our work because we can say the same for law. One of the drivers of development, alongside the causal mechanism of political event, is the application of existing legal norms to new domains of application, as we have seen in the development of dispute settlement rules at the WTO that owe a debt to tort law procedure in common law countries.

Returning to the question of how to link punctuation with the causal mechanism of political event, Tilcsik and Marquis capture the impact of political events on social behavior.[13] They examine corporate philanthropy in the wake of major political events or natural disasters. As predicted by Beach and Pederson, they show that the only way to gauge the causality of macro-scale events is to measure changes over time before and after the event. Punctuated equilibrium is now well established as the primary way to approach the question of how to think about institutional change that is the result of exogenous factors. However, institutions are not static creations without internal drivers of change. Hall argues that the best and most creative social science mixes the tools and insights of rational choice and institutionalism.[14] By this he means that social scientists must look for causal mechanisms inside institutions as well.[15] Institutions are changed by exogenous and endogenous factors as they travel along a path-dependent (or positive-feedback) trajectory of development

68   *Legal development at the WTO*

Path-dependent processes exhibit four features. First, path-dependent development is often established through multiple equilibria. Especially in the beginning of the development process, institutional momentum may shift between different sources of equilibrium. Second, we see contingent causation in which small events have very significant outcomes. Third, the timing and sequencing of events is important. We can see this in the creation of certain institutions at the end of the Second World War, at the end of the Cold War, and in the launch of a trade negotiating round following the terrorist attacks on New York in September 2001. Fourth, institutional inertia guides organizations towards a steady trajectory. Once a process begins, positive feedback "will generally lead to a single equilibrium."[16]

Moving beyond the question of which external factors are linked to institutional causality, research has begun to ask how internal factors give rise to change.[17] In the case of the WTO system, a new study was recently conducted that attempted to give shape to the rising importance of lawyers at the WTO. Marceau argued for the increasing importance of legal reasoning at the GATT and the subsequent rising importance of legal practitioners to the governance of international trade over the postwar period.[18] This work adds an important qualification to the narrative of change through multilateral consensus.

Historical institutionalism and path dependence have made their way into legal studies. Hathaway describes the way that legal development tends to move along steady tracks of path dependence.[19] She links historical institutional insights about the way that origins and internal organization shape institutional trajectories of growth with insights about how law follows a similar developmental path. In this way path-dependent arguments provide a counterpoint to a more blunt and less developed functionalist mode of argumentation in the realm of international law. Pierson shows that arguments about positive feedback suggest that institutional development cannot always be reduced to a simple functional explanation. To be fair, most functional arguments are not this simplistic, but it bears saying that path dependence ought not to be conflated with legal functionalism. Interestingly, the role of punctuated equilibrium in the development of law has not been well developed.

This study develops a shifting equilibria approach to mapping the history of postwar trade governance. Such an approach begins to develop a bridge between a punctuated equilibrium approach to theorizing change and the legal functionalism that tends to dominate in legal historical studies of the development of international economic law. In terms of method, I show a useful interplay between legal functionalism and historical institutional tools. Further, in both legal theory and the theory of political economy, this approach goes some way towards bridging the gap between rationalist and sociological modes of reasoning. The method developed here for charting political punctuation points in the equilibria of the GATT/WTO relies upon a more nuanced understanding of exogenous shock than is generally assumed in political economy. Punctuation points are not necessarily moments of macroeconomic or international political turmoil. Rather they are moments of political feedback that originate in the environment around the GATT/WTO. They are best conceptualized as insertion points in which exogenous factors make themselves felt inside the institution. These insertion points form an alternating pattern of causation at the WTO.

Political events are well established as a significant driver of institutional change, but they are not the only factor at play. From the creation of the GATT, to the creation of the WTO, we are able to see a basic continuity of approach at work in the development of the trading system. Isomorphic development is evidence of a certain internal logic guiding growth and change. In the larger context of the epistemic community of trade policy, institutional development is shaped by both a shared commitment to economic theory as well as the political logic of reciprocity, and these two conceptual poles give shape to the trade policy environment as well as some of the national strategies that influence the WTO's internal context.

Legal development at the GATT/WTO

The first section began with Howse's insight about the importance of periods of political and technocratic development at the WTO. Howse imagined larger periods, more like eras; I suggest a more structural, shifting equilibria approach to the periodization of multiple political events in order to gain a better understanding of how positive feedback (or what Pierson has termed critical junctures) drives the development of international economic law.[20] We also discussed briefly how social scientists conceptualize these critical junctures—often as large political events such as financial crises, and as such the measurement of their effects sometimes poses difficulties. Recent research, however, has shown that you can measure the impact of exogenous shocks on social behavior, although it is difficult, and works best in historical context. We then moved to the literature of Mahoney and Thelen, and Pierson, on path dependency. Here there were three important details of note. First, critical junctures are not the only way that institutions evolve.

70 Legal development at the WTO

They also evolve according to subtle shifts in internal logic and momentum. Second, institutional development processes often exhibit multiple equilibria. And finally, shifting equilibria play a role in creating positive feedback that drives institutional development.

This second section examines a number of these key political moments. Building upon the insights of Howse and the theoretical work that has taken place largely in the context of historical institutionalism, I have created a graphical representation of multilateral junctures at the GATT/WTO over the past 75 years. Figure 4.1 shows 29 major points of multilateral intervention into the development of the GATT/WTO. I have included in these critical junctures multilateral trade rounds, and in the case of multi-year rounds, the meetings that launched and concluded rounds. They also include major ministerial meetings in the later Tokyo (1973–79) and Uruguay (1986–94) Rounds. After the creation of the WTO in 1995, data points include biennial ministerial meetings, including those leading up to the launch of the Doha Round of trade negotiations in 2001. The top of the wave pattern represents time spent in multilateral trade negotiation, while the bottom of the pattern represents the time between formal negotiations. Members have been engaged in trade negotiations for 49 of the previous 76 years (see Figure 4.1). We move from here to a discussion of the substance of these critical junctures, and then an analysis in which we trace the process of change in order to show how these junctures act as causative events.

Critical junctures

We now turn to a brief examination of four sets of critical junctures that form the political context of legal development. These four sets of data points are the founding of the GATT (and the failure of the

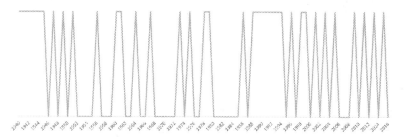

Figure 4.1 Shifting equilibria in the world trading system, 1940–2015
Source: Author's own creation.

Legal development at the WTO 71

International Trade Organization—ITO), the seven GATT negotiating rounds of the Cold War era, the Uruguay Round in which the WTO was created, and the subsequent biennial ministerial conferences that are mandated in the WTO Agreement. The data points grouped under the heading of war-era negotiations and the birth of the GATT include the Atlantic Charter, the Havana Charter, and a series of Anglo-American negotiating sessions that took place throughout the Second World War and up to the end of the ITO and the birth of a GATT-only system of trade regulation in 1947.

Irwin, Mavroidis and Sykes examined the structure and substance of Anglo-American economic negotiation in the years following the Second World War in order to develop a firm historical reading of the context, politics and economic goals pursued by the founders of the postwar trading system.[21] The world trading system is deeply rooted in British and American relations as embodied by the Atlantic Charter, the Mutual Aid Agreement, the Charter of the ITO and the General Agreement on Tariffs and Trade (GATT). Furthermore, much of the negotiating basis of the GATT rested upon the terms of lend-lease. Irwin et al. identify three main rationales for the negotiation of the GATT: first, to avoid terms of trade losses; second, to establish political and economic commitment against domestic interests; and third, to pursue foreign policy objectives related to peace and security.

In reviewing the negotiating history of the GATT, they find evidence of all three rationales but the case for a political bulwark against economic depression is actually the weakest. There is stronger evidence for terms of trade and security rationales.[22] Put another way, the preservation of terms of trade was a rationale implicit in the peace and security argument that was more important to the framers of the GATT than the academic literature has previously suggested. So the value of the GATT to its main multilateral boosters was its contribution to both global prosperity and its preservation of Anglo-American economic power. In October 1947, 23 nations met in Geneva and established the two pillars of the postwar trading system. The first was a legal frame for the negotiation of commercial policy—the GATT. The second was bilateral agreements to reduce tariffs, which were then extended to all other partners through the Most-Favored Nation (MFN) clause of the GATT. Without a dollar value attached to lend-lease, the American government, in particular Cordell Hull and the State Department, was free to extract a political price from the British—support for a new multilateral system for trade.

In this way the trading system was born of economic need, high principles and an American dislike of the British system of imperial

72 *Legal development at the WTO*

preferences, which had excluded American producers from lucrative markets in the British Empire. Canada also pushed hard to remake commercial policy in the postwar era, believing its future lay in exports to the United States, which had been growing significantly, at least since the 1930s. It was Canada's suggestion that the most effective way forward on trade multilateralism would be a smaller initial group of likeminded countries because "judging from past experience, the presence at a general international conference of the less important and for the most part protectionist-minded countries would invariably result in a watering down of the commitment."[23]

GATT was negotiated between 1946 and 1948 at the Preparatory Committee for the ITO in London, New York, Geneva, and Havana.[24] The immediate purpose of the GATT negotiations was to give the aspects of the ITO Charter dealing with trade restrictions a more definitive status. Also, the ITO itself would not deal with specific tariff reductions because that would be the purview of the GATT.[25] The ITO died when President Truman decided not to resubmit the Havana Charter to Congress in December 1950. In the nine years between the Atlantic Charter and the death of the ITO, American, Canadian and British diplomats would steadily move towards a comprehensive agreement to remove barriers to trade. The ITO was primarily an American idea. It was designed to be, in the words of Truman, "an integral part of the larger program of international reconstruction and development."[26]

According to Diebold there were three reasons the ITO eventually failed. First, changes in world affairs between 1945 and 1950, the beginning of the Cold War and the start of the Korean War. Second, changes in the political situation in the United States—with more focus on the Marshall Plan, the creation of the North Atlantic Treaty Organization (NATO), and new forms of global conflict, the last, and most complex and contentious piece of postwar planning seemed less pressing. Further, the provisional GATT had come into place in 1948. Third, American business groups were not enthusiastic about the ITO Charter. They felt it went too far in certain areas related to domestic regulation and not far enough in what they perceived to be the protectionist practices of other states, so there was no domestic pressure for Congress and the President to act. Further, the Charter's length and complexity meant that there was not much public interest.[27]

In practical terms the Charter walked a line between opening markets for commerce and protecting postwar commitments to full employment. Its combination of detailed rules and broad principles left it in the same position the modern WTO finds itself, with disciplines

Legal development at the WTO 73

that were either too rigorous or too permissive for more than 50 states that would have implemented it.[28] In Diebold's description, "the essence of this view was that the exceptions to the Charter's general rules, and the escape clauses applicable to special circumstances, were so numerous that most foreign countries could comply with the Charter without actually freeing trade from existing restrictions."[29]

The complaint was not with the principles of the Charter, but that the Charter did not go far enough to create the free trade ideal. On the other side, protectionist groups saw the ITO as a "superstate capable of directing American trade policy."[30] This is a sentiment that would not have appeared out of place among the critics of the modern trading order.[31] Following Truman's decision not to resubmit the Charter to Congress, portions of the stillborn ITO lived on in a number of definitional codes and international standards of the period, including the Code of the Liberalization of Trade, definitions of dumping, and definitions regarding customs unions in other agreements, not to mention provisions concerning intergovernmental commodity agreements.[32] And of course, many of these definitional and conceptual aspects of the ITO Charter found their way into the GATT, which had come into force in 1948. The GATT was a "narrower sphere of policy" that required little, if any, legislative action on the part of signatories, at least at the outset.[33] In the evocative words of Diebold, "GATT is the ITO manqué."[34]

The three options for multilateral trade governance that states faced in the early postwar period are the same basic options that they face today. First, ought prominent members to keep the GATT/WTO in as good a repair as possible or has it become an anachronism? Second, ought states to increase the liberalization of trade through bilateral, unilateral or plurilateral measures, or ought they to look for ways to strengthen the multilateral option? Third, ought states to revert to a more nationalistic and protectionistic set of practices if the first two options don't appear practicable? Miller thinks the GATT was revolutionary because it was successful in maintaining its demand upon the state to forgo its sovereign right to raise tariffs.[35] The first five rounds in the 1940s and 1950s focused on lowering tariffs through bilateral bargaining processes that were then generalized to the entire membership through the MFN principle. The Kennedy and Tokyo Rounds in the 1960s and 1970s added the issue of non-tariff barriers to trade, and attempted to juggle this expanded mandate along with a growing GATT membership, with greater or lesser success.

The increasing complexity of trade governance in a system with dozens of participating countries, many with special development

74 Legal development at the WTO

interests, meant that the postwar frame was coming under increasing stress by the 1970s. It was not able to deal well with agriculture, or the demands of developing countries for special treatment. The dispute settlement system was not very effective, and it was increasingly clear that the political order needed a larger mandate for dispute settlement. In the absence of effective dispute procedures, large traders such as the United States had begun to litigate trade issues in domestic courts, with predictable concerns raised about the fairness of such a practice.

Add to this changing macroeconomic climate the end of the Cold War, which left the United States as the world's only superpower. The growth of the European Union (EU) and the creation of the euro currency saw the rise of Europe as both multilateral partner and strategic counterweight to American economic supremacy. Even so, the Uruguay Round began without a firm idea to create a new trade organization despite the clear need for such an institution. By the end of the round, the so-called World Trade Organization was a full-blooded regulatory institution for global trade. It included a new focus on agriculture liberalization, safeguarding of reforms, new accession procedures, a new dispute settlement mechanism, a well-defined single undertaking for prospective members, new disciplines in intellectual property and services, and an increased awareness of participation for developing countries.[36]

Davey explains that the key new elements introduced in WTO dispute settlement were compulsory and exclusive jurisdiction on WTO-related disputes among members, automatic processes that cannot be blocked by respondents, tight timelines for each stage of the process, and an appellate body.[37] Debra Steger, the Canadian jurist tasked with setting up an appellate court, contends that Uruguay Round negotiators did not really intend to make a court because there is only one small provision—Article 17—in the Dispute Settlement Understanding (DSU) on appeals. They were, however, concerned that there might be "the occasional case in which a panel might render a 'bad report.'"[38] The Appellate Body was a quid pro quo to compensate losing the political right to block the adoption of panel reports. Most panel reports were appealed. By 2001 there were at least 12 appeals per year.[39]

In the 20 years since the establishment of the WTO the pattern of shifting equilibria is stronger than ever, with biennial ministerial conferences driving forward a liberalization and institutional development agenda, even as an overall negotiated package remains elusive. The WTO's main purpose is to secure the gains from trade for members while allowing them to maintain sovereign control over domestic regulatory and market institutions. Ministerial conference declarations act

Legal development at the WTO 75

as consolidation points in the liberalization process, road maps for future goals, and renew commitment to the multilateral process.

The terrorist attacks of September 11, 2001 were a political catalyst that drove trade policy professionals back to the bargaining table at Doha. However, without a shared commitment to embedded liberalism, and with a membership of 160 countries, it is unlikely that the multilateral process developed over the past 70 years is up to the challenge. Jones suggests that there are five basic problems facing the WTO in the Doha Round, some of which speak to the political environment, and others to the inability of the institution to deal effectively with an expansion of membership and mandate.

First, the Doha Agenda may extend liberalization disciplines too deeply behind the border for certain states. In this context the WTO set new goals without creating the capacity to reach these goals.[40] With so many members at different levels of industrial development, finding common ground (without an overarching commitment to the welfare state) is highly unlikely. Second, the single undertaking may create too high a bar for negotiating a liberalization package as large as Doha. Third, dysfunctional special and differential treatment guidelines have undercut the basic reciprocity function of the GATT/WTO.[41] Fourth, the shifting balance of economic power leads to deadlock. Combine this with the fact that now the WTO has stretched the original GATT framework in a number of ways.[42] Fifth, the dispute settlement system has increased the stakes of liberalization. Now agreements may be enforced by law. "The terms of any multilateral agreement would require implementation in the shadow of future DSU enforcement."[43]

In this changing institutional environment, Jones defines equilibrium in terms of the "achievement of consensus on achievement or supporting institutional factors or outcomes."[44] I have argued that equilibrium is a state in which the institution may make progress towards further development either at the bargaining table or through the processes governed by the secretariat. I agree with Jones that we may consider the institution to be in a state of equilibrium if members "continue to use the institution's framework in joint effort to move toward consensus."[45]

However, Franco recently remarked that "the difficulties that the Doha Round of multilateral negotiations is still facing ... have more to do with the absence of a new equilibrium in the multilateral trading system than with the specific trade matters at hand."[46] The rise of new trading powers and the proliferation of regional agreements are both causes of the WTO's malaise, as well as results of a lack of overarching consensus among the membership on the benefits of a multilateral

76 *Legal development at the WTO*

liberalization process. This debate about how to conceptualize institutional equilibrium after Doha is important because it speaks to the basic challenges inherent in legal development—the limits of consensus, the significance of legitimacy, and the crucial importance of political contestation to the entire undertaking. Yet while there is much to lament in the Doha Round, there is also a clear trajectory of institutional development.

There are several places where the current structure and process have produced significant outcomes. First, there is increasing agreement on the importance of small economies to the overall system, even if there is little consensus on how these members ought to relate to the liberalization process. This is perhaps one of the biggest outcomes at the WTO to date, and one that stands to make a very tangible mark on the institution. Second, we have also seen a marked increase in awareness of the importance of transparency in global governance, and an increased understanding of the relationship between trade and growth, especially in relation to investment, competition, capacity, and the rule of law. Third, there is also broad-based agreement on the importance of services trade to future growth and an increasing awareness of the challenges posed by services trade to small economies and poor countries. An agreement on trade facilitation at Bali in 2013 appears to be small potatoes when viewed out of context, but it was accompanied by a number of decisions on intellectual property, e-commerce, aid for trade, public stockpiling for food security purposes, and a host of other issues hardly imagined at the birth of the GATT, let alone at the end of the Uruguay Round.

When viewed in context, key decisions and the large agenda of work still left to do, ongoing negotiations suggest a subtle shift in orientation at the WTO (see Table 4.1). There are few tangible outcomes to point to as payoff for the membership at large. We may choose to read the post-Uruguay progress as stalled simply because the speed-to-progress ratio is so low, especially in relation to early GATT rounds. However, I would argue that this is the new speed of institutional development, as the WTO must not only accommodate the interests of many members, but also develop the institutional tools to effectively govern over an expanded mandate.

The space between

Considering the political economy of trade governance from the perspective of IEL offers a new analytic dimension to the well-known narrative of institutional development. It allows us to see the space

Legal development at the WTO 77

Table 4.1 Substantive decisions and future agenda, WTO ministerial conferences, 1996–2015

Year	Location	Key decisions	Future work
1996	Singapore	Declaration on Trade in Information Technology Products	Plan of action on least developed country (LDC) capacity; implementation of agreement on textiles and clothing; conclusion of telecom negotiations; continuation of financial services negotiations
1998	Geneva	Declaration on Global Electronic Commerce	Transparency improvement agreement implementation
1999	Seattle	No declaration	No declaration
2001	Doha	Launched Doha "Development Round" of liberalization negotiations; Declaration on the TRIPS Agreement and Public Health; decision on implementation-related issues and concerns; decision on subsidies procedures for developing country members; decision on waiver for EU-ACP Partnership Agreement; decision on EU transitional regime for banana imports	Continue implementation-related issues and concerns; begin negotiations on agriculture; services; non-agriculture tariff reduction; continue implementation of TRIPS Agreement; continue working groups on the relationship between trade and investment; the interaction between trade and competition policy; begin negotiations on transparency in government procurement, on clarifying and improving WTO rules, on clarifying and improving the DSU, on trade and the environment; continue work programs on electronic commerce, small economies; trade, debt, and finance; technology transfer; technical cooperation and capacity building; LDCs; special and differential treatment
2003	Cancun	No substantive agreement/no final decision	Continuation of work on outstanding issues
2005	Hong Kong	Decision on domestic support negotiations; decision on export subsidies negotiations; decision on structuring tariff cuts	Commitment to end export subsidies, domestic subsidies, and improved market access for cotton; complete services negotiations; continue negotiations on geographic indications under TRIPS; continue negotiations on trade and the environment; continue negotiations on trade facilitation; continue negotiations on DSU reform; continue negotiations on special and differential treatment; continue to resolve implementation issues
2009	Geneva	No negotiating sessions	Continuation of work on outstanding issues

78 *Legal development at the WTO*

Year	Location	Key decisions	Future work
2011	Geneva	Granted the General Agreement on Trade in Services (GATS) Art. XVI waiver to services and service suppliers of LDCs	Continue work of TRIPS Council on "non-violation and situation complaints"; continue work program on e-commerce; continue work program on small economies; direct committees to work towards streamlining accessions of LDCs; call upon the Trade Policy Review Body to continue strengthening its monitoring processes in the light of the financial crisis
2013	Bali	Agreement on Trade Facilitation; decisions on TRIPS non-violation and situation complaints, electronic commerce, small economies, aid for trade, transfer of technology, general services, public stockholding for food security purposes, tariff-rate quota administration for agriculture, export competition, cotton, rules of origin for LDCs, preferential treatment to services of LDCs, duty-free, quota-free market access for LDCs, monitoring mechanism for special and differential treatment	Implementation of all Bali Ministerial Decisions, especially with regards to the Doha Development Agenda
2015	Nairobi	The Nairobi Package—decisions on a special safeguard mechanism for developing country members (agriculture), export competition, cotton, preferential rules of origin for LDCs, extension of waiver for preferential treatment for services and service providers of LDCs	Negotiation on the creation of a permanent mechanism for public stockholding for food security purposes; continue the work program on small economies; continue TRIPS Council work on TRIPS non-violation and situation complaints; continue the work program on e-commerce

Source: Based on data from WTO Ministerial Conference Documentation.

between political events and in this way it does what Thelen and Mahoney set out to do, which is to show how internal logics play a large role in institutional development.[47] It also allows us to speculate about the future by examining the political dynamics that have facilitated legal change in the postwar trading system. I have shown how using a basic process-tracing method, we can see how multilateral meetings are causative events. The founding political process, including the creation of the GATT and the death of the ITO, set the stage for

Legal development at the WTO 79

the development of a small and tightly organized GATT secretariat. For the sake of brevity I will not break the first five GATT negotiating rounds down to their constituent meetings. With the growth of the membership in the 1960s and 1970s, the continued development of the multilateral process in this era, and the treatment of new issue areas such as non-tariff barriers, the Kennedy and Tokyo Rounds mark the beginning of a new phase of legal development at the GATT.

This process comes to a new punctuation point in the 1980s. The Uruguay Round is the clearest example of this multilateral shift because the WTO is the direct outcome of Uruguay negotiations. And then at the end of the 20th century, with an institutionalized process of biennial ministerial conferences we can see that the process of legal development makes it more difficult to determine a clear dynamic of causation. As the work of the WTO becomes more technical and complex, multilateral meetings still drive the evolution of the secretariat. However, the needs of the institution also shape the agenda of multilateral meetings. The secretariat and the ministerial conference are becoming the twin engines of causation that drive the law and politics of trade governance.

Many of the GATT's creators preferred to think of the multilateral project as a political and economic one, rather than a legal one. They desired to keep law at a distance. They believed in the idea that law, as the formal application of a system of rules, would undermine the political compromises upon which the multilateral trading system was built. Furthermore, they believed that problems should be solved by political compromise rather than recourse to law, which might create winners and losers in a way that could undermine the legitimacy of a system that had already been dealt a blow by the failure of the American Congress to ratify the ITO. Therefore, we see a basic contradiction at the heart of the GATT—distrust of "formal legalism," but a "deep commitment to rules and rules-based conduct."[48]

It was the success of the diplomatic approach that avoided lawyers which increased the legitimacy of the GATT in its early years. Even so, the move towards ad hoc dispute settlement panels in the 1950s was the first step towards the legalization of the GATT.[49] The slow shift towards legalization was necessary because the GATT had so many moving parts, each of which was incredibly important to the overall health of the entire system. Williams suggests that while the concept of a rules-based system for trade is not new—after all, bilateral trade agreements are one of the oldest forms of reciprocal agreements—the GATT was the first multilateral agreement based on the principle of one set of rules for all participants.[50] This single undertaking, coupled

80 *Legal development at the WTO*

with the principle of reciprocity, creates an institution that must move along with more than 100 other state partners, a process that seems simple in the context of economic theory, wherein the benefits of trade liberalization are clear and unambiguous, but in practicality is anything but.[51]

In a much earlier study, Hudec charts the legal development of the GATT through its increasing challenges around dispute settlement.[52] Dispute settlement had already begun by 1948, and developed along a working party (and sometime expert panel) trajectory. He calls the early panel processes a limited success in part because "the GATT disputes procedure never really succeeded in establishing and institutionalizing independent authority."[53] As a result, beginning in the 1960s the membership began to balk against the inadequate mechanisms of the GATT. Throughout the 1960s and 1970s, the GATT faced increasing challenges around dispute settlement and legal enforcement generally. The best example is the treatment of agricultural surpluses under GATT Article XI:2 (having to do with dumping). Hudec further describes "a process of legal decline" between the Kennedy and Tokyo Rounds.[54] Decline accompanied an upswing in trade discrimination across the board, an increasing blocification of trade around the development efforts of the European Economic Community, and the rising frustration of developing countries asking for both differential treatment as well as a stronger legal order.[55]

By the mid-1970s GATT legal reform was on the agenda of leading multilateral partners such as the United States, EU and Canada. The Trade Act of 1974 called for GATT legal reform, and on many other fronts the GATT's comparative legal weakness was openly discussed.[56] The Tokyo Round negotiations would have been an ideal time to discuss reform, but as Hudec tartly remarks, there was little substantive reform because liberalization rounds are "'trade negotiations' rather than 'law reform negotiations.'"[57] Further, as Ostry notes, the Tokyo Round foundered partly on Europe's unwillingness to shoulder the burden of multilateral leadership alongside the United States, and partly on a changing understanding among US policy-makers as to the substantive meaning of reciprocity. They began working towards an "export oriented protectionism" in which reciprocity is defined in terms of "market shares on a sectoral basis" rather than an "overall balance in reduction of protectionism."[58]

Perhaps the most noteworthy aspect of the early years of dispute settlement was the very large number of cases. Many of them were controversial because they were holdovers from the GATT years where cases that dealt with similar issues had been blocked.[59] The birth of the WTO brought legal scholars and social scientists together for two reasons. First, the question of how WTO law would interact with international law drew upon the bodies of knowledge in both political science and law. Second, the dispute settlement mechanism (DSM) was a prolific producer of dispute settlement reports, which could be mined by scholars in both fields for implications for governance, law, and the future success of the post-Cold War liberalization project.

Writing about the creation of the WTO, Petersmann has highlighted the significance of a developmental shift from a rule by law, to the rule of law.[60] He argues that the creation of the WTO in 1995 required a cognitive shift from the operation of the trading system according to basic rules, to the governance of the system according to the principles and procedures of international law. This move to rule of law means that members need to shift the pursuit of self-interest through a system checked by state power towards a system that recognizes that "rule-compliance ... often depends on their acceptance of law as being justifiable by 'principles of justice' and institutional 'checks and balances' restraining the passions and rational egoism of human beings."[61] As a result, for the WTO to become a more legitimate institution in the 21st century, it will have to better balance public and private interests. In particular, the interpretation of treaties in dispute settlement requires more than simple interpretation of "text, context, objective and purpose of governmental rules."[62] It also requires that interpretation of treaties "remain in conformity with the principles of justice and international law ... [including] human rights and fundamental freedoms for all."[63]

The rule of law cuts two ways. It is certainly a more effective method of rule-making because it makes compliance more certain. But it also requires that states pay more than lip service to the fundamental principles of fairness and respect for human rights. In this way Petersmann brings basic functionalist questions of institutional effectiveness into contact with larger, normative questions about the purpose of law, the cognitive factors that influence its development, and basic philosophic concepts that animate political and legal theory such as the nature of fairness and notion of right.

With the birth of the WTO, the multilateral process was further refined and institutionalized, with mandated biennial ministerial conferences established by Article IV of the Agreement Establishing the World Trade Organization. We can see now the subtle interplay between multilateral meeting and institutional development, as issues of importance are discussed and then decisions taken have an impact on the developmental trajectory of the institution. However, the interplay between meetings and the institution highlights a further question. Do the outcomes of ministerial meetings create an impetus for

82 *Legal development at the WTO*

development, or do the needs of the institution cause issues to be raised at meetings? To place this question in the wording that Howse favored, is trade regulation today driven by the needs of politics, or the requirements of technocracy? Has the legal system developed a will of its own with which to drive forward institutional development? These is a question that we cannot answer definitively, although we can suggest that if it has not done so at this point, it is likely to be the case in the future.

Shifting equilibria in the larger context

The basic question animating the last section of this chapter is, how do shifting equilibria create the momentum necessary for legal development? Shifting equilibria create political opportunities to resolve institutional challenges. Problems that are intractable from inside the institution are contextualized through the multilateral process. Further, given the importance of a broad-based buy-in from many states, the multilateral process creates legitimacy. At the same time politics creates challenges that need to be resolved. In both of these contexts, politics may be an impetus to develop novel approaches to both existing and emerging challenges. These approaches may improve upon previous approaches and in this way the evolutionary process may happen a bit faster. Ultimately, politics creates a need for law, and law responds with the framework that politics needs to operate more effectively. This is the feedback process that drives the development of not only the WTO, but the rest of the system of international economic law as well.

This concept of shifting equilibria is not without precedent. In a notable article published more than a decade ago, Helfer describes a similar dynamic unfolding in the domain of intellectual property rights governance, in which states and nongovernmental organizations identify concerns they have with the Agreement on Trade-Related Aspects of Intellectual Property Rights (TRIPS), and raise these issues in other institutional venues. Helfer calls this regime shifting, and suggests that it is a strategy for moving problematic governance issues to new contexts to achieve a better outcome.[64] Regime shifting is a similar process to that which I have described taking place inside the WTO, whereby institutional momentum shifts between multilateral and institutional footing. For Helfer, regime shifting is part of the new complexity of international economic law-making, and I would argue that it is also an effective way for states and international organizations to drive forward the process of institutional development by creating traction at multiple points in a regime complex. Positive feedback in one mechanism may drive issues forward on multiple fronts. Regime

Legal development at the WTO 83

shifting emphasizes the changing balance points and the maintenance of momentum through shifting equilibria.

Helfer also notes that regime shifting helps governance institutions keep up with the changing international political and legal environment. Increasing issue density "and the linkages it has spawned, have increased the 'demand' for international regimes to help manage these complex policy interfaces."[65] Institutional actors understand that this increased demand is not met in the first instance by an expansion of any one regime. So shifts in equilibria move issues around so that current mechanisms can "catch up," or develop responses to changing challenges. I have argued that this shifting process happens "in-house" at the WTO, and is the reason that the WTO's rapid expansion of governance scale, scope and capacity has been as successful as it has been.

This study does not intend to portray the development of law as taking place in a value-neutral environment. Leading state powers pursue multilateral strategies and the creation of international law in order to legitimize certain configurations of power and to enhance the effectiveness of governance arrangements. As Stone shows, the challenges of economic and political interdependence always require a high degree of interstate coordination.[66] The basic problem of coordination is that multilateralism does not always benefit strong and weak states equally. Small states have an obvious incentive to cooperate, but strong states do not. Why do strong states maintain multilateral institutions when they do not have the assurance that their partnership will work in their favor? Stone's answer is that the strong states that created the multilateral system, maintain back-channel mechanisms of informal governance by which they influence the outcome of multilateral processes.

One important example is the informal bilateral negotiations that take place at the WTO, by which the EU and United States seek to sway smaller states to support their vision for multilateral trade liberalization. Of course, informal governance has not become relevant recently. One could argue that informal political processes of the sort examined by Stone, created the contours of the postwar economic system, from the negotiation of lend-lease between the United States and the UK, to the last-minute machinations of Harry Dexter White at the Bretton Woods Conference.[67] Stone's understanding of informal governance gets at an important aspect of the relationship between politics and law in the international system. Legal development is always political, even as it leads to more law. Changing law is always a political process. However, once there is a legal system in place, the process by which legal mechanisms evolve, while driven by politics, is itself a piece of the legal environment.

84 *Legal development at the WTO*

Conclusion

There are four main ways to explain change in the world trading system—economic theory, game theoretic explanations of reciprocity, historical institutional approaches, and power-based theories of change. To complicate matters, conceptualizing change in the world trading system requires analysis of two cross-cutting dynamics. The first is the sharp increase in the scale, scope and complexity of political multilateralism. The second is the steady growth of the treaties and institutional processes that now form the basis of international economic law. This chapter has developed a modified historical institutional approach that makes use of insights from the theories of punctuated equilibrium and positive feedback/path dependence. In doing so I have attempted to account for both the increasing complexity of multilateralism as well as the growth of international economic law.

Over the past seven decades the global system of trade regulation has passed through many transformative moments, from the death of the proposed International Trade Organization, to the phenomenal growth of the GATT system, and the creation of the World Trade Organization. The WTO faces a number of challenges, including failure to conclude the longest negotiating round in history and, concomitantly, the rise of a number of regional agreements that attempt to jumpstart the liberalization process. All indicators point towards a continuation of a shifting equilibria pattern as the WTO attempts to come to grips with the challenges of the 21st century.

This study of the shifting equilibria that have facilitated legal development at the GATT/WTO shows in the first instance that there is still much work to be done in developing the empirical evaluation of the previous seven decades of legal development. In the second instance, it opens the possibility of thinking about the simultaneity of politics and law in rapidly growing terrain of international economic law. This research also has implications for the conceptual relationship between multilateralism and legal development—for example the relationship between consensus building and constitutionalism is under-explored, as is the comparative development of different mechanisms of international law. Further, many other legal and political challenges around economic convergence and legal densification remain unexamined. Finally, the argument above shows the basic compatibility between legal thought and IPE, and suggests that bringing these two interdisciplinary fields of study into closer proximity offers a number of new ways to think about the place of politics in the brave new world of international economic law.

Notes

1 Kathleen Thelen and James Mahoney, eds., *Explaining Institutional Change: Ambiguity, Agency, and Power* (Cambridge: Cambridge University Press, 2010).

2 Gabrielle Marceau, ed., *A History of Law and Lawyers in the GATT/WTO: The Development of the Rule of Law in the Multilateral Trading System* (Cambridge: Cambridge University Press, 2015).

3 Robert Howse, "From Politics to Technocracy—and Back Again: The Fate of the Multilateral Trading Regime," *American Journal of International Law* 96, no. 1 (January 2002): 94–117.

4 Howse, "From Politics to Technocracy—and Back Again," 94–101.

5 Howse, "From Politics to Technocracy—and Back Again," 96.

6 Howse, "From Politics to Technocracy—and Back Again," 96.

7 John Gerard Ruggie, "International Regimes, Transactions, and Change: Embedded Liberalism in the Postwar Economic Order," *International Organization* 36, no. 2 (1982): 379–415.

8 Howse, "From Politics to Technocracy—and Back Again," 98.

9 Derek Beach and Rasmus Brun Pederson, *Process-Tracing Methods: Foundations and Guidelines* (Ann Arbor: University of Michigan Press, 2013), 23–67.

10 Connie J.G. Gersick, "Revolutionary Change Theories: A Multilevel Exploration of the Punctuated Equilibrium Paradigm," *Academy of Management Review* 18, no. 1 (1991): 10–36.

11 Mark J. Roe, "Chaos and Evolution in Law and Economics," *Harvard Law Review* 109 (1996): 641–668.

12 Daniel A. Levinthal, "The Slow Pace of Rapid Technological Change: Gradualism and Punctuation in Technological Change," *Industrial and Corporate Change* 7, no. 2 (1998): 217–247.

13 Andras Tilcsik and Christopher Marquis, "Punctuated Generosity: How Mega-Events and Natural Disasters Affect Corporate Philanthropy in U.S. Communities," *Administrative Science Quarterly* 58, no. 1 (2013): 111–148.

14 Peter A. Hall, "Historical Institutionalism in Rationalist and Sociological Perspective," in *Explaining Institutional Change: Ambiguity, Agency, and Power*, ed. James Mahoney and Kathleen Thelen (Cambridge: Cambridge University Press, 2009), 220.

15 Political scientists Paul Pierson and Kathleen Thelen have separately published a lot of research on sociological and historical approaches to institutional development. Their research emphasizes the importance of subtle internal shifts in logic and institutional momentum over long time horizons. Writing about the importance of long time horizons, Pierson argues that "attentiveness to issues of temporality highlight aspects of social life that are essentially invisible from an ahistorical vantage point" (p. 2). A focus on the temporal dimension of social science cuts across the divide between rational choice and historical institutional approaches to thinking about social science (p. 8). See Paul Pierson, *Politics in Time: History, Institutions, and Social Analysis* (Princeton, N.J.: Princeton University Press, 2004). See also Kathleen Thelen, "Historical Institutionalism in Comparative Politics," *American Review of Political Science* 2 (1999): 369–404.

16 Pierson, *Politics in Time*, 44.

86 *Legal development at the WTO*

17 Thelen and Mahoney, eds. *Explaining Institutional Change.*
18 Gabrielle Marceau, "The Primacy of the WTO Dispute Settlement System," *QIL, Zoom-in* 23 (2015): 3–13.
19 Oona A. Hathaway, "Path Dependence in the Law: The Course and Pattern of Legal Change in a Common Law System" (2003), http://digitalcommons.law.yale.edu/lepp_papers/270.
20 Pierson, *Politics in Time*, 135.
21 Douglas A. Irwin, Petros C. Mavroidis, and Alan O. Sykes, *The Genesis of the GATT* (Cambridge: Cambridge University Press, 2009).
22 Irwin et al., *The Genesis of the GATT*, 197–198.
23 Irwin et al., *The Genesis of the GATT*, 63.
24 Irwin et al., *The Genesis of the GATT*, 98.
25 Irwin et al., *The Genesis of the GATT*, 74.
26 William Diebold, "The End of the ITO," Princeton University, www.princeton.edu/~ies/IES_Essays/E16.pdf (1952), 2.
27 Diebold, "The End of the ITO," 10.
28 Diebold, "The End of the ITO," 12–13.
29 Diebold, "The End of the ITO," 14.
30 Diebold, "The End of the ITO," 23.
31 Claude E. Barfield, *Free Trade, Sovereignty, Democracy: The Future of the World Trade Organization* (Washington, DC: AEI Press, 2001).
32 Diebold, "The End of the ITO," 25.
33 Diebold, "The End of the ITO," 28.
34 Diebold, "The End of the ITO," 30.
35 James N. Miller, "Origins of the GATT: British Resistance of American Multilateralism," Social Science Research Network, http://ssrn.com/abstract=256005 (2000).
36 Kent Jones, *Reconstructing the World Trade Organization for the 21st Century* (Oxford: Oxford University Press, 2015), 60.
37 William J. Davey, "The First Years of WTO Dispute Settlement: Dealing with Controversy and Building Confidence," in *A History of Law and Lawyers in the GATT/WTO: The Development of the Rule of Law in the Multilateral Trading System*, ed. Gabrielle Marceau (Cambridge: Cambridge University Press, 2015).
38 Debra P. Steger, "The Founding of the Appellate Body," in *A History of Law and Lawyers in the GATT/WTO: The Development of the Rule of Law in the Multilateral Trading System*, ed. Gabrielle Marceau (Cambridge: Cambridge University Press, 2015), 447.
39 Steger, "The Founding of the Appellate Body," 452.
40 Jones, *Reconstructing the World Trade Organization for the 21st Century*, 80.
41 Jones, *Reconstructing the World Trade Organization for the 21st Century*, 8.
42 Jones, *Reconstructing the World Trade Organization for the 21st Century*, 21.
43 Jones, *Reconstructing the World Trade Organization for the 21st Century*, 63.
44 Jones, *Reconstructing the World Trade Organization for the 21st Century*, 56.
45 Jones, *Reconstructing the World Trade Organization for the 21st Century*, 57.
46 Renzo Franco, "From the GATT to the WTO: A Personal Journey," in *A History of Law and Lawyers in the GATT/WTO: The Development of the Rule of Law in the Multilateral Trading System*, ed. Gabrielle Marceau (Cambridge: Cambridge University Press, 2015), 176.
47 Thelen and Mahoney, eds., *Explaining Institutional Change.*

Legal development at the WTO 87

48 Gabrielle Marceau, "Introduction and Overview," in *A History of Law and Lawyers in the GATT/WTO: The Development of the Rule of Law in the Multilateral Trading System*, ed. Gabrielle Marceau (Cambridge: Cambridge University Press, 2015), 8.

49 Marceau, "Introduction and Overview," 11–13.

50 Peter Williams, "Law and Lawyers in the Multilateral Trading System: Back to the Future," in *A History of Law and Lawyers in the GATT/WTO: The Development of the Rule of Law in the Multilateral Trading System*, ed. Gabrielle Marceau (Cambridge: Cambridge University Press, 2015), 85–90.

51 Williams, "Law and Lawyers in the Multilateral Trading System," 88.

52 Robert Hudec, *The GATT Legal System and World Trade Diplomacy* (New York: Praeger Publishers, 1975).

53 Hudec, *The GATT Legal System and World Trade Diplomacy*, 190.

54 Hudec, *The GATT Legal System and World Trade Diplomacy*, 214.

55 Hudec, *The GATT Legal System and World Trade Diplomacy*, 204–213.

56 Hudec, *The GATT Legal System and World Trade Diplomacy*, 239.

57 Hudec, *The GATT Legal System and World Trade Diplomacy*, 265.

58 Sylvia Ostry, *The Post-Cold War Trading System: Who's on First?* (Chicago, Ill.: University of Chicago Press, 1997), 94.

59 The best examples are EC—Bananas III, EC—Hormones, Japan—Film, and US—Shrimp. For a full description of these and all other WTO cases, visit www.wto.org/english/tratop_e/dispu_e/dispu_status_e.htm.

60 Ernst-Ulrich Petersmann, "The Establishment of the GATT Office of Legal Affairs and the Limits of 'Public Reason' in the GATT/WTO Dispute Settlement System," in *A History of Law and Lawyers in the GATT/WTO: The Development of the Rule of Law in the Multilateral Trading System*, ed. Gabrielle Marceau (Cambridge: Cambridge University Press, 2015).

61 Petersmann, "The Establishment of the GATT Office of Legal Affairs and the Limits of 'Public Reason' in the GATT/WTO Dispute Settlement System," 185.

62 Petersmann, "The Establishment of the GATT Office of Legal Affairs and the Limits of 'Public Reason' in the GATT/WTO Dispute Settlement System," 197.

63 Petersmann, "The Establishment of the GATT Office of Legal Affairs and the Limits of 'Public Reason' in the GATT/WTO Dispute Settlement System," 197.

64 Laurence Helfer, "Regime Shifting: The TRIPs Agreement and New Dynamics of International Intellectual Property Lawmaking," *Yale Journal of International Law* 29, no. 1 (2004): 5.

65 Helfer, "Regime Shifting," 8.

66 Randall W. Stone, *Controlling Institutions: International Organizations and the Global Economy* (Cambridge: Cambridge University Press, 2011).

67 Benn Steil, *The Battle of Bretton Woods: John Maynard Keynes, Harry Dexter White and the Making of a New World Order* (Princeton, N.J.: Princeton University Press, 2013).

5 Regionalism and the centralization of trade governance

- Proliferation, fragmentation and international economic law
- Incentives
- Interests
- Ideas
- Income level
- Institutional investment
- Legal fragmentation
- The WTO's exclusive jurisdiction and regional dispute settlement systems
- Recent trends in the development of regional trade agreements
- Governance value chains
- The reinsurance hypothesis
- The institutional investment hypothesis
- Conclusion

I have argued that the global political economy is moving into an era in which law, its evolution, and its purposive development, are changing international economic relations. I have described this cognitive, normative and institutional shift as a move from politics and law, to the politics of law at the global level. I have shown in the previous chapter that the process of legal development at the WTO is not necessarily typified by inertia and deadlock. Rather, the WTO is following a developmental trajectory in which multilateral politics and institutional processes interact to broaden and deepen governance capacity. This is a long process in which periods of multilateral movement set the stage for institutional growth and consolidation.

The WTO's capacity to govern complex political and economic processes is increasing. Yet in its short institutional life trade agreements have proliferated. The WTO went from being the only authoritative source of binding trade law, to being one of a number of

Regionalism and centralized trade governance 89

competitors, many of which attempt to extend and add to WTO disciplines while offering arbitral mechanisms that mimic some of the best aspects of the Dispute Settlement Understanding (DSU). This chapter turns to the question of legal fragmentation. The rapid proliferation of courts and regulatory bodies, and the increasing levels of professionalization and legal specialization required to operate them cause some scholars to wonder whether legal development may not be undermined by its own success.[1] In this chapter I ask if the proliferation of regional trade agreements (RTAs) has increased the threat of fragmentation in the growing terrain of international economic law.

This question has two dimensions. First, does the proliferation of trade agreements that reach beyond the current bounds of WTO governance raise the risk of creating silos of law? This would be an example of legal fragmentation because it undercuts the basic principle of a level playing field for all countries in terms of legal process. Second, does the proliferation of dispute settlement mechanisms, draw disputes away from the WTO system? To quote the Reverend Lovejoy of *The Simpsons*, the short answer to these questions is "yes with an 'if'" and the long answer is "no with a 'but'."[2] The major concerns are twofold. Either states will shop for the forum where they think they will get the best outcome, creating a proliferation of courts and a confusion of decisions of varying legal quality. Or, large economies will outright prefer the regional court because they offer the dominant economic partner a home court advantage. I intend to show that while both concerns are possible given the right circumstances (the yes with an "if"), they are highly unlikely outcomes (the no with a "but").

The first section of this chapter examines the issue of fragmentation as it relates to the legal process and a level playing field for governance. We first briefly discuss the history of RTA proliferation before moving to a discussion of social scientific approaches to explaining the growth of RTAs in the past two decades. I suggest that there are five basic approaches that focus on the role of incentives, interests, ideas, national income levels, and national levels of institutional development in the explanation of regional trade agreement proliferation. Next we turn to the issue of legal fragmentation. I discuss several reasons for fragmentation, including legal specialization and uneven institutional development.

The main reason why RTAs are so interesting in the context of trade governance is not because they extend legal discipline further, or in new directions per se. If this were all they did, they would be of an entirely lower order of scholarly interest. Rather we find them interesting because they contain institutional elements that mimic many

90   *Regionalism and centralized trade governance*

elements found in the WTO, and in some cases (such as the case of investor-state dispute settlement), they extend their institutional tendrils beyond the WTO's reach. In this way, they set themselves up as potential competitors and rivals to multilateral trade governance.

From this discussion of proliferation and legal fragmentation we turn to an empirical examination of court systems in regional trade agreements. The second section examines the proliferation of dispute settlement systems. In the first instance we discuss this proliferation in the context of the legal agreements that govern the WTO's exclusive jurisdiction over trading issues covered by WTO agreements. From there we turn to an empirical examination of RTA dispute settlement mechanisms and I show that there is a clear shift in the post-1995 period towards both more agreements, and agreements with full dispute settlement mechanisms. Then we move to the question of what those dispute settlement mechanisms are designed to adjudicate. By surveying the texts of all the active RTAs notified to the WTO, I show a clear pattern of dispute settlement exclusion clauses and special provisions designed to both respect the exclusive jurisdiction built into the WTO Agreement as well as to extend the reach of dispute settlement in relation to foreign investment. The largest and most controversial aspect of these regional agreements is their investor-state dispute settlement (ISDS) provisions. And it could be argued that given the careful framing of dispute settlement in RTAs, and their many exclusion provisions, that a primary role of these many agreements is to support ISDS.

The third section explores the implications of RTA proliferation for multilateral trade governance. At this point, neither of these concerns, silos of law nor the fragmentation of dispute settlement authority, has occurred in an empirically demonstrable way. The most recent concern has been that RTAs set the stage for a major reordering of the global trade governance environment. I disagree, arguing that given the ambiguous impact of RTAs on global trade governance there are two ways to consider their influence. The first approach theorizes RTAs to be a form of reinsurance and the second hypothesizes that RTAs may act together with domestic regulation and the WTO as links in a governance value chain. I show a somewhat counterintuitive pattern in which an expanding web of RTAs is the result of a centralized and increasingly legitimate organ of multilateral trade governance that decreases the opportunity costs of regional arrangements while highlighting the importance for future growth of governmental strategies that facilitate global interdependence.

Proliferation, fragmentation and international economic law

Shortly after the Second World War, J.B. Condliffe wrote, "in trading history, if enterprise is the theme, regulation is the counterpoint."[3] The history of trade is also the history of the regulation of commerce. What was true of royal control over ancient trading routes, goes doubly for the modern trading system in which markets are developed and maintained through domestic regulation and international treaty. The postwar trading system was predicated upon the vision of a multilateral system of trade regulation, and as Davey has noted, the original ITO's approach to the MFN principle would have precluded regional trade arrangements.[4]

The postwar framers of the GATT acknowledged the importance of flexibility in the service of differing national social priorities. The United States proposed an exception for customs unions, and this carve-out, known as Article XXIV of the GATT, was gradually broadened to include other forms liberalization such as regional trade agreements. In the years immediately following the Second World War preferential agreements were not used extensively and were not particularly controversial for two reasons. First, in a world of high tariffs any movement towards liberalization was welcome, although multilateralism was accorded pride of place. Second, theoretical issues around trade diversion were not fully articulated by economists, and in fact were not part of the professional lexicon of trade policy scholars until Jacob Viner published *The Customs Union Issue* in 1950.[5]

Since those early years, three main eras of postwar regionalization have been identified.[6] The first era covers the 25 years through the 1970s. In this era we see the beginnings of what became the EU when six states formed the European Economic Community (EEC) in the latter half of the 1950s. In 1960, seven other European states formed the European Free Trade Agreement (EFTA) to represent the interests of states that were unable or unwilling to join the fledgling EEC. In this period we also see the formation of early regional economic blocs in Africa and Asia, and the formation of the Generalized System of Preferences (GSP) at the GATT in 1971.

The GSP was a series of waivers that allowed GATT signatories to lower their tariff walls to incoming goods from developing countries without regard to the MFN principle.[7] As such, the GSP was designed to create incentives for producers in developing countries to sell their products on global markets. The GSP rode the wave of decolonization in 1970s, and in this period we began to see developing countries look for possible trade arrangements with developed countries, although the first developed/developing country RTA would be the North American

92 *Regionalism and centralized trade governance*

Free Trade Agreement (NAFTA), signed by Canada, the United States and Mexico in 1993.

The second era roughly corresponds to the 1980s and 1990s. During these decades at the end of the Cold War, a number of agreements were initiated by the Anglo-American countries including the Closer Economic Relations Agreement between New Zealand and Australia in 1983, the Canada-United States Free Trade Agreement of 1989, NAFTA in 1993, and expansion of the EU to 15 members in 1995.[8] More agreements were signed in this era than in the previous one, with the emphasis on expansion in Europe and the beginnings of a bilateral strategy emerging in American trade policy.

The third era might be termed the post-Uruguay Round era, or the era of the WTO. In the present period, we have seen massive growth in both the scale and scope of regional trade agreements. Crawford and Fiorentino identify four main trends in the post-Uruguay Round era.[9] First, RTAs have begun to move to the center of commercial policy in highly developed states. It is certainly the case that the negotiating momentum belongs to the new so-called mega-regional agreements such as the Trans-Pacific Partnership (TPP). Second, regional agreements are becoming increasingly complex. These are frequently full-blooded agreements that include dispute settlement provisions similar to those of the WTO. Third, this era has also witnessed a sharp rise in the number of reciprocal agreements between developing and developed countries. Finally, the general pattern among these hundreds of regional agreements is one of legal expansion and consolidation.

Social scientists ask two types of questions about regional integration. First, how are these processes possible? That is, what strategies do government officials use to create regional legal interdependence? Second, why bother? What makes regional agreements attractive in the first place? Cooley and Spruyt's theory of incomplete contracting can be used to describe the way that trade agreements are used to transfer sovereignty between states and intergovernmental institutions. Most RTAs fit this broad descriptive of "strategic incompleteness" because, like many incomplete forms of transfer, they leave many clauses "initially unspecified or deferred for future negotiation."[10]

Most RTAs include a number of clauses that express intent to cooperate or announce plans for future negotiation and as such they are in these areas (competition policy is a prime example) expressions of friendship and goodwill more than completed contracts per se. In answering the first question, Cooley and Spruyt show that the contracting that takes place in a regional trade agreement involves a reconfiguration of relationships and it is not always clear which

Regionalism and centralized trade governance 93

sovereign powers are transferred, which are not, and under what conditions these powers may revert to the state. In short, their model shows why some agreements are more comprehensive than others and why trade agreements are generally less complete than the idea of a legal agreement might suggest.[11]

Some of the recent literature has focused on how different countries with different cultures, laws, and interests have negotiated the process of regional integration. For example, Duina asks how political, social, and institutional forces made possible the process of integration, and more specifically, how national officials navigated these treacherous waters in order to create unique national strategies for regionalization.[12] Using NAFTA, the EU, and Mercosur as case studies, he argues that officials in nations with a civil law tradition tend to create comprehensive agreements and those in common law traditions tend to create agreements that were less well-specified, if only because this suits the political and institutional cultures of the participants.

We know the "how" of regional proliferation, but scholars are still undecided on the "why" question. There are five ways to explain the proliferation of regional trade agreements. I call these the five "I's" of proliferation.

Incentives

Incentives for regionalization are usually framed in terms of the gains from trade. If WTO-led liberalization got our state this far, governmental leaders might reason, perhaps a smaller regional push to drive forward WTO-extra and WTO-plus disciplines will create more wealth. This may be termed the integration-creates-opportunity-and-growth hypothesis. Are the gains from trade sufficient to justify a new regional agreement? Crawford and Fiorentino note that it is hard to empirically assess trade creation and diversion effects on an agreement-by-agreement basis. To be frank, we really cannot fully quantify the economic benefit of an agreement before it is put into place.[13] Further, evidence suggests that RTA negotiation and administration are costly.[14] These costs are infrequently factored in to calculations. By itself, the incentive argument is weak, but when combined with the interests of producers, it begins to take on more weight.

Interests

Political economy research from Open Economy Politics to the New Trade Theory suggests that domestic interests play a significant role in

94 *Regionalism and centralized trade governance*

driving economic integration. Likewise, legal scholars have picked up on this idea that integration is driven by economic interest. For example, McGinnis and Movsesian reference the legal theory underpinning American constitutionalism when they refer to the WTO as a Madisonian constitution that regulates protectionist interests.[15] Likewise, scholars of critical political economy such as Jerome Klassen theorize trade governance in terms of competing interests seeking regional stability in order to give legal expression to an expansion process already underway. Klassen argues that regionalism in general (and NAFTA in particular) has been the "spatial lynchpin of a transnational process of expansion" wherein firms have used investment as the first step in a transnationalization process.[16] In this context RTAs do not lead to foreign expansion, but rather they follow, or concretize relationships that firms have already found to be profitable. There is broad consensus that the interests of producers (and to a lesser extent consumers) drive economic integration. Interestingly, there may also be an argument that regional integration is driven by interests in government as well. After all, negotiating a regional trade agreement represents to domestic constituencies that a government is serious about expanding economic opportunity.

Ideas

Trade scholars have long known that ideas are an important driver of economic integration. Kindleberger showed how the expansion of 19th-century British free trade in Europe was at least partly driven by the power of the ideas of the Manchester School.[17] In the postwar era, Jean Monnet's vision of a Europe united by a single market was one of the driving forces behind the growth of the European Union. Similarly, other scholars have noted that the expansion of US trading networks in the 1980s and 1990s was driven by a defensive vision of American growth, in which countries in Asia were outcompeting the United States.[18] Ideas are never enough by themselves, but they give intellectual form and weight to interests and help to shape the developmental trajectory of the regionalization process.

Income level

We know that large economies tend to have intensive trade patterns. And these countries that trade a lot also tend to make more use of trade governance mechanisms. Further, wealthy countries tend to sign preferential trade agreements (PTAs) more often than countries with small economies. This is a very large and heterogeneous category of

Regionalism and centralized trade governance   95

explanation in which scholars examine the links between wealth, industrialization and trade liberalization. Factors used to explain liberalization include the size of the economies entering into agreements, their relative levels of industrial development, and the existing structural relations between the regional partners.[19] The current wave of regional integration may be driven, at least in part, by ambitious secondary powers consolidating their positions in regional markets, such as South Korea and Mexico.

Institutional investment

The institutional investment hypothesis suggests that countries with at least one trade governance membership prefer to develop more of them. It might be that uncertainty in the post-Uruguay Round era requires that states develop insurance policies against multilateral failure.[20] It may also be that once a state has taken the plunge into multilateral membership, regional memberships become a logical extension. Some economists and political scientists have theorized proliferation as a portent of multilateral weakness.[21] However, it might be possible to view proliferation another way. The WTO itself may be a portal to regional trade agreements. This chapter hypothesizes that the WTO casts something of a rain shadow behind which lies a fertile environment for regional economic development. Put another way, it could be that the existence of the WTO reduces the opportunity costs associated with trade agreement development. This is a question that we will discuss later in the chapter.

Academics and policy-makers broadly understand the how of integration, and we have a range of persuasive answers to the why of institutional proliferation. Now we must turn to the question of what all this activity means for the system of international economic law. The conventional wisdom is split on the meaning of proliferation, with most scholars agreeing that institutional proliferation carries the danger of some sort of fragmenting effect on the body of international economic regulation. While others have begun to question the conventional wisdom that the proliferation of governance institutions always leads to an increase in competition, and with it a corrosion of legitimacy and legal authority.[22]

Legal fragmentation

There are several ways to approach the issue of legal fragmentation. The traditional approach to fragmentation looks for doctrinal

96 *Regionalism and centralized trade governance*

solutions that use legal concepts as basic building blocks of law to resolve conflicts of law and bring order to an uneven system.[23] In other literature, scholarship in the broad school of legal pluralism attempts to show how pluralistic understandings of legal interaction highlight the strength of multiple legal institutions or the unity that may be found in proliferation. In the social sciences, scholarship examines institutions and their interaction in order to show how norms, processes, and organizations have been developed to address various issue areas.[24] An emerging interdisciplinary literature attempts to move beyond these debates over the relative strength and/or weakness of proliferation in order to look for areas of "normative equivalence" in international law in order to recast the debate in terms of the evolving shape of international law.[25]

Proliferation is a basic theme in the literature on legal development but scholars remain optimistic that despite the threat of fragmentation and incoherence, "diversity, experimentation, and competition have value."[26] They don't seem to unduly undermine the legal project at this point. However, there are at least two problems that scholars anticipate as the network of international economic law continues to grow. The first problem is that proliferation does not appear to be entirely rational. For example, why do states allocate resources to the development of laws that are vague or in other ways apparently ineffective? Political scientists have begun to tackle this question, as I discussed above. It may be that agreements are left purposefully incomplete in order to maintain policy space within a legal frame. Cooley and Spruyt's theory of incomplete contracting may also suggest that the relative incompleteness of an agreement may be the result of the mix of actors, with politicians preferring an incomplete agreement that leaves more room for interpretation and negotiation, while lawyers may prefer complete and comprehensive rules.[27]

The second problem revolves around how we understand the relationship between RTAs and the WTO. Are RTAs a sign of legal fragmentation or do they portend something else entirely? Koskenniemi argues that rather than pinning the blame on the growth of law, we ought to consider the rise of legal specialization and the concomitant rise of silos of knowledge in the realms of both domestic and international law. In the United Nations' International Law Commission Report of 2006, he defines fragmentation as being driven by functional differentiation, which is a feature of modern society at both the national and international levels. Fragmentation is marked by "increasing specialization of parts of society and the related autonomization of those parts."[28] For example, international law has become

Regionalism and centralized trade governance 97

increasingly complex, with lawyers and scholars specializing in trade law, investment law, human rights law, environmental law, and many other bodies of law.

There are other sources of legal fragmentation as well, such as uneven institutional development. There is also a fourth cause of legal fragmentation, which Young refers to as the conflicts that occur when different systems of law interact and conflict with each other. She examines the fragmentation hypothesis as a normal part of an international system wherein states have responded to key challenges by appealing to legal order. There is no significant pattern or overarching narrative to make sense of this call to law except the normative belief that some law is better than none.[29] Here legal scholars use the term "regime" to delineate rules that govern an issue area such as world trade, human rights, or the law of the sea.[30]

Dunoff critiques the dominant approach to regime interaction that focuses on the conflict between regimes in judicial settings. Instead he suggests that regimes interact in many large and small ways on a daily basis, and while there may be conflict, the many forms of hidden interaction outweigh the headline clashes in judicial arenas.[31] He suggests that in some places where we do see potential for conflict, international organizations have begun to undertake steps to lessen conflict. He uses the example of joint research at the WTO and International Labour Organization on conflict between trade agreements and national employment policies to highlight the way that collaboration can reduce conflict and potentially eliminate high-profile clashes between regimes of law.[32] In fact, when we look beyond the judicial arena Dunoff suggests that regimes are becoming purposive actors in their own right.[33]

In this first section we have briefly reviewed the history of regional trade agreements following the Second World War. We then turned to the questions that scholars ask about the proliferation of trade agreements. First, how is proliferation of governance institutions possible in a world where the states guard their sovereignty jealously? Second, why are regional trade agreements attractive? This is the more vexing question, and I suggested that there are a number of ways to approach this question, which I termed the Five I's of proliferation. Finally, we turned to the question of legal fragmentation, and I showed that legal scholars and political scientists approach the specialization of law and the growth of institutions a little differently, yet both agree that aggregations of rules, whether we call them regimes or institutions, are central to our understanding of the future of governance. The second section turns to the question of jurisdiction in international economic

98 *Regionalism and centralized trade governance*

law and suggests that the WTO is not losing any of its institutional weight and legal authority. In fact, the proliferation of RTAs may cement the WTO's position at the center of an expanding web of international economic law.

The WTO's exclusive jurisdiction and regional dispute settlement systems

On the face of it, there ought not to be any significant conflict between the WTO and regional arrangements because the WTO has exclusive jurisdiction over the governance of issue areas covered by the WTO Agreement and associated treaties. According to the WTO's dispute settlement training module, "Article 23 [of the DSU] not only excludes unilateral action, but also precludes the use of other fora for the resolution of a WTO-related dispute."[34] So the first element of compulsory jurisdiction is the requirement that WTO-related disputes are settled at the WTO. The second element of compulsory jurisdiction has to do with the negative consensus rule for WTO dispute settlement. Under the pre-1995 GATT system, there had to be consensus between the complainant and respondent to settle their dispute at the GATT. In the current system, when one party files a complaint, the respondent must respond at the WTO. As Chaisse and Chakraborty suggest, the automaticity of panel establishment means the WTO "effectively has compulsory jurisdiction."[35]

Marceau agrees, although she notes that there is no general rule that requires states to choose one dispute settlement forum over another. Even so, Article 3.8 of the DSU provides that members bringing a dispute do not have to prove an economic or legal interest in the dispute and do not have to provide evidence of negative trade impacts.[36] This is the third dimension of exclusive jurisdiction. That said, members still have a choice of forum and if both parties decide to take a case to an RTA rather than the WTO, they may do so because Article XXIV of the GATT and Article V of the GATS allow for the formation of regional agreements.

Further, Artiran adds that Article XXIV offers a certain amount of leeway because even though it regulates the formation of RTAs, it does not regulate their structure or operation.[37] Importantly, Marceau points out that while the WTO does not regulate the function of other trade agreements, those agreements do not limit the WTO's oversight powers. "The WTO-DSM cannot be restrained from exercising its jurisdiction given the quasi-automatic access and compulsory nature of the WTO's DSM, even if the governments concerned are using or have

Regionalism and centralized trade governance 99

used the parallel RTA-DSM."[38] Basically, just because two parties agree to take a dispute to a regional DSM, such a decision does not preclude one of them, or even another member entirely, from raising the same issue at the WTO. There is no such thing as double jeopardy at the global level.

How might the WTO's dispute processes be constrained in favor of an RTA? As clarified by the Appellate Body in *Peru-Agricultural Products* in 2015, "the language of the understanding must clearly reveal that the parties intended to relinquish their rights."[39] This is the fourth dimension of compulsory (exclusive) jurisdiction, that in order to relinquish WTO jurisdiction, states have to actively relinquish their rights; perhaps by building an exclusion clause into their regional arrangements in order to signal intent to refuse redress at the WTO. The WTO's jurisdiction is exclusive unless both parties relinquish these rights, a highly unlikely but not impossible scenario.

There is a stickiness to the WTO's exclusive jurisdiction that accounts for lack of usage when it comes to RTA dispute settlement. Marceau suggests that nothing stops a dispute brought to an RTA to be reconsidered at the WTO. So choosing the WTO over an RTA may be a way to avoid dispute proliferation. She also notes that 25 percent of the cases that have come to the WTO could have gone to regional bodies, so the choice of forum, although still political, is also a question of both state legal strategy as well as institutional legitimacy.[40] Until this point states have overwhelmingly chosen to litigate at the WTO, and it is not clear what it would take to change this pattern.

Some scholars have suggested that the WTO ought to limit its oversight in order to create an orderly hierarchy of trade arbitration. Henckels argues that the WTO's broad jurisdiction may unnecessarily complicate the issue of forum choice and so the WTO should use its "inherent power of comity" to decline jurisdiction in certain cases, such as when a case may be effectively resolved by an RTA.[41] Such a move might cast the WTO as a sort of supreme court for trade but it is not clear from a reading of the relevant texts if this is even possible. It would certainly require a very different reading of the DSU than has been done by panels and the Appellate Body to date. It is also not clear what concrete benefit there would be for members. Yang argues that members ought to build a forum choice clause into the WTO's DSU, a project that seems both politically difficult and potentially unnecessary given the flexibility built into the current system.[42]

The WTO's exclusive jurisdiction over a great majority of the body of trade regulation has a double impact on regional trade agreements. On the one hand, it offers an order and legitimacy to trade arbitration

100   *Regionalism and centralized trade governance*

that may provide a template for regional efforts. On the other, the WTO's DSU covers such a large terrain of regulation that much of what might be litigated in regional arrangements, in practice goes to the WTO. What impact then does the WTO's exclusive jurisdiction have on the empirics of RTA development? In one dimension, it explains the pattern we see in RTA DSM usage. Very few cases have gone to regional trade bodies. But in another way, exclusive jurisdiction would seem to suggest that there is very little need for other dispute settlement bodies, and yet, as I will show below, states continue to build such mechanisms into their preferential arrangements.

Recent trends in the development of regional trade agreements

The concern about proliferation is really a concern about the proliferation of regional dispute settlement mechanisms. If RTAs were simply sideline agreements that looked to tailor trade regulation to regional interests, we would not bother to think about them. However, the fact that they create other mechanisms to enforce existing rules makes them interesting. I am far more concerned with the creation of legal mechanisms that might compete with the centralized system of the WTO than we are about states creating regional agreements to extend WTO disciplines in new directions or to take up liberalization issues not dealt with at the WTO per se.

The empirical study below shows the growth of RTAs with full DSM provisions and in particular the rise of these provisions after 1995. Then we turn to a discussion of what these mechanisms cover and what they exclude. Exclusions give us some sense of the legal limits of the regional dispute settlement mechanisms. We then turn to special procedures in order to get some sense of the focus of regional mechanisms. Special procedures are the areas of dispute settlement where particular rules have been laid out for certain issue areas. Most importantly, these procedures cover investor-state dispute settlement. Finally, we turn to a brief regional comparison of the use of exclusions and special procedures in order to get some sense of how RTAs in North America, Europe, Latin America and Asia organize these rules.

Figure 5.1 give us some sense of the proliferation of dispute settlement arrangements. Of the 261 active preferential agreements notified to the WTO by 2014, only 28, or a little over 9 percent, had no dispute settlement provisions at all. Some 91 percent have some form of DSM, although 90 of these contain only a consultations clause or another form of basic provision. Some 143, or 55 percent contain a full dispute settlement mechanism. And as Figure 5.2 shows, the completion of the

Regionalism and centralized trade governance 101

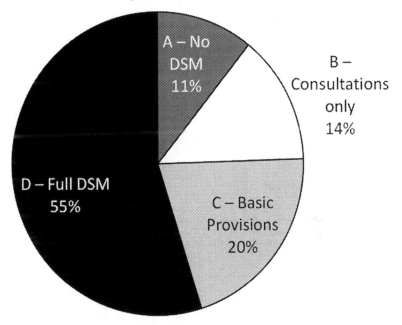

Figure 5.1 Dispute settlement arrangements in regional trade agreements
Source: Adapted from Marc D. Froese, "Regional Trade Agreements and the Paradox of Dispute Settlement," *Manchester Journal of International Economic Law* 11, no. 3 (2014): 367–396.

Uruguay Round was the spark that ignited this proliferation of DSMs, most of which are patterned on the WTO's DSU to a greater or lesser extent.

Figure 5.2 shows the phenomenal growth of RTA dispute mechanisms in the postwar period. We see that before the end of the Cold War, not only were regional trade agreements relatively sparse, but the most common form of dispute settlement mechanism was a simple clause promising diplomatic consultations should trading frictions arise. After 1995 we see a marked rise in preferential agreements, but the biggest spike in agreements containing complete dispute settlement mechanisms occurs during the Doha Round, post-2001. In the years since, overall growth in RTA development has slowed, and with it the development of full-service DSMs. The rise of larger, more complex mega-regional agreements, such as the negotiations between Canada and the EU, the United States and the EU, and the Pacific rim nations, may account for some of this slow-down, as these larger agreements are much more time-consuming to develop. It almost goes without saying that all contain comprehensive dispute settlement provisions.

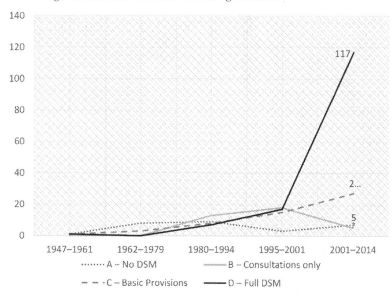

Figure 5.2 The development of RTAs, 1947–2013
Source: Adapted from Marc D. Froese, "Regional Trade Agreements and the Paradox of Dispute Settlement," *Manchester Journal of International Economic Law* 11, no. 3 (2014): 367–396.

Next, we turn to the substance of dispute settlement provisions in RTAs. We saw above that more than half of the RTAs in force contain comprehensive dispute settlement provisions. Now we must unpack that box, describe what a suite of comprehensive provisions looks like, and examine the special provisions and exclusions by which each agreement tailors its mechanism to regional requirements. In a previous article, I developed a set of five boxes that contain all the elements of a modern preferential trade agreement.[43] Not every agreement contains all these elements, but most agreements developed after 1995 contain language dealing with almost all of these clauses. In fact, an agreement that did not deal with all of these issues would be something of an outlier in an early 21st-century history of trade deals.

As Table 5.1 shows, there are five basic themes across which states negotiate preferential deals. Trade in goods tends to include standard issues like duties and rules of origin, as well as customs procedures, and specific arrangements that deal with the particular goods of concern to the trading partners, like cars or electronics. Trade in services is dominated by financial services, telecommunications, transportation services, and it is usual to include a clause specifying how the parties wish

Regionalism and centralized trade governance 103

Table 5.1 Legal clauses in RTAs

Trade in goods	Duties, quotas, rules of origin, quantitative restrictions, customs procedures, sector-specific arrangements, e-commerce
Trade in services	Services, financial services, telecommunications, temporary entry for business purposes, transport (including maritime and air transport)
Investment	Investment provisions, including ISDS
Intellectual property	Intellectual property rights provisions
Competitive environment	SPS, TBT, safeguards, antidumping procedures, government procurement, competition policy, transparency, economic cooperation, state-trading enterprises and monopolies, subsidies, trade facilitation, labor standards, environmental standards, sustainable development

Source: Adapted from Marc D. Froese, "Mapping the Scope of Dispute Settlement in Regional Trade Agreements: Implications for the Multilateral Governance of Trade," *World Trade Review* 15, no. 4 (2016): 563–585.

to deal with the movement of people across borders for the purposes of delivering these services. A majority of these newer RTAs also include investment provisions, with special rules for investor-state dispute settlement taking a prominent place in the text. The final box is something of a catch-all category, dealing with the many ways that states use behind-the-border measures to support and protect domestic industry. Many of these provisions, such as sanitary and phytosanitary standards (SPS), technical barriers to trade (TBT), and antidumping provisions, are taken straight from the WTO's playbook. Others, such as competition policy, are not yet formalized at the WTO, and as such, the RTA provisions tend to be somewhat vague, more in the vein of a promise to consider the issue in the future than a complete and binding set of provisions regulating appropriate standards for competition.

Now that we know what is in an average trade agreement, we need to turn to a discussion of how dispute settlement provisions in such an agreement apply to each legal clause. In a perfectly ordered legal universe, the DSM of each RTA would apply equally to each of the clauses. However, we can already anticipate the complications that can arise. For example, a number of these clauses duplicate regulation at the WTO, and as a result, placing them under the jurisdiction of an RTA would be a waste of resources, especially in issue areas such as SPS and TBT where there is already a significant body of dispute settlement at the WTO. Further, there are a number of clauses relating to

104   Regionalism and centralized trade governance

trade facilitation, environmental standards, and competition policy that are incomplete, and therefore most states prefer to exclude them from dispute settlement. Figure 5.3 shows the most common dispute settlement exclusion clauses ranked by prevalence in RTAs notified to the WTO.

Alongside dispute settlement exclusions, most agreements set aside special arrangements for the settlement of disputes in significant areas. Figure 5.4 breaks down the most common arrangement by thematic category. In those arrangements dealing with the competitive trading environment, labor and environmental standards are subject to provisions that limit access to dispute settlement. Likewise, government procurement provisions similarly narrow the scope of potential complaint in order to protect the integrity of democratic choice while maintaining the intent of the agreement. Intellectual property (IP) rights are also the subject of several general modifications designed to enhance openness while protecting IP rights; these may be intended to clarify rights rather than raise the bar for using the DSM.

RTAs increasingly contain enhanced investment clauses. Most investment provisions contain sector-specific modifications, most importantly investor-state dispute settlement provisions that allow foreign economic actors to sue governments under the agreement.

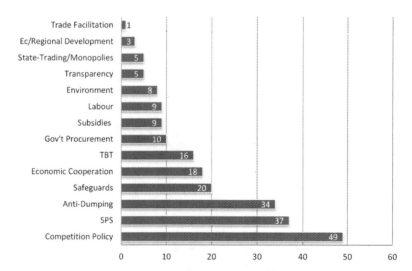

Figure 5.3 Excluded clauses in RTA dispute settlement
Source: Adapted from Marc D. Froese, "Mapping the Scope of Dispute Settlement in Regional Trade Agreements: Implications for the Multilateral Governance of Trade," *World Trade Review* 15, no. 4 (2016): 563–585.

Regionalism and centralized trade governance 105

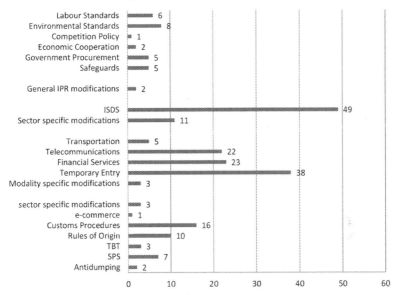

Figure 5.4 Special provisions in RTAs
Source: Adapted from Marc D. Froese, "Mapping the Scope of Dispute Settlement in Regional Trade Agreements: Implications for the Multilateral Governance of Trade," *World Trade Review* 15, no. 4 (2016): 563–585.

Importantly, non-state actors do not have the standing to bring a case to the WTO, which makes ISDS a potentially significant step beyond the postwar consensus around the place of states in international law. Turning to services, the most important changes state that parties may not litigate the denial of temporary entry for business purposes unless they can make a case for a pattern of denied entry. Various other modifications tailor the dispute provisions for cases involving financial services and telecommunications. Finally, turning to special provisions covering dispute resolution around trade in goods, the most important carve-out creates policy space for customs procedures and rules of origin for the reasons specified above related to maintaining the integrity of national choice in a liberalized market environment.

Finally, we move to a brief examination of exclusions and special provisions in regional context. Table 5.2 offers a breakdown by region, with an emphasis on the most prominent actors signing RTAs. Turning first to North America, we have 18 RTAs signed by the United States and Canada, with the most common exclusions related to SPS, antidumping measures and competition policy, reflecting a broadly liberal policy frame that maintains the WTO's exclusive jurisdiction over SPS

106 *Regionalism and centralized trade governance*

Table 5.2 Exclusions and special provisions in RTAs, sorted by region

	Exclusions		Special procedures	
United States (11 RTAs)	SPS	8	Competition policy	1
	TBT	1	Financial services	7
	Antidumping measures	4	Telecommunications	8
	Competition policy	4	ISDS	7
	Economic cooperation	1	Investment	1
	Labor standards	6	Temporary entry	2
	Environmental standards	5	Labor standards	2
			Environmental standards	2
Canada (7 RTAs)	SPS	3	Investment	2
	Competition policy	5	Financial services	2
	Temporary entry	2	Antidumping measures	1
	Antidumping measures	4	SPS	1
	Labor standards	2	TBT	1
	Environmental standards	2	Temporary entry	2
	Subsidies	2	Telecommunications	1
	Safeguards	2		
	Investment	1		
Europe (EU and EFTA— 49 RTAs)	Competition policy	9	Rules of origin	2
	SPS	5	Financial services	2
	TBT	4	Investment	3
	Subsidies	3	Labor standards	1
	Antidumping measures	13	Environmental standards	1
	State-trading enterprises	3	ISDS	1
	Government procurement	1	Finance cooperation	2
	Safeguards	8	Customs procedures	7

	Exclusions		Special procedures	
	Intellectual property rights	1	Telecommunications	2
	Sustainable development	2	SPS	3
	Transparency	1	Services	1
	Economic cooperation	1	e-commerce	1
			Intellectual property rights	2
			TBT	1
			Sustainable development	1
			Sector-specific procedures	2
			Safeguards	1
Japan (11 RTAs)	SPS	5	Temporary entry	2
	TBT	5	ISDS	6
	Economic cooperation	1	Telecommunications	2
	Financial services	1		
	Competition policy	5		
	Government procurement	1		
	Promotion of an economic relationship	2		
BRICS (9 RTAs)	SPS	1	Temporary entry	3
	TBT	1	ISDS	2
	Transparency	1	Investment	1
	Competition policy	1	TBT	1
	Economic cooperation	2		
	Safeguards	1		
Chile (11 RTAs)	Safeguards	5	Temporary entry	5
	Antidumping measures	2	Labor standards	1
	MFN clause/ investment	1	Environmental standards	2

108 *Regionalism and centralized trade governance*

	Exclusions		Special procedures	
	Temporary entry for business purposes	1	Transportation	3
	Competition policy	2	ISDS	2
	SPS	1	Investment	1
	TBT	1		
	Economic cooperation	1		
	Transportation	1		
Korea (5 RTAs)	Safeguards	2	ISDS	2
	Antidumping measures	4	Telecommunications	3
	Competition policy	4	Temporary entry	2
	SPS	3	Financial services	2
	TBT	1	Customs procedures	1
	Subsidies	1	Labor standards	1
	Economic cooperation	1	Environmental standards	1
	Investment	1		
	Government procurement	1		
Turkey (11 RTAs)			Customs procedures	7
			Rules of origin	7

Source: Adapted from Marc D. Froese, "Mapping the Scope of Dispute Settlement in Regional Trade Agreements: Implications for the Multilateral Governance of Trade," *World Trade Review* 15, no. 4 (2016): 563–585.

and antidumping. Competition policy is excluded because its discipline is not well developed in international economic law. The most common special procedures relate to services, most importantly investor-state dispute settlement.

In the European context we have 49 RTAs signed by the EU and the EFTA. Exclusions and special procedures largely conform to the pattern laid out above, with exclusions tending to support the WTO's exclusive jurisdiction and special procedures designed to protect democratic choice while preserving the incomplete nature of clauses that are not yet fully defined by treaty and precedent. Japan's RTAs also follow this general pattern. The BRICS countries (Brazil, Russia,

India, China and South Africa) have notified the WTO of nine RTAs, and the most prominent dispute settlement exclusions relate to economic cooperation clauses, presumably for reasons related to policy autonomy. These agreements tend to maintain the standard language for the settlement of disputes related to the denial of temporary entry. Two of the nine contain special provisions for ISDS and one more breaks with the tradition of excluding TBT from dispute settlement by creating a modification of dispute settlement parameters for the purposes of resolving TBT disputes.

This second section began with a discussion of the WTO's exclusive jurisdiction for the settlement of trade disputes arising from multilateral agreements. Next we turned to an empirical examination of the scope and scale of dispute settlement in RTAs. I showed the rise of complex dispute settlement mechanisms, their importance following 2001, and then we considered the ways that these DSMs exclude certain clauses from dispute settlement and create special procedures for others. The general pattern is one in which RTAs respect the exclusive jurisdiction of the WTO while creating mechanisms to settle disputes that may arise from areas of WTO plus/extra regulation, such as investor-state claims. I suggested in the first section that one of the underdeveloped explanations of RTA development was the level of institutional sophistication of the parties involved, with the idea being that states that build capacity in international trade governance may be more likely to use that expertise in other ways in the future.[44] I further suggested that there might be something about WTO membership that makes it easier to develop secondary nodes in the network of interdependence. Next we turn to an analysis of what these empirical patterns of RTA development mean, using a combination of insights gained from legal theory and from social science literature on global value chains.

Governance value chains

In a recent volume of essays, Fabbricotti offers a sustained attempt to build a political economy approach to international law, noting "political economy brings a theoretical framework that helps to capture a problem's underlying structure."[45] In order to bring political economy into international law, she asked van Aaken and Trachtman to develop a model of the political economy of law that would be of use to legal scholars who require an overview of the subject. They noted that the basic merit of IPE is that it "empirically constructs the outcome (of a problem to be solved) by focusing as a first step on the interests of the

110   *Regionalism and centralized trade governance*

actors."[46] The focus on interests opens up a number of avenues of legal research, particularly among international law scholars more comfortable with textual and doctrinal research, which often assumes that interests may be absorbed into a larger discussion of legal interpretation.

In response, van Aaken and Trachtman developed a standard approach to political economy rooted in Lake's open economy politics in which they theorize that "IL is made by strategic states willing to reduce their autonomy along certain dimensions in order to increase the satisfaction of their preferences along other dimensions, where after the commensuration of these two dimensions, each state's government counts itself as better off."[47] Governments hope to gain from the sacrifice of sovereignty that occurs when order is created beyond the state. This may be Political Economy 101, but it bears repeating that governments form RTAs because they believe them to be in their best interest. Even so, it is the shape of that interest that engages us here.

There are two main ways to proceed; both are rooted in basic assumptions about the interests of governments and their states. I call these the reinsurance hypothesis and the institutional investment hypothesis. They overlap in certain ways, but ultimately each hypothesis rests upon different assumptions, although both ways of thinking about the place of the state in the multilateral system may operate in the same place (and sometimes in the same research) simultaneously. The first assumes that the multilateral system is fragile and prone to decomposition, and therefore looks to multiply its successes while they still remain as a template. The second assumes that the multilateral system is robust and looks to build upon its strengths to replicate them in the regional context.

The reinsurance hypothesis

The reinsurance hypothesis rests upon two ideas. The first is that multilateralism is inherently fragile, and given the stresses it has endured in the past two decades, its best days may be in the past. The second is that trade protectionism is always more politically popular than market openness, so policy-makers must guard against the creeping tide of protectionist sentiment. Muzaka and Bishop chart the fascination with the end of trade multilateralism, noting that it has been a prominent theme in the literature since at least the 1980s.[48] In fact, we might consider the fragmentation literature to be a more subtle form of this popular leitmotif. They show that the reason why scholars often mistake the end of multilateralism is because despite the narrative of

Regionalism and centralized trade governance 111

progress that underpins the postwar principle of non-discrimination, trade multilateralism has not been a straight line of falling tariffs and the blunting of non-tariff barriers.[49]

I have suggested elsewhere that there are three reasons why states, which are already heavily invested in the WTO dispute system, may wish to reinvest in a regional trade agreement.[50] I termed this the reinsurance hypothesis because all three reasons refer to the WTO, and attempt to ensure against its failure, in certain ways. First, regional dispute arrangements are a way of showing confidence in the new agreement by blessing it with the main endowments of the WTO. Governments can assure vested interests that the regional system will have all the strengths of the multilateral system with few of the weaknesses of big tent multilateralism. Second, they are a reasonable attempt to protect arrangements in places where the RTA exceeds the negotiations at the WTO. Third, they are a constructive commitment to the principle of judicial independence. Economic actors may be certain that disputes will be adjudicated with impartiality. This refers back to both the basic concerns about judicial impartiality that led to the Canadian/European argument for a dispute settlement mechanism at the Uruguay Round, as well as the fact that in a large-scale comparison of modern RTAs, almost every agreement lacking dispute provisions is found among the former Soviet states. Dispute mechanisms are a statement of regulatory autonomy as well as an expression of confidence in regional expertise.

The second issue is the perception of a rising tide of protectionism. Aggarwal and Evenett take a broad approach to considering the growth of global protectionism since the financial crisis of 2008. They term the rising protectionism a fragmentation of the global economy. "Here, fragmentation should be taken to mean departures from nationality-blind treatment of commercial interests that creates differences across rivals in the profitability of serving some customers."[51] This is a different understanding of fragmentation than we see in the legal literature. This fragmentation of markets is caused by the financial crisis, the existence of effective non-tariff barriers to trade, and the pushing of domestic interests at the expense of multilateral interests. Multilateral causes include political clashes at the WTO over the rapid growth of regional traders such as China, and an abandonment of the WTO for mega-regional negotiations by the United States and the European Union.

Scholars working under the assumptions of the reinsurance hypothesis often view the successes of the multilateral system as either in the past, or heavily contingent upon institutional externalities in the present. It would be an oversimplification to imagine that they view

112 *Regionalism and centralized trade governance*

multilateralism only in terms of forward momentum. Even so, there is something of a declinist undercurrent to literature that views regional arrangements as a death knell for multilateralism. In contradistinction, Muzaka and Bishop offer a more fulsome definition of trade multilateralism that emphasizes the fitful, complex and sometimes contradictory nature of multilateral progress. "The institution of trade multilateralism ... is best seen as an enduring—although changeable—structure with both material and symbolic properties ... It is, moreover, an arrangement that is produced, maintained, and transformed through social construction and interaction amongst actors and groups that, importantly, have different normative and unequal power positions ... far from being *orderly* arrangements, institutions like multilateralism are better understood as *dynamic* arenas of conflict and contest" organized around the key principle of non-discrimination.[52]

The reinsurance hypothesis, with its emphasis on backstopping multilateralism and the steady pressures of protectionism is not an unconvincing approach to thinking about the place of law in regional governance. The reliance upon this perception of fragility in the multilateral system is a weakness, but it also admits to the fact that multilateral success is always contingent upon a number of complex political factors. The externalities that beset multilateralism continue to make it a risky undertaking. Even so, the reinsurance hypothesis is perhaps a second best approach to explaining state behavior during the Doha Round.

The institutional investment hypothesis

The institutional investment hypothesis posits that governments are becoming convinced that they must invest in governance and collaborative market regulation endeavors, both to gain the benefits of multilateral liberalization as well as to benefit from new business strategies such as global value chains. RTAs are a low-cost, low-risk signal that a state is willing to invest in the institutional infrastructure required to take advantage of opportunities afforded by global markets. Even so, this thesis begs the question, do RTAs do what they set out to do? Are they the best next step?

Baldwin and Seghezza attempt to answer this question with an empirical examination of tariff levels in multilateral and preferential agreements.[53] Their research is an intervention in the literature developed by Limao and others that asks if RTAs are building blocks of liberalization or stumbling blocks.[54] The research that Baldwin and Seghezza critique suggests that RTAs may be stumbling blocks, and looks for evidence that countries cut tariffs less at the WTO in areas

Regionalism and centralized trade governance   113

where there are regional preferences in place. If this were the case, "we should observe the highest MFN [multilateral] tariffs in products where PTA tariffs are the lowest."[55] However, Baldwin and Seghezza find exactly the opposite. "The products where nations have chosen high MFN tariffs they have granted few preferences ... In fact, the data show that MFN and PTA tariffs are complements, not substitutes."[56] So RTAs are not necessarily stumbling blocks. Nor are they always building blocks of multilateral liberalization. Rather, they seem to act as complements, at least to the extent that state tariff preferences are similar in both.

How ought we then to triangulate RTAs in the system of international economic law? Baldwin and Seghezza think the answers lie in the forces "that simultaneously influence the selection of MFN and PTA tariffs," which they identify as domestic sectoral vested interests.[57] However, while the argument for domestic interests is not necessarily off the mark, it does not answer the basic question of why an RTA at all, if it largely complements the MFN system? Blanchard offers a convincing answer.[58] A domestic firm may lobby its government for a preferential trade or investment agreement with a country in which the company has a vested interest. The example she gives is a Canadian firm that produces shoes in Thailand and wants preferential tariff access for the shoes produced by their Thai contractor. Rather than lower the MFN tariff rate, the government may prefer a bilateral or regional deal. So RTAs may also signal the presence of corporate ties and in this way act as a rationalization of government regulation for the benefit of domestic firms. This is a second dimension to the institutional investment hypothesis.

Governments use the RTA model to develop the infrastructure required to take advantage of modern production methods while simultaneously building upon the existing relationships that domestic firms have with foreign partners. Hoekman agrees, noting that both the rise of regional powers and the "increasing complexity of the policy agenda affecting international production networks and supply chain trade" are reasons behind the rise of RTAs.[59] Similarly, Wolfe notes that the rise of exogenous structural factors slowed down negotiation at the WTO and made regional deals more attractive because, as he puts it, "the trading system is no longer a transatlantic bargain."[60] RTAs appear to be a more agile strategy to address the many regulatory issues that typify value-chain production. However, whether they address the changing needs of value-chain production is another question altogether.

114 *Regionalism and centralized trade governance*

There are a number of benefits to thinking about RTAs in the context of value chains. The Organisation for Economic Co-operation and Development (OECD), WTO and World Bank released a joint study on the policy implications of global value chains in which they argued that there are a number of trade-related requirements for countries attempting to aid domestic firms seeking to integrate into global value chains. Three of these are germane to our discussion. First, it is necessary to move beyond traditional thinking about trade that values exports over imports because finished goods are likely to move across multiple borders before they are consumed. RTAs may benefit value chains by further lowering barriers to trade, although as we saw above, they do not tend to lower tariffs more than the WTO does.

Second, multilateral market opening may be preferred over preferential arrangements because markets upstream and downstream from production can matter as much as barriers between direct trading partners. This may be a reason why states have begun to attempt to improve upon RTAs with mega-regional agreements that may provide a better intermediate link in the governance of value chains than have traditional bilateral arrangements. Third, trade facilitation continues to be important, as are improved logistics and regulatory cooperation, because they reduce delays and bureaucratic uncertainty. It is unclear the extent to which RTAs reduce bureaucracy. They may have that potential, but it is not their stated goal. Even so, more research is required.

I would go a step further and suggest that there are also benefits to using the value-chain methodology to consider the place of RTAs in global governance. We might term the network of trade regulation that extends from the state, through regional arrangements and to the multilateral system, a governance value chain. Gereffi and Fernandez-Stark suggest that there are four dimensions to global value-chain analysis: input-output structure, geographical considerations, governance structure, and institutional context. Most important for us is the analysis of governance, because it "allows one to understand how a chain is controlled and coordinated when certain actors in the chain have more power than others."[61] Gereffi, Humphrey and Sturgeon argue that more research is necessary to explain how value chains are governed.[62] It may be that RTAs are only the beginning of a process by which states develop the tools necessary to effectively govern global production networks in the context of a multilateral approach to international economic law.

Another inducement to the development of RTAs may be the existence of the WTO itself. I suggested earlier that the existence of the WTO may reduce the opportunity costs associated with trade

Regionalism and centralized trade governance   115

agreement development. The WTO provides the right ingredients for RTA development with a ready template for most agreements in its own institutional contours. For example, there is no need to haggle over how a dispute settlement mechanism might work when both parties are members of the WTO and its methods are now uncontroversial. Further, the WTO has already negotiated low tariffs, and partly as a result of multilateral success and partly as a result of the evolving global economic environment, tariffs are less of an issue in many areas of production. Also, many of the most contentious issues such as antidumping and countervail, and technical barriers to trade have been regulated by the WTO and there is no need to duplicate them at the regional level. Finally, the WTO's own travails in the Doha Round make RTA development that much easier because the stakes of failure are higher at the WTO, while RTAs remain a relatively low-cost, high-return investment, at least in theory.

Even so, the RTA model is clearly a blunt instrument, and numerous studies have shown that better approaches might include directly targeted agreements on trade facilitation and mutual regulatory recognition. RTAs are a quick and dirty way to build upon the WTO's success at a time when the WTO seemed to have lost momentum. It is very likely that the post-Cold War wave of RTAs is an historically unique phenomenon born of flagging multilateral momentum and an incomplete understanding on the part of states as to what 21st-century production patterns require in terms of regulation. In this way, RTAs may be the weakest link in the governance value chain.

Conclusion

This chapter examined the development of RTAs in the context of both legal and political economy literature. Inside this ongoing argument about the mutually inclusive significance of legal literature to IPE research, I made an argument about the relationship of RTAs to the World Trade Organization. Conventional wisdom suggests that RTAs are competitors and rivals to the WTO system, but I argue that they are better viewed as flawed attempts to develop a governance value chain with which to better regulate global production networks and capture the economic benefits that accrue from these value chains.

The first section examined the history of RTAs, paying particular attention to their proliferation after the Cold War. I suggested that there are five main approaches to the study of proliferation, and that the literature on legal fragmentation offers a different (and promising) lens through which social scientists may think about institutional

116 *Regionalism and centralized trade governance*

development. The second section began with a discussion of the WTO's exclusive jurisdiction over disputes involving its agreements. I showed that the discussion over the place of RTAs vis-à-vis the WTO may be a concern about the duplication of juridical mechanisms. We turned to an empirical examination of the scope and scale of dispute settlement in RTAs. I showed a pattern in which RTAs respect the exclusive jurisdiction of the WTO while creating mechanisms to settle disputes that may arise from areas of WTO plus/extra regulation, such as investor-state claims. I also suggested that there might be something about WTO membership that makes it easier to develop secondary nodes in the network of interdependence.

The last section builds upon the literature introduced in the first section and the empirical study of the second section to suggest two ways to think about RTAs in the context of the growing web of interconnection that typifies international economic law. I suggested that going forward, two hypotheses about the place of RTAs in IEL will likely dominate. The first is the reinsurance hypothesis that argues for RTAs to be interpreted as backstops to an uncertain multilateral process. This approach has a number of strengths, but it is also freighted with the assumptions of declinist thinking about multilateralism that tend to assume the best days of cooperation are in the past, despite the fact that there is no evidence of a golden age of multilateralism. I then argued for the development of an institutional investment hypothesis, which makes the case that RTAs are easy to develop in the context of the WTO due to the reduction of opportunity costs. I further argue that just because they are a low-cost, low-risk approach to developing a governance network to both regulate and promote value-chain production, they are not necessarily the best tool. Or at least they are a product of their era, and are likely to be eclipsed in the future by better-targeted solutions to the challenges of value-chain governance.

This brief study of RTAs suggests that legal proliferation has a number of implications for future research. There are two things we know: RTAs are likely to be an intermediate step in an expanding web of legal interconnection. We will turn to other forms of regulation presently. Second, RTAs do not necessarily undermine the centrality of the WTO. There is one big thing we do not know. If RTAs are not a very strong link between national and multilateral trade governance, what ought governments to do to effectively govern global production networks? We might see renewed movement towards plurilateral and mega-regional agreements (such as the Transatlantic Trade and Investment Partnership—TTIP, and the Comprehensive Economic and Trade Agreement—CETA), even though these are a harder sell for national

Regionalism and centralized trade governance 117

publics. However, we are also seeing mega-regional projects such as the TPP begin to falter.

We would be naive to believe that the structures to govern trade today will remain with us, in their present form, for the rest of the 21st century. We have up until very recently thought of economic integration as a one-way street. But the British vote to exit the EU raises the question of de-integration. "Brexit" may be the first of a series of steps away from the regional integration model. It might be that the future holds smaller regional agreements that are tightly oriented towards the needs of production networks—agreements with greater direct economic benefit and fewer political drawbacks. Perhaps a renegotiation of NAFTA promised by the Trump Administration will be a back-to-the-future moment.

Notes

1 Martti Koskenniemi, "The Politics of International Law—20 Years Later," *European Journal of International Law* 20, no. 1 (2009): 7–19.
2 *The Simpsons*, "Hurricane Neddy," Season 8, Episode 8, Dir. Bob Anderson, Written by Matt Groening, Fox, 29 December 1996.
3 J.B. Condliffe, *The Commerce of Nations* (London: George Allen and Unwin Ltd., 1951), 27.
4 William J. Davey, *Enforcing World Trade Rules: Essays on WTO Dispute Settlement* (London: Cameron May, 2007).
5 Jacob Viner, *The Customs Union Issue* (New York: The Carnegie Endowment for International Peace, 1950).
6 Richard Pomfret, "Is Regionalism an Increasing Feature of the World Economy?," *The World Economy* 30, no. 6 (2007): 923–947.
7 Valbona Muzaka and Matthew Louis Bishop, "Doha Stalemate: The End of Multilateralism?," *Review of International Studies* 41, no. 02 (2015): 383–406.
8 Pomfret, "Is Regionalism an Increasing Feature of the World Economy?"
9 Jo-Ann Crawford and Roberto V. Fiorentino, "The Changing Landscape of Regional Trade Agreements," in *WTO Discussion Papers* (Geneva: World Trade Organization, 2005).
10 Alexander Cooley and Hendrik Spruyt, *Contracting States: Sovereign Transfers in International Relations* (Princeton, N.J.: Princeton University Press, 2009), 5, 9.
11 Cooley and Spruyt, *Contracting States*, 182–184.
12 Francesco Duina, *The Social Construction of Free Trade: The European Union, NAFTA and Mercosur* (Princeton, N.J.: Princeton University Press, 2007).
13 Ferdi De Ville and Gabriel Siles-Brugge, *TTIP: The Truth About the Transatlantic Trade and Investment Partnership* (Cambridge: Polity Press, 2015).
14 Crawford and Fiorentino, "The Changing Landscape of Regional Trade Agreements," 16.

118 *Regionalism and centralized trade governance*

15 John O. McGinnis and Mark L. Movsesian, "The World Trade Constitution," *Harvard Law Review* 114, no. 2 (December 2000): 511–605.

16 Jerome Klassen, *Joining Empire: The Political Economy of the New American Foreign Policy* (Toronto: University of Toronto Press, 2014), 152.

17 Charles P. Kindleberger, "The Rise of Free Trade in Western Europe, 1820–1875," *Journal of Economic History* 35, no. 1 (1975): 20–55.

18 Crawford and Fiorentino, "The Changing Landscape of Regional Trade Agreements."

19 Duina, *The Social Construction of Free Trade*, 30–46.

20 Marc D. Froese, "Regional Trade Agreements and the Paradox of Dispute Settlement," *Manchester Journal of International Economic Law* 11, no. 3 (2014): 367–396.

21 Jagdish Bhagwati, *Termites in the Trading System: How Preferential Agreements Undermine Free Trade* (New York: Oxford University Press, 2008); Daniel W. Drezner, "The Tragedy of the Global Institutional Commons," in *Back to Basics: States Power in a Contemporary World*, ed. Martha Finnemore and Judith Goldstein (London: Oxford University Press, 2013).

22 Jeffrey L. Dunoff, "A New Approach to Regime Interaction," in *Regime Interaction in International Law: Facing Fragmentation*, ed. Margaret A. Young (Cambridge: Cambridge University Press, 2012).

23 C. Wilfred Jenks, "The Conflict of Law-Making Treaties," *British Yearbook of International Law* 30 (1953): 401–426.

24 Margaret A. Young, ed., *Regime Interaction in International Law: Facing Fragmentation* (Cambridge: Cambridge University Press, 2012).

25 Tomer Broude and Yuval Shany, eds., *Multi-Sourced Equivalent Norms in International Law* (Oxford: Hart Publishing, 2011).

26 Jonathan I. Charney, "The Impact on the International Legal System of the Growth of International Courts and Tribunals," *International Law and Politics* 31 (1999): 707.

27 Cooley and Spruyt, *Contracting States*.

28 Martti Koskenniemi, "Fragmentation of International Law: Difficulties Arising from the Diversification and Expansion of International Law," in *Report of the Study Group of the International Law Commission* (Geneva: United Nations International Law Commission, 2006), 11.

29 Margaret A. Young, "Introduction: The Productive Fiction between Regimes," in *Regime Interaction in International Law: Facing Fragmentation*, ed. Margaret A. Young (Cambridge: Cambridge University Press, 2012), 2.

30 In IPE we have generally moved on from the concept of the regime, in which scholarly interest peaked around the end of the Cold War, and subsumed it in the larger concept of institutions. This newer conception brings together rules, norms, and modes of decision-making with a social scientific understanding of the logic of institutional growth and trajectories of development. See Young, "Introduction: The Productive Fiction between Regimes," 10.

31 Dunoff, "A New Approach to Regime Interaction," 138.

32 Dunoff, "A New Approach to Regime Interaction," 168.

33 Lim and Mercurio believe that the ongoing fragmentation of international economic law, as both a move towards legal expertise as well as a proliferation of institutions, is a drift away from the original intent of the

Regionalism and centralized trade governance   119

Bretton Woods institutions. In that context, recent developments that seem to accelerate this trend, such as the 2008 global financial crisis, are examples of quantitative rather than qualitative change (p. 529). Even so, the financial crisis underscores the enduring concern of the fragmentation thesis, which is the possibility of a loss of coherence in international law, which in turn undercuts the legitimacy of IEL. See Dunoff, "A New Approach to Regime Interaction," 168; C.L. Lim and Bryan Mercurio, "Conclusion: Beyond Fragmentation?," in *International Economic Law after the Global Crisis*, ed. C.L. Lim and Bryan Mercurio (Cambridge: Cambridge University Press, 2015); see also Steven Bernstein and Erin Hannah, "The WTO and Institutional (In)Coherence in Global Economic Governance," in *Handbook on the World Trade Organization*, ed. Amrita Narlikar, Martin Daunton, and Robert M. Stern (Oxford: Oxford University Press, 2012).

34 For an overview of the main provisions of the Dispute Settlement Understanding go to www.wto.org/english/tratop_e/dispu_e/disp_settlement_cbt_e/c1s3p3_e.htm.

35 Julien Chaisse and Debashis Chakraborty, "Dispute Resolution in the WTO: The Experience of India," in *Beyond the Transition Phase of WTO: An Indian Perspective on Emerging Issues*, ed. Dipankar Sengupta, Debashis Chakraborty, and Pritam Banerji (New Delhi: Academic Foundation, 2006), 509.

36 Gabrielle Marceau, "The Primacy of the WTO Dispute Settlement System," *QIL, Zoom-in* 23 (2015): 4.

37 Pinar Artiran, "A Different Approach to the External Trade Requirement of GATT Article XXIV: Assessing 'Other Regulations of Commerce' in the Context of EE Enlargement and its Heightened Regulatory Standards," in *International Economic Law and National Autonomy*, ed. Meredith Kolsky Lewis and Susy Franckel (Cambridge: Cambridge University Press, 2010).

38 Marceau, "The Primacy of the WTO Dispute Settlement System," 5–6.

39 WT/DS457/AB/R at Para. 5.25. For a copy of the Appellate Body ruling, go to www.wto.org/english/tratop_e/dispu_e/457abr_e.pdf.

40 Marceau, "The Primacy of the WTO Dispute Settlement System," 13.

41 Caroline Henckels, "Overcoming Jurisdictional Isolationism at the WTO-FTA Nexus: A Potential Approach for the WTO," *European Journal of International Law* 19, no. 3 (2008): 571.

42 Songling Yang, "The Solution for Jurisdictional Conflicts between the WTO and RTAs: The Forum Choice Clause," *Michigan State Journal of International Law* 23, no. 1 (2014): 107–152.

43 Marc D. Froese, "Mapping the Scope of Dispute Settlement in Regional Trade Agreements: Implications for the Multilateral Governance of Trade," *World Trade Review* 15, no. 4 (2016): 563–585.

44 Marc L. Busch, Eric Reinhardt, and Gregory C. Shaffer, "Does Legal Capacity Matter? A Survey of WTO Members," *World Trade Review* 8, no. 4 (2009).

45 Alberta Fabbricotti, "Introduction," in *The Political Economy of International Law: A European Perspective*, ed. Alberta Fabbricotti (Cheltenham: Edward Elgar, 2016), 2.

46 Anne Van Aaken and Joel Trachtman, "Political Economy of International Law: Towards a Holistic Model of State Behavior," in *The Political*

120   *Regionalism and centralized trade governance*

Economy of International Law: A European Perspective, ed. Alberta Fabbricotti (Cheltenham: Edward Elgar, 2016), 13.

47 Van Aaken and Trachtman, "Political Economy of International Law," 41.

48 Muzaka and Bishop, "Doha Stalemate."

49 Muzaka and Bishop offer four reasons for the continuation of this perception of decline—the perceived Doha stalemate, the proliferation of free trade agreements (FTAs), the WTO's architecture, sometimes called the wrong rules for the 21st century (including continuation of the GATT "club model," the single undertaking and the consensus model), and finally the global financial crisis. See Muzaka and Bishop, "Doha Stalemate," 6–14.

50 Froese, "Regional Trade Agreements and the Paradox of Dispute Settlement."

51 Vinod K. Aggarwal and Simon J. Evenett, "A Fragmenting Global Economy: A Weakened WTO, Mega FTAs, and Murky Protectionism," *Swiss Political Science Review* 19, no. 4 (2013): 553–554.

52 Muzaka and Bishop, "Doha Stalemate," 15.

53 Richard Baldwin and Elena Seghezza, *Are Trade Blocs Building or Stumbling Blocks? New Evidence* (Geneva: World Trade Organization, 2007).

54 Nuno Limao, "Preferential Trade Agreements as Stumbling Blocks for Multilateral Trade Liberalization: Evidence for the US," *American Economic Review* 96 (2006): 896–914.

55 Baldwin and Seghezza, *Are Trade Blocs Building or Stumbling Blocks?*, 2.

56 Baldwin and Seghezza, *Are Trade Blocs Building or Stumbling Blocks?*, 11.

57 Baldwin and Seghezza, *Are Trade Blocs Building or Stumbling Blocks?*, 12.

58 Emily Blanchard, "A Shifting Mandate: International Ownership, Global Fragmentation, and a Case for Deeper Integration under the WTO," *World Trade Review* 14, no. 1 (2015): 87–99.

59 Bernard Hoekman, "Sustaining Multilateral Trade Cooperation in a Multipolar World Economy," *European University Institute Working Papers* (2013), 15. http://cadmus.eui.eu/bitstream/handle/1814/28962/RSCAS_2013_86.pdf;sequence=1.

60 Robert Wolfe, "First Diagnose, Then Treat: What Ails the Doha Round?," *World Trade Review* 14, no. 1 (2015): 1; see also pp. 13–15.

61 Gary Gereffi and Karina Fernandez-Stark, *Global Value Chain Analysis: A Primer* (Center on Globalization, Governance and Competitiveness, Duke University, 2011), 8.

62 Gary Gereffi, John Humphrey, and Timothy Sturgeon, "The Governance of Global Value Chains," *Review of International Political Economy* 12, no. 1 (2005): 78–104.

6 Legal development without multilateral coordination

- **The proliferation of international investment agreements**
- **Legal convergence and the question of multilateralization**
- **A global marketplace for law and the problem of social cost**
- **Conclusion**

The previous two chapters explored the significance of international economic law to the study of the political economy of trade governance by examining the increasing centralization of regulation in the post-1995 period. We have discussed the significant development of international economic law and argued that it compels scholars of international political economy to re-evaluate their approach to thinking about law, moving from a position in which law exists alongside political economy, to a place where markets and politics operate within the frame of law. Then I began to show what that sort of approach looks like, discussing the implications of legal insight for our understanding of multilateral institutional development and for the way we think about regional trade agreements, which I suggest ought to be analyzed within a larger web of legal relations.

Chapter 4 began with the insight of legal scholar Robert Howse about the periodic shift in institutional footing in the trade governance system and used it to develop a thicker description of institutional development at the WTO. I showed that contra the conventional wisdom that argues the WTO is losing its grip on the issues, the WTO is in fact broadening and deepening its governance competencies through a political process of shifting institutional equilibrium from multilateral meeting to the secretariat and back again. Likewise Chapter 4 began with a common concern shared by law and political economy scholars that RTAs are undermining the multilateral system. I showed how the WTO as a developing institution is increasingly embedded at the center of a rapidly growing global economic governance network.[1]

122 *Legal development and multilateral coordination*

This chapter turns to another node in the densification of the web of law, international investment agreements (IIAs). I examine the multilateralization hypothesis, whereby a number of legal scholars have wondered whether the growing web of IIAs comprises a multilateral answer to the apparent and potential incongruities of the current hybrid model of bilateral-global investment regulation. They argue that IIAs are an example of multilateralism from below. The multilateralization hypothesis offers a way for political economy scholars, with their emphasis on the interconnection of ideas, interests and institutions, to contribute to the debate about the future of legal development.

I argue that the legal literature on multilateralization lacks an appreciation of the role of political agency and collective intentionality in developing the multilateral system. I make a case that what we are seeing in the web of investment treaties is legal convergence without multilateral coordination. This process is driven by market forces and maintained in its basic legal and institutional forms by the problem of social cost. The transaction costs associated with a shift in regulatory form and function are further compounded by the proliferation of these agreements between 1990 and 2010. The first section reviews literature pertaining to the proliferation of international investment agreements. I will begin with a brief history of the use of stand-alone agreements for the protection and promotion of investment and then move to a discussion of convergence around a legal standard.

The second section argues that the convergence of legal form may seem to be a promising basis for a future multilateral project, but we cannot ascribe coordinated political agency to this shift. I then use the data from the United Nations Conference on Trade and Development's (UNCTAD) IIA Mapping Project to show how the legal form of investment agreements has grown over the past 50 years. When making a case for legal convergence, it would be useful to show a pattern wherein legal standards develop over time, converging around a common regulatory model. But this is not the case for international investment agreements. Rather we see that most agreements have, over the course of this period, contained most of the basic elements of a standard IIA most of the time. If this is convergence, it is primarily in the sense that proliferation tends to make a basic standard of protection more generally available to more investors. It is only secondarily in the sense of a legal model for regulation emerging over time.

The final section examines this empirical study of legal convergence in the light of recent literature on the economics of international law. I suggest that the shifting sands of legal convergence look like an economy where actors' moves are coordinated by market forces and the

Legal development and multilateral coordination 123

norms of the marketplace. Rather than the early stages of a political project, we are more likely witnessing the movement of supply and demand towards a certain price point, which for our purposes is defined as a particular model of investment regulation. In this market for law, the question of multilateralization must be considered alongside the problem of social cost.[2] The Coase Theorem goes a significant length toward explaining the reluctance of states to shift from a bilateral to a multilateral footing for the purposes of further development of the terrain of investment law.

The proliferation of international investment agreements

Investment protection is deeply entwined with the history of colonialism, political revolution, and globalization. Clauses protecting investment in international agreements go back to the 18th century, when they began to appear in American Friendship, Commerce and Navigation (FCN) treaties.[3] The main goal of these agreements was the protection of property rather than other forms of investment that are important today such as financial instruments.[4] In the 19th century expropriation was relatively rare due to the prevailing economic and political conditions; most magnet jurisdictions were colonial dependencies. Few capital-importing countries were independent. Yet in the relatively few cases where expropriation did occur, it happened through the seizure of property and capital-exporting states asserted their rights under international law for compensation. Vandevelde describes this as a network of treaties with a narrow scope and relatively weak protections.[5] Miles suggests that in this period the assertions of investor states that they maintained commercial rights under international law was a common refrain. Further, due to the political inequalities of the colonial era, capital-exporting states were largely free to define these rights for themselves.[6]

By the early 20th century, the political context of investment regulation had shifted as Latin American and Eastern European states began to seize land in the name of agrarian reform. Within 30 years, in the aftermath of the Second World War, post-colonial states were using similar rhetorical methods to gain control over natural resources.[7] The basic issue was whether these new states were bound by the decisions of previous colonial administrators. We also see in this era the first attempts by post-colonial states to reshape investment law as well.[8] In the immediate decades following the Second World War, the failure of the ITO left the GATT as a basic multilateral frame for trade, but provided no similar frame for investment regulation. The United States

124 *Legal development and multilateral coordination*

continued to use FCN agreements in this era, concluding 21 between 1946 and 1966, before abandoning the bilateral approach for a focus on multilateralism thereafter.[9]

Several attempts were made on the part of investor states to develop a multilateral frame for investment regulation. There were calls for investment protections in the stillborn ITO in the late 1940s. Following its failure, the International Chamber of Commerce drafted a Code of Fair Treatment for Foreign Investment in 1949. A similar draft statute from the International Law Association called for a foreign investment court. Two draft conventions on the protection of investment were put forward by the OECD in 1961 and 1967.[10] In this era of distrust, decolonization, and the non-aligned movement, multilateral cooperation for global investment regulation was for the most part a non-starter because investment flows by wealthy countries drew comparisons with colonialism and older, predatory forms of foreign control over wealth and the means of producing it.

In the context of the Cold War and expropriations carried out by socialist states, North American and Western European states were equally suspicious of the aims of developing countries. The first modern investment treaty was signed by Germany in 1959. A small but significant number were signed throughout the 1960s. These so-called bilateral investment treaties (BITs) were unique in that they dealt exclusively with investment and were negotiated primarily between developed and developing countries.[11] Developing countries saw these as a way to attract foreign investment; developed countries used them to protect investment. Even so, relatively few were signed in this era due to the skepticism of developing countries, who worried about the neocolonial possibilities of investment treaties that were not reciprocal; their protections and responsibilities went in one direction.

The convention establishing the International Centre for the Settlement of Investment Disputes (ICSID) was a product of this polarization in the post-colonial era, and was the first substantive multilateral success for the global regulation of investment in 1965. Within a decade the United Nations (UN) adopted the *Declaration for the Establishment of a New International Economic Order* (NIEO) and a Charter of the Economic Rights and Duties of States (CERDS), both of which contained language around investment protection that appeared to some wealthy member states to weaken international investment protections. For example, neither text explicitly repudiated nationalization and expropriation without market-value compensation. Miles notes that despite the failure of the NIEO to redevelop norms and rules around foreign investment protection, the populist character

Legal development and multilateral coordination 125

of social movement activism around the issue has remained until today "an enduring source of pressure" for international investment law reform.[12]

Developed countries responded to the action of developing countries at the UN with a wave of bilateral investment agreements. Between 1959 and 1989, 400 BITs were concluded. This is a significant number of treaties, but it was dwarfed by the 2,000 treaties signed in the following two decades.[13] Miles wonders why developing countries agreed to a rising number of international investment agreements, both in the form of BITs and RTAs, when they had largely eschewed multilateral options. Historians agree that changing ideas about the place of open markets in driving growth and development had an appreciable effect on the global policy environment. There was a general move by the 1980s towards freer markets and shifts in International Monetary Fund and World Bank policy towards funding programs that promoted investment liberalization. This victory for market ideologies was accompanied by a loss of other alternative forms of capital for developing country growth and development. American borrowing after 1980 absorbed a significant amount of capital; the United States simultaneously began to make less aid available for the public financing of development.[14]

By the 1980s and 1990s the biggest change in investment protection was the increasing linkage between trade and investment.[15] In this context the creation of the WTO and the conclusion of the GATS were particularly important. Services trade deals to a great extent with investment because "GATS explicitly applies to delivery of services through a 'commercial presence.' Thus a GATS commitment to allow trade in a certain service sector through a commercial presence amounts to a commitment to allow the establishment of a foreign investment."[16] In the post-Cold War era, investment is no longer an alternative to trade flows but rather a means of promoting trade, and this is the biggest qualitative shift in the investment environment in the past century[17]

Further, the post-Cold War democratization processes underway in Eastern Europe, Asia and Latin America contributed to greater openness to foreign direct investment (FDI). Recent research has shown that democratization increases the influence of national groups (such as workers) that benefit from FDI inflows.[18] Even so, a multilateral investment agreement has been on the horizon for at least two decades (Multilateral Agreement on Investment, or MAI, negotiations were suspended in December 1998). The WTO's General Council decided not to negotiate a multilateral agreement during the Doha Round, effectively shelving the multilateral project indefinitely in August of

126 *Legal development and multilateral coordination*

2004. Even so, the increasing complexity of investment regulation means that such a deal is not likely to happen outside the WTO; the question remains one of political will and institutional capacity.

Between 1990 and 2010 the number of IIAs exploded. At the end of 2016 there were a total of 2,625 international investment agreements in force, 2,321 of which were bilateral investment agreements and a further 294 were other treaties with investment provisions, such as regional trade agreements. This proliferation raised the question of whether the future of investment regulation lies in bilateral or multilateral institutions. The issue of different levels of rule-making has been approached by international law scholars through an interdisciplinary approach to theorizing the interaction between law and politics.[19] Leal-Arcas examines the convergence of IIAs around a basic treaty model and standard of legal protection—what he and others refer to as the multilateralization of investment law.[20] Much of what this literature refers to as the development of multilateralism is more properly considered in terms of softer forms of convergence, or what Ruggie refers to as a generic multilateral order.[21] Even so, he recognizes the importance of political commitment to developing a multilateral frame for investment regulation. He argues for the necessity of creating a framework for investment organized around the functionality of BITs and possibly coordinated by the WTO.

Chalamish assumes the necessity of a multilateral agreement for investment and he shows the inability of the WTO to host such a governance forum at the present time. He argues that the network of BITs is already a well-developed governance environment that may provide the tools necessary to institute a multilateral system for investment regulation for a number of reasons. The first has to do with historical shifts in the normative economic environment. By the 1990s we saw a general convergence between developed and developing countries over the importance of foreign investment to economic growth as well as an emergent consensus under customary international law on the formula devised to pay fair market value for expropriated property. Further, while BITs have succeeded where multilateral negotiations failed, their success has "reinforced the importance of investment regulation as a bargaining chip in international economic negotiations."[22] Second, most model BITs use substantially similar definitions to identify investments and investors. They also tend to be reasonably sensitive to the changing terrain of investment protection, quickly recognizing new methods for investment and incorporating them into existing treaties.[23]

Third, multilateral economic governance institutions such as UNCTAD and the World Bank help to bring together investors and

Legal development and multilateral coordination 127

host states, and even help to initiate BIT negotiations. Moreover, the legal texts themselves contain a multilateralization dynamic because MFN clauses assure investors that where a host country signs a more favorable treaty with another country, investors from other countries (with BITs with the host) are entitled to claim a substantially equal level of investment protection. Finally, BITs provide a limited and well-defined set of investors' rights influenced by both trends in treaty drafting as well as trends in FDI. Nevertheless, Chalamish is somewhat hesitant to go all-in on the multilateralization thesis. Rather, he argues that the network of BITs are steadily evolving towards a customary international law form and that in their evolution beyond traditional concepts of international law, they "may offer a substantive legal frame for future multilateral investment regulation."[24]

Schill notes that the development of investment law on a bilateral basis following the Second World War is very different from the multilateral processes developed for the governance of trade and monetary relations. As a result, he suggests that we have seen an unbalanced system in which bilateral investment regulation is the shortest leg on the stool of the global economy, producing an imbalance where global economic regulation is "supported only by international trade and monetary law."[25] Schill believes that this imbalance has been corrected to some degree in recent years by a multilateralization from below, by which the convergence of standards of protection, treaty language, and dispute settlement mechanisms in BITs have created a *de facto* multilateral order for the protection of investment. He suggests that this order is multilateral as opposed to some other form of order because convergence has created generalized rules and extended the principle of non-discrimination to most participating actors.[26]

In arguing that the convergence towards a common model of bilateral investment regulation is a *de facto* multilateralization of international investment law, Schill uses Ruggie's definition of multilateralism as an institution coordinating relations among three or more states based upon agreed-upon rules of conduct.[27] Despite Schill's relatively comprehensive glossing of Ruggie's work, he avoids two significant points. The first concerns the definition of terms. The second concerns the historical specificity of US-led postwar multilateralism, which Ruggie believes to be a demanding institutional form in which significant political commitments are necessary to generalize the benefits of multilateralism. I will deal with these challenges in the next section.

The argument that legal convergence creates multilateral community is novel and interesting. Schill presses forward, arguing that the densification of the web of investment treaties "can be interpreted as an

128 *Legal development and multilateral coordination*

expression of the intention of states to establish a framework based on uniform standards."[28] Indeed, the web of treaties does form a larger system that backstops global investment markets and, as I will show, legal convergence is a significant step forward in the broadening and deepening of IEL. Even so, I would argue that it is not multilateralism, although it may be something different yet similarly effective at weaving dense networks of mutual obligation. In fact, it might be that the use of bilateral treaties stresses the contingent nature of investment rights and the centrality of the state in guaranteeing these rights. Further, the proliferation of IIAs will not necessarily make it easier for states to agree on a multilateral mechanism in the future.

The multilateralization thesis has deep roots in legal theory and history, and is an important moment in the development of the theory around economic law because it brings together insights from IR and IPE as well as insights from law and economics to speculate about the future of law in a way that moves beyond doctrinal debate. In an extension (and perhaps reformulation) of his basic ideas in a more recent article, Schill articulates an approach to enhancing international investment law's legitimacy through a recognition that multilateralization requires a collective commitment to public law principles including the rights and duties of citizens, the rule of law and, concomitantly, the idea of the public interest.[29] He acknowledges that to reap the benefits of multilateralism, actors must recognize the costs of regulation and work to generalize its benefits. Speaking to the backlash against certain aspects of investment law, such as ISDS, he recommends the articulation of public law reasoning as a frame for investment law and a way to increase its international legitimacy. He argues that "at the heart of the criticism of international investment law is what can be called the 'public law challenge.'"[30] Because investment treaty arbitration impinges upon state autonomy and affects the relationship between individuals and their governments in critical areas, it ought to internalize questions of public law-related procedural fairness and substantive equity.[31]

Because international investment law fills an important space in commercial regulation, it requires a common intellectual frame with which to engage with investment law. This is a constructive way to engage with an area of law increasingly suffering from a lack of legitimacy, even as it is increasingly common and of growing importance to value-chain production and other forms of cross-border flows of goods, services, people and money. The main political problem with IIAs is that in comparison to other traditional aspects of international law, states maintain less direct control over the enforcement of investment treaty obligations, especially as they relate to dispute settlement. At the

Legal development and multilateral coordination 129

same time, decisions by arbitral bodies increasingly "affect the fabric of the host state."[32]

This is a functional argument for the treatment of international investment law as public international law because it shares essential similarities to domestic and international legal review processes. A comparative public law approach "views issues of state responsibility and investor-state dispute resolution not as isolated phenomena of international investment law, but in context with analogous problems that arise elsewhere at the domestic or international level."[33] This suggests that the past 20 years of legal development at the WTO have created a standard for legitimate commercial arbitration, even though the WTO system is not as flexible or accessible for commercial interests as the network of ISDS mechanisms in BITs. More to the point, perhaps because the WTO engages in a state-to-state model of dispute settlement, it eases some of the concern about the lack of transparency and predatory practices attributed to ISDS.

There are two main themes in the multilateralization literature that I highlight in order to compare them with Ruggie's understanding of substantive multilateralism below. The first is the generalizability of the benefits of investment treaties, whether through MFN clause or dispute settlement decisions, and the relation of these evolving legal frames to the multilateral form.

The second is the idea that a coordinated effort to create bilateral treaties, alongside the basic multilateral enforcement mechanisms such as those of the ICSID Convention, create not only a vision of order, but a novel approach to multilateralization—an institution of order from below. Next we turn to a closer theoretical and empirical examination of these questions, with the intention of clarifying the links between the political economy and legal literatures.

Legal convergence and the question of multilateralization

The multilateralization argument is interesting for the theoretical questions it poses, but it stumbles against the empirical evidence because multilateralism requires political intent on the part of parties involved. The basic definition of multilateralism that is trotted out at times like these is the coordination of national policies or priorities by at least three states.[34] Ruggie offers a finely qualified definition of multilateralism beyond this nominal descriptor. He is concerned with the substantive, "qualitative dimension," arguing that multilateralism is predicated upon collective action "on the basis of certain principles" for the ordering of international relations.[35]

130 *Legal development and multilateral coordination*

Ruggie, like most other political scientists after him, differentiates between generic multilateral forms of order and the use of multilateral organizations, which are a specific creation of the 20th century. He argues for a substantive political basis of modern multilateralism, suggesting that there are other forms of multilateral coordination, such as the hub-and-spoke model of Nazi Germany's economic treaties, and these may be somewhat effective but they differ substantively from a multilateralism rooted in an understanding of collective action and generalizable benefits for all participants—what Ruggie calls collective action "against an unknown enemy" and on behalf of an "unknown victim."[36]

Multilateralism embodies collective political will that may be initially negotiated bilaterally, as in the case of early rounds of GATT negotiations, but which rises above a simple calculation of the sum of its parts because of its collective commitment to the generalization of benefit and a political pledge of a collective response to future challenges. Schill and others are interested in finding some form of collective will in the convergence of international investment agreements towards a recognizable legal standard. But as I have shown, the web of BITs does not fit easily alongside Ruggie's definition of multilateralism. It is perhaps too much to describe the web of BITs as a post-multilateral form. But it is equally difficult to describe it in the terms of multilateralization.

There are two corollaries to Ruggie's definition of multilateralism as coordination of interstate relations based on certain generalized principles of conduct. First, "generalized organizing principles logically entail an indivisibility" among members of the collective relating to the issue in question.[37] The best example is the norm of most-favored nation status embraced by the international trading system. But legal theorists ought not to get caught up the similarities of MFN as an organizing principle in the network of BITs and its use as an organizing principle in the trading system. Secondly, the real point of significance, as Ruggie goes on to write, is the idea that "indivisibility is a *social construction* not a technical condition" (original emphasis).[38] The italics suggest an intentionality on the part of the political actors constructing the multilateral institutional order.

Note also the contrast with bilateralism that is "premised on specific reciprocity, the simultaneous balancing of specific quid pro quos by each party with every other at all times."[39] The densification or intensification of these relations do not meet the standard for collective intentionality, even if these many relations do converge in form and function. Multilateralism cannot come about by accident or by subtly indirect means. Even though Ruggie uses the MFN principle and early GATT negotiating rounds as an example of bilateral negotiations that

Legal development and multilateral coordination   131

were generalized to a larger collective, it bears repeating that those bilateral negotiations took place within the context of a multilateral trade round, and were undertaken with the express purpose of generalization to the collective. Collective gain was their stated purpose, not a happy accident. In this way multilateralism is difficult to separate from the principled and intentional action that creates it.

Schill makes an important point that dense networks of bilateral relations may create the conditions necessary for a shift to multilateral negotiation; the multilateralization argument holds in the generic sense of the term, but fails in the substantive sense. There is a tendency in the BIT system to converge around a more generic multilateral impulse for order, but no collective will at the present time to move towards a purposive multilateral organization. The multilateralization thesis therefore adequately describes the place of the network of international investment agreements in the liberal economic order, and may even partly fulfill the definition of a multilateral regime if we take for granted that the decision-making procedures that raise a regime above an order are fully decentralized and occur at a remove through tribunal decisions and thereby lack a collective deliberative basis. However, we must note that this only partly fulfills the definition of a regime and falls far short of a multilateral organization.[40]

The second corollary to Ruggie's argument states that 20th-century institutional multilateralism is an American cultural form.[41] He notes that the United States did not seek to endow international organizations with independent powers per se. But the multilateral processes in the postwar years were driven by an intentionally multilateralist agenda.[42] Ruggie makes the explicit distinction between functional theories of institutions and their focus on cooperation to limit transaction costs on the one hand, and his understanding of multilateralism predicated upon political intentionality and rooted in the political values of the New Deal on the other.

Further, the success of substantive multilateralism is tied to the credibility of commitments made by leading states. Ruggie calls multilateralism a demanding institutional form, and notes that the hegemon has less expensive (both in terms of political and economic capital) strategies at its disposal. In most cases, multilateral negotiating strategies are less credible (and effective) than bilateral strategies for this reason. But in the American context, multilateralism became a trusted negotiating form. The American commitment to multilateralism was only credible for reasons that are inherent in the American political system, such as an electoral system geared to the median voter (and an electorate wishing to capitalize on America's leadership position), a

132 *Legal development and multilateral coordination*

separation of legislative and executive powers that made policy reversal difficult, and the general transparency of the political arena. As a result, the United States was in a unique position to capitalize on a demanding institutional form that offered higher dividends for success than did bilateral or unilateral means on their own.[43]

Ruggie completes his study of the anatomy of multilateralism with a brief historical tour, where the example of the development of the International Telegraph Union is a case study in what is missing in the legal literature's indirect and decentralized understanding of multilateralism. This development consisted of three parts: the collective agreement on the rules of telegraphy, the establishment of a permanent secretariat to administer the implementation and coordination of the system, and the provision of periodic conferences to revise the system as necessary. Of course bilateral relations may have multilateral consequences, a good example being the Cobden-Chevalier Treaty. However, British free trade featured a hegemon to guarantee stability through unilateral or bilateral means.[44] It is very interesting that pre-20th-century examples of multilateral ordering line up more closely with the multilateralization thesis. Even so, the 20th century represents a move to multilateralism organized on an institutional basis and here the multilateralization thesis lags.[45]

I have shown above that at least in theoretical terms multilateralism and legal convergence are very different processes. The first is a strategy to harness broadly convergent interests for political purposes, while the second may be the result of many different forces, all, some, or none of which may be intentional. To put a spin on a hackneyed truism of social science, convergence is not causation. Furthermore, multilateralism is not necessarily the only natural outcome of converging interests (or converging laws), so much as it is one possible process by which interests may be harnessed for political effect. Perhaps one may answer by arguing that the multilateralization thesis posits a functionalist understanding of the place of law in the development of political order. I would argue that if this is the case, it still puts the cart before the horse in that it posits law as prior to collective intentionality. Even so, while I disagree with the chain of logical inference in the multilateralization thesis, I would agree that the substantive focus on convergence is very useful.

Having considered the theoretical aspects of legal convergence, we must now turn to an empirical examination of the substance of the thousands of investment agreements signed over the past several decades. The goal is to examine the use of legal language in these agreements, looking for trends in the use of certain types of clauses. If we are to find convergence towards a single model of investment regulation, we will see it in the shift in the language used in agreements signed since 1959. The body of IIAs is vast, and unlike the WTO, which acts as a global knowledge base for trade regulation, there are no complete databases of international investment agreements. The closest we have is UNCTAD's Investment Policy Hub that coordinates the IIA Mapping Project, which has analyzed the main provisions in almost 2,000 IIAs.[46] I use this database to map the development of investment protection provisions over time. Figure 6.1 shows the hump of investment treaty proliferation that looks a great deal like the curve of RTA proliferation that has been much cited in that literature.

A couple of points ought to be made. First, there was a massive surge in treaty proliferation between 1990 and 2010. After those decades new signings dipped significantly, a pattern that suggests a post-Cold War peace dividend. It also suggests that the most active years of IIA proliferation are over, either because nations have spent the political capital of the post-Cold War period, or because the needs of the global economy are changing, the perceptions of global publics are shifting, the priorities of leading states are changing, or perhaps the proliferation of treaty-making itself has within it a dynamic of diminishing returns. Nevertheless, in governance terms, the long tale of the post-Cold War period will be with us for decades to come, but the boom in IIA creation is likely over.

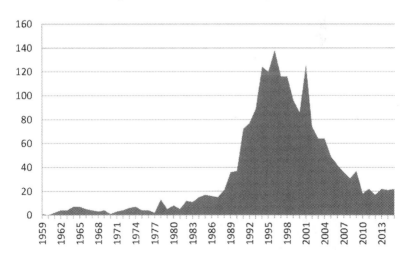

Figure 6.1 The proliferation of international investment agreements, 1959–2015
Source: Based on data from UNCTAD Investment Policy Hub.

134 *Legal development and multilateral coordination*

Figure 6.2 shows the use of clauses relating to standards of treatment over the same period. We might expect to see a developmental curve over the 50-year period, with the use of MFN, national treatment (NT) and fair and equitable treatment clauses gaining in popularity as investment treaties proliferated. But this is largely not the case. The use of MFN, NT, fair and equitable treatment clauses, and prohibitions against unreasonable, arbitrary and discriminatory measures closely map to the overall shape of the curve of investment treaty proliferation. Put simply, these clauses have been used all along, and their use proliferates as treaties proliferate, rather than as a function of regulatory convergence per se.

The one outlier may be a well-defined explication of indirect expropriation, which was very rare in treaties prior to 1995, and remained a relatively rare phenomenon during the boom years of treaty proliferation, even though its use has increased significantly in the past ten years. Even so, Figure 6.2 suggests that we do not see a convergence around a model so much as we see the proliferation of a basic model, which has been refined over time. This is indeed a form of convergence, but perhaps one that is entirely subtler than the literature has suggested.

Figure 6.3 shows a similar pattern for dispute settlement clauses. Both state-to-state dispute settlement and investor-state dispute settlement provisions have existed in IIAs from the earliest years. These clauses proliferated with the surge in IIA signings we have discussed above. In the context of dispute settlement, the question of convergence becomes a bit more complex because with the proliferation of dispute settlement mechanisms, comes a surge in their use, and this proliferation

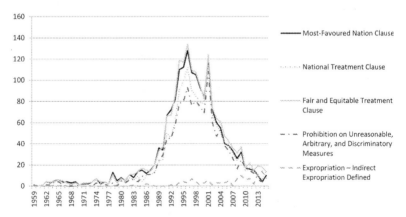

Figure 6.2 Clauses relating to standards of treatment, 1959–2015
Source: Based on data from UNCTAD Investment Policy Hub.

Legal development and multilateral coordination 135

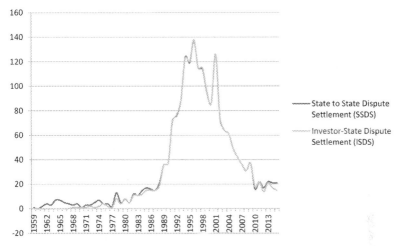

Figure 6.3 Dispute settlement clauses, 1959–2015
Source: Based on data from UNCTAD Investment Policy Hub.

of treaty arbitration has driven the development of a significant body of law concerning investment protection. This growth of legal decision-making, like the surge in cases during the first two decades after the creation of the WTO, has created a significant body of jurisprudence that has broadly defined the parameters of investment regulation.

In Figure 6.4 we see a marked increase in use of language that affirms the rights of host states to regulate industry, and an increase in statements regarding public health and the environment, labor standards and corporate social responsibility. Here we see a much clearer pattern of convergence. These clauses proliferate over time, and taken

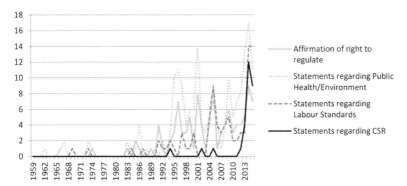

Figure 6.4 Legal language affirming state regulatory space, 1959–2015
Source: Based on data from UNCTAD Investment Policy Hub.

136 *Legal development and multilateral coordination*

with the previous figures, we can see a trend towards convergence around the language used to evoke the flexibility of these agreements. This might be a response to increasing politicization of bilateral investment treaties, but it is more likely a measure of the evolving norms around state responses to globalization.

The use of language concerning the state's right to regulate, the protection of public health, the environment and labor standards, and statements affirming corporate social responsibility map easily onto the rise of concerns around these domains in public discourse. For example, statements regarding corporate social responsibility are almost completely absent from BITs until around 2010, when that language proliferates while the academic literature begins to focus on the issue.[47] Statements regarding public health and the environment arise around the time those issues became connected to the trade liberalization debates in the United States. It is likely that this language reflects the evolving concerns of public interest groups in investing states.

The time-series study confirms that the main trend in the development of investment treaties is proliferation, which has in turn driven a trend of legal convergence by the means of amplification. At the end of the day, proliferation and amplification are not multilateralization. Even so, the idea of generating order from below makes a sort of progressive sense while simultaneously satisfying the need to account for political order in the process of legal development. Secondarily, it makes an intuitive sense because multilateral processes are still conceptualized as being guided by states in the legal literature, but in a post-imperial, post-hegemony, dare we say, a more European way. Yet thinking more concretely about the typological placement of the BIT system in the global system of cooperation suggests a way forward.

Ruggie's differentiation of organizations, regimes and orders suggests a way to triangulate the BIT system in the global network of international economic law. First, the multilateralization thesis does not extend the theory of multilateral institutionalism because it cannot adequately deal with the problem of collective intentionality, and therefore cannot meet a substantive definition of multilateral institutionalism. Second, a regime is less concrete than an organization and refers to "common, deliberative though often highly asymmetrical means of conducting interstate relations."[48] The BIT system does not look like a multilateral regime because it lacks a mechanism for self-conscious change, what Ruggie calls a consultation mechanism. As a result, we can see places where the fabric of multilateralization wears thin, particularly around contentious forms of dispute settlement such as ISDS.

Legal development and multilateral coordination 137

Third, the simplest form of multilateralism, the multilateral order, refers to the "architectural dimension" of the rules that order relations.[49] The legal convergence associated with proliferation of international investment agreements best resembles a form of multilateral order—a general agreement among political actors on what the rules ought to look like most of the time. However, the slowing pace of BIT creation suggests that we contextualize this order in the post-Cold War era because in the absence of clear evidence of leadership and intentionality it is largely the result of consensus driven by the political economic context. Defining the BIT system as a basic form of order also suggests a developmental trajectory of law heavily influenced by economic factors. Comparatively less work has been done in law on the economic basis of international law, which I will discuss below.

A global marketplace for law and the problem of social cost

In this final section I make a three-part argument for a politics of international economic law that benefits from the insights of the economics of law literature.[50] In doing so, I show how emerging legal theory interacts with social scientific methods to offer several new and important insights about the dynamics of legal development. In the first part, I briefly discuss the relationship between rational choice insights and international law scholarship. In the second, I examine the literature around the "market for law" thesis as it relates to our discussion of international investment law. In the third part, I argue that legal convergence is the result of a growing global market for law. Furthermore, the lack of a multilateral dimension to investment regulation may also be explained using rational choice methods. The problem of social cost, first articulated by R.H. Coase in 1960, explains how the proliferation of IIAs may undermine, rather than support a multilateralization dynamic, or at the very least may make multilateralism a more difficult choice for contracting states.

Political scientists have developed many insights about the international legal system but have failed to explain why states obey international law when there is no obvious enforcement mechanism.[51] Guzman attempts to answer this question using a rational choice method developed at the intersection where economics and political science methods meet. He argues that the three R's of compliance—reputation, reciprocity, and retaliation—work together to the norms of cooperation in international law. Put very simply, a rational choice explanation of international law argues "states must experience some gain as a result of their engagement with the international legal system

138 *Legal development and multilateral coordination*

and that gain must be larger than what they invest."[52] The preference for cooperation is rational. States see a bigger return on cooperation than they do on non-cooperation.

The rational choice model has implications for how we understand all forms of international law, and how we understand courts. Guzman argues that the role of courts at the international level is not compliance enforcement but rather compliance inducement by using rulings for information purposes. Court decisions provide states with input that can guide their analysis of how other governments perceive their policies and how certain actions will be met by other states, in terms of impact on reputation, future reciprocal interactions and possible future retaliation. The rational choice approach also suggests that legal form matters less than some scholars have thought because forms of international law exist on a continuum of potential state action. As a result, the legal instrument developed in any given context may serve as a signal about the relative importance of an issue to the bargaining state.

This places the question of bilateral versus multilateral strategy into sharp relief because both reciprocity and retaliation mechanisms are more effective in the bilateral context.[53] While bilateral relationships stress reciprocal behavior, the basic goal of multilateralism is to overcome collective action problems and thereby enhance treaty effectiveness through monitoring. This question of the effectiveness of multilateralism raises the issue of agreement scope. Bilateral agreements are generally narrower in scope than multilateral agreements because increasing the number of participants increases the number of concerns that must be addressed in the agreement and in turn increases transaction costs. Bilateralism has a narrow scope and lower transaction costs, which means that the benefits of multilateralism must be large enough to outweigh the greater costs of a larger scope of agreement.[54]

Guzman's argument about the usefulness of rational choice approaches for explaining the effectiveness of international law allows us to shift focus from a demonstration of the functional importance of social science methods to the study of international law, to an argument about the role of markets in the creation of treaties. Building upon this theoretical literature, O'Hara O'Connor and Franck use the work of Larry Ribstein on jurisdictional competition to develop a number of insights in the realm of international investment law.[55] In *The Law Market* (2009), O'Hara and Ribstein provide a way of thinking about jurisdictional competition in which "private parties on the demand side shop for governing laws supplied by states."[56] The best examples of jurisdictional competition in the international economic law literature are forum shopping (discussed extensively in the literature on regional

Legal development and multilateral coordination 139

trade agreements) and the ways that multinational corporations shop for appropriate investment agreements among a number of host countries.

In this approach to understanding the dynamics of law, "states actively seek to attract foreign investment through a variety of legal and economic incentives."[57] The market pressure that states, as law-makers, operate under may lead to legal convergence as states seeking to attract assets compete to create attractive legal environments. States compete in different ways. Some are active competitors, some passive competitors, some strategic non-competitors if they have other attractive factors that may tip investment decisions in their favor. The end result is that "not only is foreign investment law driven by state efforts to attract foreign assets—fueling the supply side of the market—but these laws enhance asset mobility more generally, which works to motivate states to provide attractive commercial law more generally."[58]

States, like other market actors, are limited in their ability to compete in global markets by imperfect information.[59] Furthermore, a perfectly competitive environment is impossible when states have different economic capacities and differential access to hard power resources. As a result, market-based activities are as much a function of perception, imperfect information and cognitive/behavioral factors, as they reflect supply and demand.[60] I showed above that not every instance of actors working together to greater efficiency ought to be categorized as collective action. Buyers and sellers seeking to participate in the market converge on the price of a good or service. In many ways the legal convergence that typifies patterns of IIA proliferation looks more like the interaction between supply and demand that occurs around the pricing of assets, than it does the political coordination of states for collective action. There is no intentionality on the part of treaty-makers to coordinate effort beyond the rational action of actors seeking the effective protection of investments in a host state.

The market for law approach shares certain commonalities with another critique of the multilateralization thesis posed by Muchlinski. He argues that the multilateralization thesis misses the larger point that the BIT system is less an organic body of law than it is "a process of practitioner-led treaty interpretation that allows for a creative approach to investor and investment protection."[61] He suggests that four factors undercut the generalizability of BIT dispute settlement decisions. First, awards handed down by investor-state tribunals are not always made public. Second, there is certainly some use of precedent, but tribunals are not obligated to cite previous cases. Third, without an appellate body, there is no way to resolve conflicts that arise

140 *Legal development and multilateral coordination*

from tribunal decisions. Finally, nobody knows the extent to which tribunal decisions influence investors or states, but there appears to be a fear that government action is hindered by an inability to map the implications of BITs, and therefore some states are reviewing their obligations, and in certain cases, backing away from investor-state dispute settlement mechanisms.[62]

There is a second, and potentially more significant challenge posed by thinking about the costs associated with investment protection. It is not only a trade-off between effective market governance and state autonomy, but also a trade-off between the relative inefficiency of current approaches and the potential costs of adopting another system for global investment regulation. The Coase Theorem can help explain the failure of the multilateral option for investment governance. The Coase Theorem is often stated as "under perfect competition private and social costs will be equal."[63] But stated this way it misses Coase's main point, which is that an analysis of the transaction costs associated with social protection is always necessary because in the real world of imperfect competition, these costs are never nil.

Coase begins by examining the actions of firms that may have a negative effect on other actors. However, his analysis is equally prescient for us if we are to consider law in the same micro-economic terms of supply, demand, competition and price. Coase argues that the common approach to social cost is one in which A inflicts harm on B and, as a result, the question is how to restrain A. However, he suggests that this only elucidates half the problem. All things being equal, restraint will be harmful to A, so the question becomes, "should A be allowed to harm B, or should B be allowed to harm A?"[64] Looking at social cost in this way allows us to see the true problem, which is that corrective change will have a price beyond the marginal costs associated with the immediate corrective, and "change may produce more harm than the original deficiency."[65] Therefore, making a choice between different social arrangements in broad terms ought to take into the final calculation "the total effect of these arrangements in all spheres of life."[66]

The problem of social cost—that the transaction costs associated with change are never cost-neutral—means that changes in the system of IIAs must be considered in terms of the total effect rather than their marginal costs. In our context, states must consider the cost of multilateralism in terms of its total effect. Is it better to move to the multilateral system? We do not know, but the fact that such a move has been a political non-starter for the past two decades gives some clue as to the cost/benefit calculations happening at the state level. Put another way, in the current calculus of bilateral investment treaty-making, the

Legal development and multilateral coordination 141

loss of legal legitimacy that comes from the use of less effective bilateral negotiations and dispute settlement processes is at least partially offset by symbolic (and possibly real) gains in certain forms of state autonomy vis-à-vis foreign investors.

The ways that states weigh autonomy against the benefits of multilateral action has been recently explored in the political economy literature. A number of studies confirm the basic outline of this research—that states remain the primary forces behind deeper economic integration, that they use law as a tool to develop those interconnections, and that intentionality on the part of governments is the most important factor in the development of international economic law.[67] Cooley and Spruyt's work on contracting states that I discussed in a previous chapter also has important implications for the law market literature. The marketplace in which treaty-taking states meet the requests of investing states through the bilateral investment treaty speaks to an important dynamic in the way that sovereignty is transferred among states. It can further allow us to develop bridges between political economy and security studies by allowing us to examine investment bilateralism alongside other bilateral relationships, from decolonization to bilateral security agreements.[68]

Jupille, Mattli and Snidal show that states remain the primary actors behind global commercial regulation, in that they choose the institutions that they work through. And yet while states are free to choose their governance options, "institutional choice in global commerce is molded to a large extent by the institutional status quo: already existing venues shape responses to new cooperation challenges."[69] We do not have a multilateral investment regime because states have not chosen to create one, and this failure to address the multilateral option must be considered to be deliberate. While states are somewhat conservative in their choices relating to regulation, Stone has shown that there are other strategic reasons for preferring the status quo over a new and unproven system.[70] Leading powers tend to use carefully constructed political backdoors in international institutions to maintain control over certain mechanisms that are essential to the functioning of the institution. This may increase the legitimacy of the institution by guaranteeing outcomes to a certain extent. It could be argued that this is precisely the strength of the network of BITs. Treaty-offering states are able to maintain a certain amount of control over the regulation of investment through both the transactional process of offering and signing BITs as well as the bilateral frame of political relations, although the process multiplies the transaction costs associated with global governance.[71]

142 *Legal development and multilateral coordination*

Conclusion

Until very recently, it has been mostly lawyers who were interested in the politics of international law. At the national level, political scientists are interested in political strategies pursued in legal environments, such as the courts, but did not consider the international economy to be a terrain wherein legal strategies were of first-order importance. The proliferation of IIAs, RTAs, and even WTO dispute settlement has changed that perception. I argued in this chapter that what is missing from the multilateralization literature is an appreciation of the role of intentional agency and leadership for collective action in developing the multilateral system.

In the first section we paid particular attention to the literature arguing that the remarkable similarity of investment agreements may be considered a case of multilateralism from below, or the multilateralization of this legal issue area. The multilateralization thesis posits the inevitability of multilateralism when state interests align with a general consensus on the substantive elements of law. However, this functional understanding of postwar multilateralism tends to ignore the role of political values and ideas in the development of the political leadership necessary for such a collective endeavor.

While the question of multilateralization is important in theoretical terms, the real-world application of this idea is a dead letter for four reasons. First, BITs will likely never become a dense enough network to create demand for a multilateral agreement that stands apart from the ICSID Convention and the WTO because densification is both a source of convergence and a cause for maintaining the status quo. More law is never a one-way street to deeper political interdependence. Second, the MAI failed, suggesting that while there was political will in the post-Cold War period for a multilateral trade project, little was left over for investment. It is difficult to say when (or if) the political stars will align in a way that states demand a multilateral investment governance mechanism. Third, ISDS, which had been considered a crowning achievement of investment bilateralism, is increasingly contentious and unpopular with global publics.[72] This could be a spur to multilateralism, or it could corrode and walk back the deep reach of investment law. Time will tell. Fourth, the multilateralization literature tends to gloss over the importance of intentionality and leadership to the development of multilateral mechanisms.

Nevertheless, the fact that we can ask if multilateralization is immanent suggests both the vast growth of the terrain of law as well as the important convergence of legal templates, ideas about regulation, and jurisdictional models. In fact, I would go so far as to argue that

Legal development and multilateral coordination 143

while the multilateralization thesis is based on a less than completely fulsome application of the concept of multilateralism, it is still important because it is a serious attempt to grapple with the implications of the growth of IEL, something that IPE scholars have been slow to do.

I made a case in the second and third sections that what we are seeing in the web of bilateral investment treaties is legal convergence without multilateral coordination. This process is driven by market forces and maintained in its basic legal and institutional forms by the problem of social cost, and further complicated by the proliferation of these agreements between 1990 and 2010. Perhaps in this context we could say that a market for bilateral agreements is both the best of all available options and the worst of options. As the best option, it offers lower transaction costs with most of the benefits of a generalized multilateral system through the legal convergence associated with MFN clauses and ICSID dispute settlement. As the worst option, these clauses may create perverse incentives for firms to seek profits through the courts—a process that can be interpreted as a form of reverse expropriation. At the very least, it is appropriate to suggest that in the context of states with well-developed court systems, ISDS may be a counterproductive regulatory strategy.

Finally, I argued that despite the obvious problems associated with relying upon legal convergence through a market for law to create some form of regulatory consistency, there are likely to be significant unanticipated costs associated with moving to a multilateral form of global investment regulation. The problem of social cost (not to mention the fallacy of sunk costs) begins to explain why states doubled down on the bilateral strategy in the field of investment regulation even as they shifted to a deeper form of multilateral engagement in the field of trade regulation.

Our discussion of the bilateral strategy for investment governance and its prospects for evolutionary development towards the multilateral form has significant implications for the trade multilateralism literature where scholars are divided on whether values or interests play a deciding role in multilateral success. I have suggested one way to think about proliferation and legal convergence without multilateral coordination and in doing so this discussion adds a much needed dimension to the trade multilateralism literature in which one often gets the sense that legal development proceeds in a somewhat straightforward and orderly fashion. I have shown in this chapter and the previous one, two very different ways that bilateral and regional arrangements can work together, both to reinforce a set of multilateral relationships, as well as to reinforce a bilateral dynamic. The common thread seems to be an

144 *Legal development and multilateral coordination*

historical institutional trajectory of development in each case (RTA and BIT), as well as a political commitment on the part of governments to engage in a variety of treaty processes in order to simultaneously benefit from deeper economic integration while maintaining some form of institutional and political status quo.

Notes

1 Carlos A. Primo Braga and Bernard Hoekman, eds., *Future of the World Trade Order* (Fiesole, Italy: European University Institute, 2016).
2 Erin A. O'Hara and Larry Ribstein, *The Law Market* (Oxford: Oxford University Press, 2009); R.H. Coase, "The Problem of Social Cost," *Journal of Law and Economics* 3 (1960): 1–23.
3 Wolfgang Alschner, "Americanization of the BIT Universe: The Influence of Friendship, Commerce and Navigation (FCN) Treaties on Modern Investment Treaty Law," *Goettingen Journal of International Law* 2 (2013): 455–486.
4 Kenneth J. Vandevelde, "A Brief History of International Investment Agreements," *U.C.-Davis Journal of International Law and Policy* 12 (2005): 158.
5 Vandevelde, "A Brief History of International Investment Agreements," 161.
6 Kate Miles, *The Origins of International Investment Law: Empire, Environment and the Safeguarding of Capital* (Cambridge: Cambridge University Press, 2013), 69.
7 Miles, *The Origins of International Investment Law*, 75–78.
8 Miles, *The Origins of International Investment Law*, 81.
9 Vandevelde, "A Brief History of International Investment Agreements," 162.
10 Miles, *The Origins of International Investment Law*, 85.
11 Vandevelde, "A Brief History of International Investment Agreements," 171–173.
12 Miles, *The Origins of International Investment Law*, 100.
13 Vandevelde, "A Brief History of International Investment Agreements," 179.
14 Vandevelde, "A Brief History of International Investment Agreements," 177.
15 Surya P. Subedi, *International Investment Law: Reconciling Policy and Principle* (Oxford: Hart Publishing, 2008), 87–92.
16 Vandevelde, "A Brief History of International Investment Agreements," 176.
17 Investment agreements are effective when it comes to protecting investment but not very effective at promoting investment. Like regional trade agreements, they tend to formalize existing commercial relations rather than provide incentives for new investment patterns. See Eric Neumayer and Laura Spess, "Do Bilateral Investment Treaties Increase Foreign Direct Investment to Developing Countries?," *World Development* 33, no. 10 (2005): 1567–1585.
18 Sonal S. Pandya, "Democratization and Foreign Direct Investment Liberalization, 1970–2000," *International Studies Quarterly* 58 (2014): 475–488.
19 Stephen Woolcock, ed., *Trade and Investment Rulemaking: The Role of Regional and Bilateral Agreements* (New York: United Nations University Press, 2006).

Legal development and multilateral coordination 145

20 Rafael Leal-Arcas, "The Multilateralization of International Investment Law," *North Carolina Journal of International Law and Commercial Regulation* 35 (2010): 34–136.

21 John Gerard Ruggie, "Multilateralism: The Anatomy of an Institution," in *Multilateralism Matters: The Theory and Praxis of an Institutional Form*, ed. John Gerard Ruggie (New York: Columbia University Press, 1993).

22 Efraim Chalamish, "The Future of Bilateral Investment Treaties: A De Facto Multilateral Agreement?," *Brooklyn Journal of International Law* 34, no. 2 (2009): 317.

23 Chalamish, "The Future of Bilateral Investment Treaties," 320.

24 Chalamish, "The Future of Bilateral Investment Treaties," 353.

25 Stephan Schill, *The Multilateralization of International Investment Law* (Cambridge: Cambridge University Press, 2009).

26 In arguing for a multilateralization dynamic, Schill distinguishes the multilateral form from what he calls hegemonic order, in which the will of the hegemon is paramount and rules correspond to the hegemon's interest. This is something of a false dichotomy and differs markedly from the political literature on the postwar history of multilateralism. Further, his emphasis on the communitarian elements of multilateralism somewhat downplays the role of powerful states in creating and sustaining multilateral orders, both in the context of historical orders of the 18th and 19th centuries, as well as in the cases of the United States in the global trading system, and Germany and France in the European Union today. See Schill, *The Multilateralization of International Investment Law*, 9.

27 Schill, *The Multilateralization of International Investment Law*, 3; Ruggie, "Multilateralism," 3–11.

28 Schill, *The Multilateralization of International Investment Law*, 364.

29 Stephan Schill, "Enhancing International Law's Legitimacy: Conceptual and Methodological Foundations of a New Public Law Approach," *Virginia Journal of International Law* 52, no. 1 (2011): 57–102.

30 Schill, "Enhancing International Law's Legitimacy," 67.

31 William W. Burke-White and Andreas von Staden, "Private Litigation in a Public Law Sphere: The Standard of Review in Investor-State Arbitrations," *Yale Journal of International Law* 35 (2010): 283–346.

32 Schill, "Enhancing International Law's Legitimacy," 76.

33 Schill, "Enhancing International Law's Legitimacy," 100.

34 Julia C. Morse and Robert O. Keohane, "Contested Multilateralism," *The Review of International Organizations* 9, no. 1 (2014).

35 John Gerard Ruggie, "Multilateralism: The Anatomy of an Institution," *International Organization* 46, no. 3 (Summer 1992): 566–567.

36 Ruggie, "Multilateralism," 569.

37 Ruggie, "Multilateralism," 571.

38 Ruggie, "Multilateralism," 571.

39 Ruggie, "Multilateralism," 571–572.

40 It is important to note that this study of multilateralism as a concept and as a theoretical construction improves on older theories of regimes and their reliance on Hegemonic Stability Theory by problematizing the fact that the hegemon chooses an multilateral option despite the rationality of bringing power to bear through unilateral or bilateral means. "In short, it may be true—but uninteresting—that regimes are created by the powerful. Power

146   *Legal development and multilateral coordination*

alone can explain neither the choice of rules nor the distributional implications of a particular regime." This does not mean that great powers are unnecessary, but rather points out that multilateral failure is not the result of the inefficiencies associated with big-tent multilateralism. Judith Goldstein, "Creating the GATT Rules: Politics, Institutions, and American Policy," in *Multilateralism Matters: The Theory and Praxis of an Institutional Form*, ed. John Gerard Ruggie (New York: Columbia University Press, 1993), 223. See also Miles Kahler, "Multilateralism with Small and Large Numbers," in *Multilateralism Matters: The Theory and Praxis of an Institutional Form*, ed. John Gerard Ruggie (New York: Columbia University Press, 1993).

41 Andrew Moravcsik, "Liberal Theories of International Law," in *Interdisciplinary Perspectives on International Law and International Relations: The State of the Art*, ed. Jeffrey L. Dunoff and Mark A. Pollack (Cambridge: Cambridge University Press, 2013).

42 Ruggie, "Multilateralism," 589–590.

43 Anne-Marie Burley, "Regulating the World: Multilateralism, International Law, and the Projection of the New Deal Regulatory State," in *Multilateralism Matters: The Theory and Praxis of an Institutional Form*, ed. John Gerard Ruggie (New York: Columbia University Press, 1993).

44 Ruggie, "Multilateralism," 577–581.

45 According to Ruggie, the move to institutions had three important consequences. First, it complicated the simpler ends-means relationship that typified earlier multilateral orders. Second, multilateral forums themselves began to share the "agenda setting and convening powers of states." And third, "multilateral diplomacy has come to embody a procedural norm in its own right," and conveys an international legitimacy all its own. Ruggie, "Multilateralism," 584.

46 Some 1,959 of the 2,625 agreements in force have been mapped. While this still leaves 664 outside our study, the overwhelming majority of IIAs have been mapped, offering a large and representative sample of the language used in investment treaties.

47 Adam Sneyd, *Governing Cotton: Globalization and Poverty in Africa* (London: Palgrave Macmillan, 2011).

48 Ruggie, "Multilateralism," 572.

49 Ruggie, "Multilateralism," 572.

50 Nicholas Mercuro, and Steven G. Medema, *Economics and the Law: From Posner to Post-Modernism* (Princeton, N.J.: Princeton University Press, 1997).

51 Andrew Guzman, *How International Law Works: A Rational Choice Theory* (Oxford: Oxford University Press, 2008), 8.

52 Guzman, *How International Law Works*, 12.

53 Guzman, *How International Law Works*, 63.

54 Guzman, *How International Law Works*, 161.

55 Erin A. O'Hara O'Connor and Susan D. Franck, "Foreign Investments and the Market for Law," *University of Illinois Law Review* 5 (2014): 1617–1662.

56 O'Hara O'Connor and Franck, "Foreign Investments and the Market for Law," 1618; O'Hara and Ribstein, *The Law Market*.

57 O'Hara O'Connor and Franck, "Foreign Investments and the Market for Law," 1619.

Legal development and multilateral coordination   147

58 O'Hara O'Connor and Franck, "Foreign Investments and the Market for Law," 1660.
59 Gene M. Grossman, *Imperfect Competition and International Trade* (Cambridge, Mass.: MIT Press, 1992).
60 Lauge N. Skovgaard Poulsen, "Bounded Rationality and the Diffusion of Modern Investment Treaties," *International Studies Quarterly* 58 (2014): 1–14.
61 Peter Muchlinski, "Corporations and the Uses of Law: International Investment Arbitration as a 'Multilateral Legal Order'," *Onati Socio-Legal Series* 1, no. 4 (2011): 3.
62 Muchlinski, "Corporations and the Uses of Law," 7.
63 R.H. Coase, *The Firm, the Market, and the Law* (Chicago, Ill.: University of Chicago Press, 1990), 174.
64 Coase, *The Firm, the Market, and the Law*, 96.
65 Coase, *The Firm, the Market, and the Law*, 153.
66 Coase, *The Firm, the Market, and the Law*, 154. Further, when we consider factors of production (including law), we must consider them in the context of existing law and regulation. For example, we often speak of the ownership of land, when what we really mean is the purchase of certain rights to carry out a "circumscribed list of actions" on the land (p. 155). The same may be said of many other factors of production and this draws the mind to regulation that ensures the right to carry out one set of actions or another in a foreign context. In this sense, BITs may be considered factors of production and their use subject to the analysis of private and social costs, to use Coase's terminology.
67 Thomas G. Weiss and Rorden Wilkinson, "Rethinking Global Governance? Complexity, Authority, Power, Change," *International Studies Quarterly* 58 (2014): 207–215.
68 Alexander Cooley and Hendrik Spruyt, *Contracting States: Sovereign Transfers in International Relations* (Princeton, N.J.: Princeton University Press, 2009), 186–187.
69 Joseph Jupille, Walter Mattli, and Duncan Snidal, *Institutional Choice and Global Commerce* (Cambridge: Cambridge University Press, 2013), 199.
70 Randall W. Stone, *Controlling Institutions: International Organizations and the Global Economy* (Cambridge: Cambridge University Press, 2011).
71 Alexander Thompson and Daniel Verdier, "Multilateralism, Bilateralism, and Regime Design," *International Studies Quarterly* 58 (2014): 15–28.
72 Lauge N. Skovgaard Poulsen and Emma Aisbett, "When the Claim Hits: Bilateral Investment Treaties and Bounded Rational Learning," *World Politics* 65, no. 2 (2013): 273–313.

7 Creating international economic law beyond the state

- Precedent and the articulation of law beyond the state
- Precedent in international investment arbitration
- Precedent at the WTO
- Mapping case citation at the WTO
- Question 1: How many separate WTO and GATT cases are cited as precedent?
- Question 2: Is the number of cases cited increasing over time?
- Question 3: Which cases are cited most often?
- Question 4: Do some complainants and respondents rely on precedent more than others?
- Law-making, legitimacy, and moments of rapid legal development
- Precedent as law-making
- Legitimacy and authority
- Moments of rapid development in international law
- Conclusion

This book has been making two arguments, one about the increasing centrality of law in international economic relations, and the other about the potential for bringing legal concepts and insights into contact with the study of global political economy. This chapter further develops these arguments by examining a relatively new area of interest to governance experts—the use of precedent by international courts and tribunals. Previous chapters examined the way that international law scholarship can elucidate the political economy of regulation. This chapter turns to a foundational question in the international economic law literature: how ought we to think about the citation of previous cases in international dispute settlement? Are they precedent, as we conceive it in the common law context? If so, what are the implications for the politics of international economic law?

International economic law beyond the state 149

I argue that in the context of the WTO, the development of a body of precedent and its extensive use by all disputing members, make it a primary indicator of the growing authority of trade law and perhaps international economic law generally.[1] Legal scholars debate the relationship between precedent and legal legitimacy. It may be that the use of precedent requires a substantially legitimate legal system to operate effectively. Or it may be that the referencing of previous cases reinforces the authority of the law in the present by drawing links with decisions in the past. In either case, a stable and broadly legitimate and authoritative body of law goes hand in hand with a well-functioning system of precedent across the terrain of international economic law.

While precedent in IEL does not operate in quite the same ways that the principle of *stare decisis* operates in the common law system, it nevertheless creates a body of legal decision that must be consulted when national legal experts and international panelists examine new cases.[2] In doing so it maintains the same legitimating function as that of *stare decisis* in the Anglo-American tradition. There is a small but growing body of empirical studies of precedent citation in international economic law.[3] Following the work of Pauwelyn on precedent citation at the WTO's Appellate Body (AB) and Stone Sweet and Grisel on case citation patterns in international investment arbitration tribunals, I develop an empirical study of citation trends at the WTO in which I show not only an upward trend in citation, but an increasingly confident institution wherein WTO cases are cited more, and GATT cases less.[4]

The question of precedent has been minimized by lawyers and diplomats for many years. Following the creation of the WTO, scholars of governance and economic law downplayed the possibility that WTO dispute settlement panel decisions would create legal precedent. In discussions of the many new dispute settlement panels at work, they focused on the political benefits of removing trade friction, the novel application of rules, and the flexibilities built into the system. For example, the literature of the WTO's first decade contains much discussion of forum shopping and little of compulsory jurisdiction. There was a good reason for this circumspection. The dominance of the international legal system by Anglo-American scholars, lawyers and judges reminded many members of the bad old days of Western European colonialism in which economic domination was frequently cloaked in the rhetoric of law. At the WTO, scholars avoided too much talk of law, and by extension, avoided discussion of whether the decisions made by panels were meant to build upon one another.

Another reason for reticence over the possibility of precedent at the WTO was that domestic constituencies (not to mention governments)

150 *International economic law beyond the state*

in the largest trading jurisdictions, the United States and European Union, were uncertain about the future implications of dispute settlement. In the American context, these and other new institutional commitments triggered a messy debate in the mid-2000s over whether a supranational legal body could make law that constrained the policy autonomy of the United States.[5] In Europe, the idea of supranational legal power was less problematic, yet it remained a thorny issue, especially following the failure to ratify the Treaty Establishing a Constitution for Europe in 2005.

However, it has become hard to ignore the fact that interpreting economic law in both its investment and trade variants, requires recourse to the decisions of earlier arbitrators. Whether we call it precedent or not (and increasingly we do), judges and arbitrators at the international level rely heavily upon past decisions. For example, at this point the activity of the WTO's Dispute Settlement Body has evolved far beyond a simple application of rules. We are well and truly on the road of law, legal decision-making, and legal rationality. The first section reviews the most important literature on precedent in international economic law, paying attention to its relation to the legitimacy and stability of the legal system. The second section develops an empirical study of the use of precedent at the WTO. The final section examines the implications of precedent for how we think about the place of law in global politics and how we study law's influence on global political and economic activity.

Precedent and the articulation of law beyond the state

The literature on precedent is broad and heterogeneous in the sense that it covers many aspects of law, from human rights, through the private arbitral tribunals that decide in certain investment disputes. However, it is unified in the sense that scholars across this terrain document a widespread citation of previous cases in the decisions handed down by modern international courts and tribunals. For our study of precedent in the context of international economic law, I divide the literature into three pools. The first subsection reviews literature on the significance of new court mechanisms, with an emphasis on the use of precedent in international law, broadly construed. In the second I review literature on the use of precedent in international investment arbitration, and then I move to a growing body of literature on the use of precedent at the WTO.

The new design of international courts emphasizes compulsory jurisdiction, which makes it harder for states to block the cases they wish to avoid. When the spread of compulsory jurisdiction is coupled with

International economic law beyond the state 151

the expanded content of international law and increased opportunities to contest state practice, we see courts begin to adjudicate issues that used to be the prerogative of the state. As Alter puts it, "the existence of an international legal remedy empowers those actors who have international law on their side," be they states or non-state actors.[6] Of course, international courts cannot force compliance. Rather they work with other actors to create indirect costs for the political actors that try to ignore international law.[7] Usually these are other states that have an interest in the issue at play, whether that is a material interest or an ideological interest in upholding the concept of the rule of law.

Alter goes on to emphasize that the most important reason to develop international courts is that they entrench politics across time and space, by which she means that "States delegate authority to an international court so as to ensure that subsequent governments do not walk away from the set of policies inscribed in the law."[8] Law locks in political progress by preventing the potential backsliding of future governments—a particularly significant achievement in the context of democratic party politics wherein the policies of one political party are sometimes unwound by subsequent political competitors and rivals.

Precedent is the use of previous decisions and previous legal reasoning in deciding cases in the present. In common law jurisdictions, precedent is used very often. For example, criminal law, contract law, and tort law (the law that governs civil liability), all rely heavily upon precedent. It is generally believed that precedent offers stability and transparency to legal decision-making that is necessary for effective economic and social governance. Detractors argue that the precedent principle may lock courts into sub-optimal decision-making by placing too much emphasis on the reasoning of the past. Some legal systems, such as those in Continental Europe and parts of Africa and Asia, place less emphasis on precedent than do Anglo-American courts, which frequently operate according to the principle of *stare decisis*, a Latin phrase meaning to stand by previous decisions. *Stare decisis* is often described as the highest standard of precedential adherence.

In the international context precedent creates expectations that are on the one hand, the result of a signed treaty, but on the other hand, the result of practices that the original signatories did not necessarily foresee. As the engine of an evolving system of rules, precedent sits at the nexus of enlightened self-interest, political will, and legal authority. In the national context, citizens expect the back and forth between courts and the legislative arm of government. But they are less enthusiastic about the prospect of court systems that exist beyond the reach of national governments. Further, the ongoing precedential

152 *International economic law beyond the state*

development of international law raises the question of whether the mechanisms designed to facilitate state interdependence may also create some of the rules by which states interact.

Bogdandy and Venzke use precedent as a lens through which to understand the contribution of international courts to the law-making process.[9] It is a significant factor in making law because rules can never fully determine their own application. Furthermore, the meaning of a norm at play in a particular case is never discovered, but rather created.[10] This is why international law scholars tend to refer to international adjudication as a process of developing the law. International law may not formally adhere to a principle of *stare decisis*, but precedent acts as a focal point in adjudication because actors expect cases that are alike to be treated alike. Some scholars have gone so far as to suggest that the pull of precedent is so strong in the WTO's Appellate Body that it "almost makes a mockery" of international law's circumspection about the weight of legal judgment.[11]

Even without a formal legal principle, precedent remains an unavoidable form of international law-making because courts need to create authoritative reference points for future legal discourse. Yet even though the use of precedent is inevitable, in certain ways it can complicate or undermine the legitimacy of international law because international legal authority is expected to flow from the consent of states rather than the constitutional authority of courts because such authority does not exist at the international level, at least not in a formal sense. As a result, international courts must work harder than national courts to develop multiple bases of legitimacy, such as rules pertaining to transparency, the use of amicus curiae briefs, and fora for public participation.[12]

Other scholarship has explored the relationship between precedent and professional practice. Cohen argues that to understand the use of precedent in international law, we need to understand how the law operates day to day because the use of precedent springs as much from the practice of lawyers as it does from the preferences of state actors. The daily practice of law therefore provides ground rules that structure the pattern of legal argumentation, and precedent is critical to that process.[13] Communities of legal practitioners may be as important, and in some cases more important, than state actors in the creation of norms of legal argumentation that lays the ground rules for the development of international law.

One result is that by and large, the use of precedent is "a function of specific communities of practice rather than formal state decisions."[14] The relationship between professional expectation and legal authority

International economic law beyond the state 153

is an important dimension for further study because professionalization and judicialization tend to reinforce each other. In a recent working paper, Cho theorizes precedent as a social phenomenon in order to explain its legal power in terms of its role in the legal system, in legal language, and its place as a symbol of legal authority.[15] Judges and lawyers view precedent as their legal reality. It operates therefore as a social fact that emerges out of community consensus. Precedent is the product of legal actors in much the same way that policy is the product of government. For legal actors, precedent is an archaeology of the epistemic community—it structures narratives about the past and gives meaning to activity in the present.

The question of precedent in international law is therefore much more than a basic question of the appropriate role for an international judiciary in treaty interpretation. It becomes a question of how to think about the fact that legal professionals take their culture, mindset, and modes of reasoning with them when they step into the international context. Scholars have discussed the porous membrane between the state and the international in the governance of global economy, and now we must also consider the artificiality of that divide in professional communities as well.

Precedent in international investment arbitration

The literature on the development of precedent in investment arbitration begins the difficult task of ascertaining whether case citation is a factor in the development of a larger body of law. Until quite recently investment law was a large and heterogeneous collection of treaties and arbitration bodies, typified as much by its disunity as by the similarities of treaty language. Even ten years ago it was somewhat novel to imagine that arbitrators in investment tribunals were constrained by precedent, as Cheng suggests. He concludes that precedent citation is on the rise because the high transaction costs associated with treaty negotiation mean that states only renegotiate trade and investment treaties periodically, making precedent in arbitral awards a stable and transparent way to approach the regulation of new and emerging areas of treaty application, such as e-commerce.[16]

In a system with no meaningful appeals oversight, precedent also offers a way to increase the overall legal authority of arbitral decisions, and for these reasons its use is on the rise. Even so, it is hard to map the impact of precedent in such a decentralized system. It appears most often in clusters of awards that address similar points of law. In fact scholars who watch investment litigation suggest that there are

154 *International economic law beyond the state*

significant variations in precedent citation across the broad field of economic law. Kaufmann-Kohler, for example, sees very little "precedential value" in commercial arbitration, a strong reliance on precedent in sports arbitration, and in investment arbitration, "a progressive emergence of rules through lines of consistent cases on certain issues."[17] Yet even here she concludes that consistency is blurred by a number of contradictory decisions.

Franck has suggested that these inconsistent decisions may ultimately undermine the authority and legitimacy of investment arbitration, and wonders if they are more common than scholars may expect, if only because of the continuing proliferation of international investment agreements.[18] Rather than calling for a more rigorous use of precedent as Cheng does, she explores the possibility for a multilateral appeals body, suggesting that multilateral institutional development would have a salutary secondary effect of creating greater awareness of the proliferating body of investment arbitration among judges, lawyers and policy-makers.

Yet other scholars disagree altogether with the idea that precedent and the judicial control it exerts are a good thing for investment arbitration. Ten Cate argues that arbitrators should not make consistency with previous awards a primary goal. Investment law is a fragmented and dynamic terrain that by its very nature is not a good vehicle for harmonizing law. Further, "giving weight to consistency in decision-making inevitably leads to a decrease in accuracy, sincerity, and transparency" in the arbitral process.[19] Her argument that a focus on precedential control inordinately constrains judges is not new, but it is a useful antidote to the scholarship which may get a little ahead of itself in arguing for an emerging consistency in the treatment of previous cases by arbitral tribunals.

In questioning the desirability of a system of precedent that may slow the pace of change in a relatively young field of law, it seems prudent to anticipate a possible future of less consistency but more autonomy for arbitrators; a system in which legal legitimacy is found in awards that are sensitive to their context. Ten Cate is right to emphasize the difficulties around qualifying the desirability of a scholarly focus on precedent. Even so, her argument may be already overtaken by event. There is an emerging body of new research that quantifies the use of precedent in international investment arbitration.

Stone Sweet and Grisel have compiled a database of citation in investment disputes, counting all instances in which a tribunal cited a prior case.[20] They found that the average number of citations per decision has doubled since 2000. In a database of all cases cited in investor-state arbitration between 1977 and 2014, 97 percent of all precedent (2,108 citations in total) were cited since 2000. Some 84 percent (1,827 citations) were added since 2005, and almost half of all case citations (971, or 45 percent) took place between 2010 and 2014. The average number of citations per award also doubled in the same period, from an average of nine citations per award in the late 1970s to an average of 18 citations per award after 2010. Further, in the period before 2000, tribunals tended to cite the International Court of Justice most often, but in the post-2000 period, tribunals tended to cite other investor-state tribunals. In fact, since 2005, 90 percent of all awards cite prior awards, with emphasis placed on awards handed down by the ICSID.

The study in section two of this chapter finds a similar pattern of citation at the WTO. While the citation of prior cases was a regular occurrence in GATT panels by the 1980s (something that appears to not have been the case in investor-state arbitration), the increasing trend towards citation of prior panel decisions over the same period closely resembles the pattern of prior award citation discovered by Stone Sweet and Grisel. In both areas of economic law, arbitrators are becoming increasingly confident that the body of law to which they are contributing is sufficiently robust to allow the development of a precedential system.

Precedent at the WTO

In the absence of little movement on liberalization targets and no new multilateral trade agreements, the decisions of panels and the Appellate Body become more important because they are now a main driver of legal development at the WTO. This turn of events raises a number of questions. Is the law beyond the state capable of creating more law? Is precedent that is created beyond the direct mandate of national governments legitimate? How ought scholars and the legal community to think about compliance in a case where a state is found to be in breach of a rule that it did not explicitly agree to? We do not yet have answers to all of these questions, but the pace of legal development at the WTO suggests that we ought to be considering these and other emerging implications that arise from the adjudication of international economic law.

The principle of *stare decisis* is often used to differentiate between the stricter use of precedent favored by Anglo-American legal systems and others used by French Napoleonic and Germanic systems of law. The degree to which courts rely on previous decisions varies across national jurisdictions, state legal systems and levels of governance. Generally reliance upon precedent is weakest in international tribunals

156 *International economic law beyond the state*

where arbitrators must reconcile different treaty interpretations (often rooted in different systems of law) in order to arrive at an authoritative interpretation of state obligations. Yet even here prior cases have a considerable impact upon panel reasoning. As Professor Jackson has noted, "[t]he general perception under international law is that, although there is a 'precedential effect' that seems to be operating de facto and in practice, there is certainly not *stare decisis*, and in some cases, not a very strong precedential effect."[21] At the WTO, however, we can see a fairly strong precedential effect, which is rooted in the history of the GATT.

GATT evolved based on a scant legal text, at least by modern standards. However, the GATT signatories developed a set of dispute settlement procedures which recognized prior cases early on. Strategic treaty interpretation was crucial to the development of the dispute settlement system. Article XXIII states that a member may file a complaint if it "considers that any benefit accruing to it directly or indirectly under this agreement is being nullified or impaired."[22] At first the membership took this to mean that a breach of obligation was not enough reason to file a complaint. There had to be a material nullification or impairment of benefit. Eventually nullification and impairment came to mean any harm that could not have been reasonably anticipated when concessions were negotiated.

Bogdandy and Venzke note that by the early 1960s, a panel determined that any violation of the GATT could be considered "a prima facie nullification or impairment."[23] This decision created a much broader window for bringing complaints to the GATT. The GATT established early-on both a culture of legal interpretive development through precedent as well as a central role for the panel in interpreting treaty obligations. Towards GATT's later years some scholars suggested that panel reports were to a limited extent, "new law."[24] This idea that panels may modify settled GATT interpretation never gained traction at the WTO, however. The WTO Charter provides for the power of the Ministerial Conference to adapt interpretations of multilateral agreements by a 75 percent majority vote. As a result, there is less room for precedential impact because panel interpretation is now distinct from the unique power of the Ministerial Conference to issue a definitive interpretation.

With the birth of the WTO in 1995 we see a new, softer precedential approach enshrined in Article XVI (1) of the Agreement Establishing the World Trade Organization, which reads in part: "Except as otherwise provided under this Agreement or the Multilateral Trade Agreements, the WTO shall be guided by the decisions, procedures, and

International economic law beyond the state   157

customary practices followed by the CONTRACTING PARTIES to GATT 1947 and the bodies established in the framework of GATT 1947."[25] This guidance clause provides a basis for WTO dispute settlement processes giving a certain amount of deference to prior GATT decisions, and by extension, the decisions of the WTO's panels as well.

The language of precedent may structure the social world of judges and lawyers, but there is also a reasonable, functional rationale for its use. Precedent contributes to court legitimacy by increasing the transparency of decision-making as well as its predictability and stability. Back in the early days of WTO dispute settlement in 1996, the Appellate Body found in *Japan—Alcoholic Beverages II* that adopted panel reports "create legitimate expectations among WTO members and, therefore should be taken into account where they are relevant to a dispute."[26] By the late 1990s legal literature had begun to describe the practice at the WTO as non-binding precedent and in certain cases as *de facto stare decisis.* [27]

Within the first ten years of dispute settlement, the practice of relying upon previous cases became well established. The softer use of precedent, in which panels did not bear a burden associated with refining a definitive interpretation of the agreement in question, freed panels to use precedent without fear of undermining the political position of contracting states. I would go so far as to suggest that shifting the responsibility for definitive interpretation away from dispute settlement allowed for a more traditional use of precedent, by which I mean the use of precedent for developing authoritative arguments. This freedom was fully on display when in 2003 the AB stated in one of its reports that panels ought to consider AB reports as having "a precedent effect." The panel went on to explain that "indeed, following the Appellate Body's conclusions in earlier disputes is not only appropriate, but is what would be expected from panels, especially where the issues are the same."[28] Following precedent was no longer a simple shorthand for referencing past debates or an effective way to leverage the wisdom of previous panels; it was now a basic expectation of legal argumentation at the WTO.

In a recent working paper, David examined *US—Stainless Steel (Mexico)*, in which the Appellate Body raised the precedential standard by requiring panels to justify their departure from appellate reasoning if their decisions disregard precedent.[29] The European Communities (EC) asked the Appellate Body to clarify and confirm the binding effect of its reports on future panel decisions. The panel decided that in the interest of "ensuring security and predictability" as required by DSU Art. 3.2, "absent cogent reasons, an adjudicating body will resolve

158   *International economic law beyond the state*

the same question in the same way in subsequent cases."[30] The membership is somewhat divided on the desirability of a higher standard for precedent, with the EU preferring the greater stability offered by tighter adherence to precedent, and the United States remaining skeptical about the possible impacts of precedent on state autonomy.[31]

Pelc uses rational choice theory to study the way that states are drawn to the logic of precedent and that past decisions shape governmental expectations. He examines the rationale behind membership support for precedent at the WTO. On the face of it, rational states ought not to employ the use of precedent in legal argumentation because it empowers courts at the expense of states. It stands to reason that they would be especially wary of firm rules of precedent such as *stare decisis*, as it is employed in common law jurisdictions. However, his findings seemingly fly in the face of rational expectation. Pelc has found that members invest in precedent by initiating disputes that may tilt the rules in their favor in the future.[32] This is interesting because it explains to some extent why states litigate certain cases where the value of trade is relatively low. He has also found that member states choose to behave as if the principle of *stare decisis* operates at the WTO's dispute settlement system. Further, the use of precedent is a deliberative strategy on the part of governments to empower trade courts.[33]

Members systematically invest in precedent despite continuing concerns about the potential for judicial activism because they wish to empower courts that might otherwise acquiesce to political demands. The concerns about political backsliding on global economic commitments therefore outweigh the fear of judicial overreach. This empowering of the court system is not a new phenomenon. Pauwelyn uses a precedent mapping method similar to the one employed in this study in order to show the influence of the Appellate Body on subsequent decisions. He finds that the rule of precedent has been present in Appellate Body adjudication from the very beginning in 1995.[34]

Next, we turn to a mapping study of case citation at the WTO. The WTO's dispute settlement system has dealt with many cases; more than 500 have been introduced since 1995, and approximately 60 percent of those entered the panel process. This multi-stage process resolved more than 200 cases, although not all of those ended in a panel report. Furthermore, there is a pattern of participation across large and small economies. At least 100 members, or about two-thirds of the membership, have participated in dispute settlement, either as complainants, respondents, or third parties intervening in, or observing cases. Close to 200 panel reports have been issued and these form the basis of what has been hailed as a "balanced and consistent" case law.[35] Further, the

International economic law beyond the state   159

dispute settlement system has been somewhat sensitive to non-trade issues like public health, although more can be done to better integrate legal reasoning in the domain of trade law with the larger terrain of international law.[36]

Mapping case citation at the WTO

Sacerdoti has recently outlined three basic challenges facing the WTO's dispute settlement system, and all three have a bearing upon the development of precedent. First, while the system itself is short on resources, states are putting more resources into their cases. Members brought a large number of cases to the Dispute Settlement Body (DSB), and these, coupled with the increasing complexity of the issues litigated and the increasing sophistication of arguments presented, have strained the resources of the panel system. We see the same issue at the Appellate Body, where larger and more complex panel reports mean more challenges raised and issues appealed. In theory the panel process should not take more than six months, but in practice it is taking between one and a half and three years. Furthermore, most panelists are not professional judges or arbitrators. Sacerdoti estimates that about half of them are "trade diplomats based in Geneva who do not have a legal degree and normally work for their government."[37]

Second, there are ongoing challenges around compliance. It is not uncommon for the losing party to drag out effective implementation. Slow compliance means more secondary compliance and retaliation proceedings (notated as "other" in the figures below). Finally, the fact that the membership has been unable to agree on the Doha Round means no new rules to deal with new economic realities such as the green economy and e-commerce. As a result, panels need to do what Sacerdoti refers to as "gap-filling" and "law-making," for which they were not designed.[38] While some scholars may consider the expansion of the DSB's informal mandate in this regard to be a weakness, I would suggest that national governments frequently use legal decisions to mold existing legislation so that it conforms to the needs of emerging issue areas. The fact that we are seeing this at the WTO may suggest a maturing system of international economic law.

Precedent implies more than just the recognition of legal context in a panel report or Appellate Body decision. It suggests reliance on previous decisions when making a determination in the present. As I discussed above, WTO panels cannot use precedent to change official interpretation of agreements or to strike down certain interpretations of law (or even the law itself) as sometimes happens at the national

160 *International economic law beyond the state*

level. But panelists do use previous decisions to interpret fact and evidence; previous decisions provide ways of knowing and deciding in the present case. There are several ways to measure the use of precedent. Most straightforward is to map the use of previous cases at WTO, as this study does. However, future studies may wish to examine the use of general principles from international law in panel reports, the use of previous cases from other international tribunals, and reference made to previous cases decided in national courts, for which some panels report data, although most do not.

This study uses a basic precedent mapping method that emphasizes trends over time. The WTO lists the cases cited in a report in the front matter of all panel reports, Appellate Body reports and other arbitration (such as DSU Art. 21.3 reports, Art. 21.5 panel and AB reports, and Art. 22.6 reports), starting with cases completed in the latter half of 2003 and early 2004. Of more than 500 disputes filed, 282 were successfully concluded in either a panel report or a mutually agreed-upon diplomatic solution. Of these completed cases, 191 ended in a panel report being adopted by the DSB. Of these 191 cases for which there is at least one complete panel, the WTO has compiled case citation information for 119, or approximately 62 percent. I focus on these cases, showing trends for precedent citation for the past 13 years. Clearly this database is not exhaustive because it doesn't include the citation information for panel reports issued between 1995 and the first half of 2003. Nevertheless, it offers a large and representative sample wherein we can see a number of trends in precedent citation over the past decade.

I ask four basic empirical questions about case citation. First, how many GATT and WTO decisions are cited as precedent? This question gives some sense of the generalizability of the citation phenomenon. Do new panels cite only certain prominent cases, or do they cite broadly across the breadth of completed panel reports? Second, is the number of cases cited increasing over time? The answer to this question gives some sense of whether the use of precedent has become a basic approach to creating a stable and transparent system of legal decision-making. Third, which cases get cited the most? Are there certain authoritative cases, or do panels cite cases that occurred most recently? This is a question that strikes toward a basic pattern in precedential systems, often referred to as precedential path dependence. This is a pattern in which courts prefer to cite cases that previous courts have cited, creating an historical institutional trajectory of legal reasoning. Finally, do some complainants and respondents rely on precedent more than others? This question attempts to understand the way that different litigants cite to support their case. While I will not examine the

International economic law beyond the state 161

substance of legal reasoning, I will show in empirical terms the quantity of citations between the United States and the EU and all other litigants.

Question 1: How many separate WTO and GATT cases are cited as precedent?

By the end of 2016 there were 191 completed cases at the WTO; the adoption of a panel report by the DSB is here considered evidence of successful completion. Some 96 percent of these panels, or 183 separate cases, are subsequently cited as precedent. Only nine cases have not been cited in a subsequent case, and eight of these were adopted in the latter half of 2016, making them too new to be completely digested by legal talent and member governments. Only one long-standing case has not been cited in a subsequent panel, *US—Textiles Rules of Origin*. [39] An average of 37 GATT/WTO cases have been cited per panel report, and an average of 22 GATT/WTO cases cited per AB panel report, with an average of seven cases cited in other arbitration reports. Figure 7.1 shows the citation numbers for all completed panels, sorted by year. I should note that citation lists for several of the cases in the years 2002–2004 are incomplete. I have nevertheless included them here. This database mirrors the fact that the WTO's citation lists are a work in progress.

Question 2: Is the number of cases cited increasing over time?

Figure 7.2 shows the overall number of cases cited in all dispute settlement action, sorted by year. The trend line suggests that the anecdotal evidence produced by Sacerdoti of more cases producing longer,

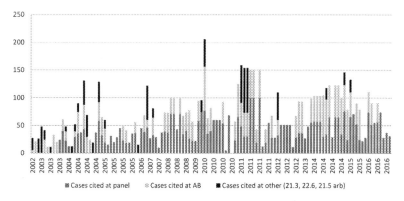

Figure 7.1 Cases cited, all completed panels, sorted by year
Source: Based on data from the WTO Dispute Settlement Database.

162 *International economic law beyond the state*

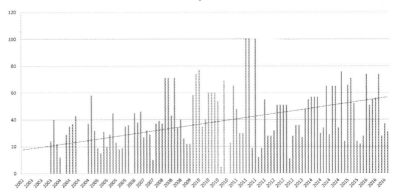

Figure 7.2 WTO cases cited, sorted by year
Source: Based on data from the WTO Dispute Settlement Database.

more complex panel reports, is in fact the case. By 2008, most panel reports are citing more than 40 previous cases. This number ought not to be confused with the overall number of citations. Cases are cited multiple times across a number of different documents in a single case. An average report has anywhere from several hundred to several thousand footnotes.

Similarly, Figure 7.3 shows an upward trend in the number of cases cited in Appellate Body reports on an annual basis. Again, each line represents an AB report. By 2011 we can see a noticeably higher average number of case citations per AB report.

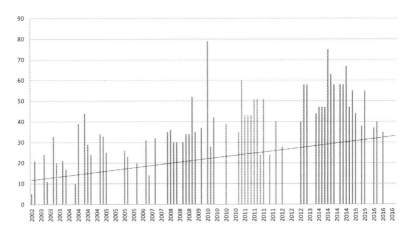

Figure 7.3 WTO cases cited, Appellate Body reports, sorted by year
Source: Based on data from the WTO Dispute Settlement Database.

Interestingly, we see a downward-sloping trend line for case citation in all other arbitration. However, this is likely due to the fact that we see more of this secondary arbitration occurring between 2003 and 2005, which pushes the average up at that end of the spectrum. As you can see in Figure 7.4, secondary arbitration occurring after 2005 tends to cite more cases, with six of 12 reports citing more than 40 separate cases each.

Another interesting feature of precedent citation in this period is the trend towards citing GATT panel reports less often (Figure 7.5). GATT dispute settlement reports (that predate the birth of the WTO) are cited a total of 339 times. Of the 126 dispute panels completed at the GATT, 64 (or 51 percent) are cited in subsequent WTO reports. The trend to rely upon the precedent of the GATT less is not surprising given the fact that many of the old panel reports remained officially "unadopted" because the dispute settlement body of the GATT required consensus. Conversely, the WTO mechanism requires consensus to void the adoption of a panel report. This reverse-consensus mechanism ensures that all completed panels are adopted. With 191 completed panels to consider, it is little wonder that the case law of the GATT is given proportionately less weight.

Question 3: Which cases are cited most often?

Almost every case has been cited, but some are cited much more than others. This research does not attempt to ascertain which case has been cited most often in absolute terms because any method used to count

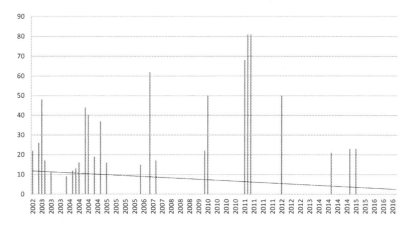

Figure 7.4 WTO cases cited, all other arbitration, sorted by year
Source: Based on data from the WTO Dispute Settlement Database.

164 *International economic law beyond the state*

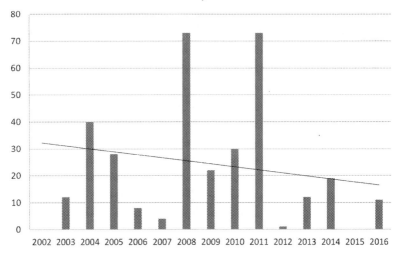

Figure 7.5 GATT cases cited, sorted by year
Source: Based on data from the WTO Dispute Settlement Database.

the sheer number of citations devoted to any single case would ultimately fall apart around the facts that many cases are cited in a perfunctory manner along with a number of other cases, and there are multiple reports within each of these cases to cite. So throwing out a number and saying this case or that one is cited the most would obscure more than it illuminates. Rather, I show in Table 7.1 a range of cases, most of which occurred during the first five years of dispute settlement. Together they suggest the breadth of citation and the reasoning behind citation patterns.

Table 7.1 shows a range of prominent early cases that have been heavily cited. It is important to note that while I suggest the context in which these cases are frequently cited in the far right cells of the table, in point of fact, these cases are cited across a wide variety of contexts. *India-Patents (US)*, which is cited in 103 DSB reports, is a good example. The case is cited in the *US—Upland Cotton* Appellate Body report where the panel discusses the need to interpret multiple treaty provisions "harmoniously."[40] In the panel report for *EC—Selected Customs Matters* it is cited when discussing the limitations of a panel's terms of reference with regards to the entire body of EU customs law.[41] In the Appellate Body report for *China—Rare Earths (EC)*, it is cited as the basis for a previous finding in *US—Gambling*, which is being used in this context to determine the appropriate weight to place on a responding member's (in this case China) characterization of the trade

International economic law beyond the state 165

Table 7.1 The citation of selected prominent early cases

Case	Short title	Date	Reports containing at least one citation	Legal issue to which citation refers
WT/DS27	EC—Bananas III	1997	219	MFN obligation
WT/DS213	US—Carbon Steel	2002	143	Requirements for the establishment of a panel
WT/DS33	US—Wool Shirts and Blouses	1997	137	Burden of evidence falls upon the complainant to make a case for inconsistency with treaty obligations
WT/DS8/10/11	Japan—Alcoholic Beverages II	1996	125	Use of the Vienna Convention on the Law of Treaties in dispute settlement
WT/DS207	Chile—Price Band System		113	Distinction between claims and arguments in context of establishing a panel
WT/DS2 and DS4	US—Gasoline	1996	111	Justification of less favorable treatment under GATT Art. XX (D)
WT/DS50	India—Patents (US)	1997	103	Standard of review
WT/DS141	EC—Bed Linen	2000	101	Interpretation of certain provisions in the Anti-Dumping Agreement
GATT Case	EEC—Parts and Components	1990	18	Role of dispute settlement in establishing generalizable rules and norms
GATT Case	Belgium—Family Allowances	1952	9	Interpretation of the term "like"

Source: Based on data from the WTO Dispute Settlement Database.

166   *International economic law beyond the state*

measure in question.[42] Clearly, prominent early cases are cited very broadly, a fact which speaks to their legitimizing function.

In the national context, legal scholars have wondered why some cases are cited more than others with regard to general principles of law. Hathaway suggests that there is a strong knowledge trajectory in precedent citation (in common law legal systems) because "the doctrine of stare decisis … creates an explicitly path dependent process."[43] Referring to American constitutional law, Gerhardt cautions against the use of a strongly path-dependent theoretical model when studying court decisions, suggesting rather a "limited path dependency," may better explain the use of previous cases "in the absence of rules for construing precedent."[44] A similar argument may be made for the theorizing of precedential citation in dispute settlement at the WTO, where early cases are cited often and in a variety of contexts to illustrate a variety of reasoning processes.

Question 4: Do some complainants and respondents rely on precedent more than others?

It stands to reason that some members of the WTO use the citation of previous cases in their complaints and responses more than other members. Given the legal resources of the United States and the EU, for example, and their use of top-flight legal talent, it stands to reason that we would observe a legal style that more heavily relies on precedent citation. Do the United States and EU rely on precedent more than other countries? The somewhat surprising short answer to this question is, not really. Of the 119 cases in this dataset, the United States and/or the EU were respondents in 61, leaving 58 cases with non-US/EU respondents. An average 37 cases were cited in each report to which the United States or the EU responded. An average 41 cases were cited in reports in which other parties responded. When defending trade measures, WTO members tend to use previous cases to a similar extent.

Figure 7.6 shows case citation averages broken down by respondent across the three categories. The four columns show case citation averages across panel reports, AB reports and other arbitration in which the United States and EU respond to each other, the United States and EU respond to other members, other members respond to the United States/EU, and other members respond to members not the United States/EU. These four columns looks broadly similar, with 106, 116, 133 and 111 cases cited on average in cases corresponding to each category, respectively. Perhaps the biggest outlier is cases· in which

International economic law beyond the state 167

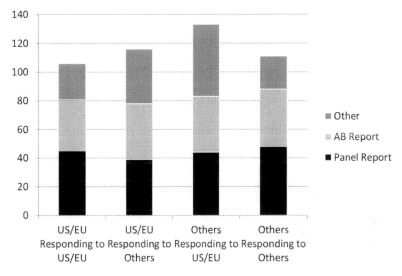

Figure 7.6 Case citation averages broken down by respondent
Source: Based on data from the WTO Dispute Settlement Database.

other members are responding to the United States/EU. But even here the average number of cases cited in panel reports and AB reports is very similar to all other cases. The biggest difference is the average number of cases cited in compliance reports (50). Anecdotally, American and European compliance remains an issue at the WTO, which may account for the fact that when other countries attempt to gain compliance through the WTO, they tend to cite more precedent. Once the law is on their side, they use it a little more heavily to attempt to gain compliance.

To better focus on our question of whether litigation of large economies relies more heavily on precedent, we need to isolate those cases in which the United States and EU are the complaining parties. These cases may cast a different light on the issue. Again we have four columns, one in which the United States and EU complain against each other, one where they complain against someone else, one in which others complain against the United States/EU, and one where others complain against others. In Figure 7.7, again the gross averages are broadly similar, with 106, 115, 122 and 117 cases cited on average in cases corresponding to each category, respectively. The first column, in which the United States/EU complains against the other is exactly the same as the first column having to do with respondents in Figure 7.6. Beyond that, we can see that when averages are broken down by

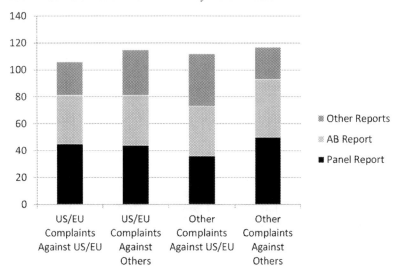

Figure 7.7 Case citation averages broken down by complainant
Source: Based on data from the WTO Dispute Settlement Database.

the type of complainant, we don't see any standout differences in the use of citation by the United States/EU and other members.

In summary, citation of WTO cases is up across panel reports and AB reports, and a little down across other arbitration reports. Overall, the trend is to cite fewer GATT decisions, suggesting that as we move further from the birth of the WTO and as the numbers of WTO cases increase, WTO reports will continue to be cited to a far greater extent. It is not an exaggeration to suggest that the training wheels are coming off the WTO's dispute settlement system and it is becoming self-sufficient in terms of the application of legal precedent. The third question had to do with the extensive citation of prominent cases, and I showed that early cases tend to be more heavily cited and they are cited across a range of contexts, suggesting a certain path dependence to precedent citation at the WTO, much like the use of precedent in common law jurisdictions.

In examining the last question having to do with whether the largest economies use precedent differently than other members, I showed that when it comes to case citation, the United States and EU are not substantially different from other members of the WTO. This suggests a (fairly) uniform increase in legal expertise across the members that use the dispute settlement system. At least when it comes to precedent citation there are no huge gaps in legal practice between the largest

International economic law beyond the state 169

economies and the rest of the membership, perhaps because large and small economies now tend to hire the same firms specializing in international trade and investment law. This also suggests that the judicialization of trade dispute settlement, with its many new and often technocratic practices, has been embraced by the membership at large, presumably because the benefits outweigh the disadvantages.

Much of the empirical research presented so far applies basic time-sequence and process-tracing methods to areas of knowledge that are usually of most interest to legal scholars. This empirical dimension is rooted in a theoretical concern with the growing world of international economic law and a methodological concern with the place of law in the study of political economy. We now turn to these theoretical concerns in order to better understand the implications of this development of a precedential system.

Law-making, legitimacy, and moments of rapid legal development

The pace at which the WTO has developed a full-bodied court complete with an authoritative system of precedent is impressive. In this section, we will consider several implications. First, we turn to a basic question that animates theorists of international law: what is the law-making potential of international precedent? It is widely assumed that the combination of judicial review and precedent citation give courts formidable quasi-legislative powers at the national level. Such powers could potentially reshape our expectations of international organizations. Next we turn to the role of legitimacy and authority in accelerating or undercutting the current trajectory of legal development. When scholars of international economic law talk about its legitimacy and authority, they are really talking about the relationship between *political* legitimacy and *legal* authority, or politics and law. In a system that lacks an overarching governmental frame, this relationship has developed according to a recognizable pattern. Furthermore, the logic of the legitimacy/authority equilibrium ought to be considered in the context of the postwar order, from which it gains its normative powers.

Finally, we will ask whether the recent era of intensive legal development at the WTO amounts to what some scholars refer to as a Grotian moment, a period of intensive legal development, that broadens and deepens state engagement with international law. I argue that the concept of a Grotian moment loses some of its explanatory power when considered in historiographical terms. Even so, the idea that certain events affect institutional momentum is interesting and bears further scrutiny. When considered in the context of shifting equilibria

170   *International economic law beyond the state*

(first discussed in Chapter 4), the idea of a Grotian moment maintains a great deal of its analytic potential. It may be that when we look back on this moment from a future vantage point, we will consider the rise of precedent at the WTO to be one of these formative moments in the development of international economic law.

Precedent as law-making

In theory, international organizations carry out a mandate according to the powers delegated by member states and spelled out by international treaty. In practice, carrying out a mandate requires that organizations develop policy, create rules, and in some cases create new obligations for their membership. In short, international organizations increasingly have a part in creating international law. Precedent is one such form of law-making. Johnstone examines law-making in international organizations.[45] His study revolves around the concept of delegation, whereby states transfer some of their sovereign autonomy for regulation to international organizations.

There are three types of delegated authority. Explicit delegation occurs when states mandate a delegation of authority, above and beyond treaty obligations. There are relatively few examples of explicit delegation. Implied delegation occurs where the nature of the mandate dictates an expansion of authority. Most delegation is implied by the fact that some law-making is required in order for international organizations (IOs) to carry out their mandates. Attenuated delegation speaks to the arm's-length relationship between many states and IOs, and suggests that some law-making such as the decisions of international courts, results from this arm's-length relationship. This may be considered an undesirable side-effect of delegation, or a logical outcome of organizational independence.[46] In either case, attenuated delegation, and the law-making it entails, is an entirely foreseeable consequence of sovereign delegation.

The extent to which international courts make law is contested.[47] But Johnstone's work suggests that even when states protest the legitimacy of law-making at IOs, the process is a necessary outgrowth of the increase in institutional coordination happening at the transnational level. For example, the WTO's guidance clause was an explicit attempt to limit the law-making potential of dispute settlement panels. Even so, panels continue to refine rules, and in so doing create standards for state behavior. In *US—Stainless Steel*, the Appellate Body stated that its job was to end the debate over zeroing, and in doing so, end the practice once and for all. The AB was making law, both in terms of

International economic law beyond the state 171

creating precedent for future disputes as well as in the sense that it self-consciously reinforced a standard for future state behavior. It is entirely likely that if zeroing becomes an illegitimate protectionist practice, it will be in no small part due to the efforts of dispute settlement panels.

If delegation is an unintended, but entirely foreseeable, outcome of international regulation, one wonders why states don't either look for ways to curb it or admit its usefulness and actively seek to guide the process of delegating authority. Johnstone notes that in the literature, rational choice theory and discourse analysis are best suited to forwarding the study of law-making by IOs. Rational choice theory helps explain why states voluntarily give away their authority to regulate. The example in our context is Pelc's research on state litigation strategies at the WTO, described above. Further, rational choice theory also sheds light on the democratic deficit, which grows as the autonomy of IOs increases. However, democratic deficit research also highlights the fact of IO autonomy because the democratic deficit would only increase if the autonomy of IOs were a practical reality.[48] The democratic deficit literature may also help to explain why states (at least democratic ones) cannot explicitly support the growth of organizational autonomy. Governments would have to admit that on some level, they are consciously trading some democratic accountability for international legal stability. Discourse analysis delves into that complex of relational practices. It also has something to say about the legitimacy of law-making, suggesting that inclusive deliberations are a way to counteract the democratic deficit.

This idea that precedent is a strategy (whether intentional or not) by which international organizations may make, or in some way form or contour, international law, has significant implications for the way we think about law's legitimacy and authority. The relationship between legitimacy and authority is as old as the most basic questions of political philosophy. Who governs? How do they govern? Why do they govern? In democratic theory, we argue that the authority to govern springs from the legitimacy of those who would rule—either in terms of the divine right of kings or the integrity of the democratic process.[49] In the context of international law, authority is delegated by states, as we discussed above. However, when delegation is often implied and the relationship between the authority of the state and the mandate of the organization is somewhat attenuated, the questions arise again of what legitimates the process of international law, and in what context are the decisions of international courts authoritative? Or more to the point, perhaps, what are we to make of the complex relationship between legitimacy and authority?

172 *International economic law beyond the state*

Legitimacy and authority

The past 20 years have witnessed significant growth in the reach of international law. Jemielniak et al. estimate that approximately 90 percent of the entire historic output of international courts has occurred since the mid-1990s.[50] They see a complex relationship between legal authority and political legitimacy. It has not always been the case that the two go hand in hand. If it were, we would see that the more authority an institution has, the more legitimacy it would also enjoy. But that is not always the case; sometimes as authority grows, so does responsibility for past mistakes. When authority attaches to responsibility, legitimacy may decrease. However, they go on to suggest that both the arbitral system for investment law and the WTO have managed to avoid the pitfall of authority/responsibility.

This is at least partly because early adoption by member states established their legitimacy, and usage over time has increased their authority. Miller adds another dimension to the discussion of place of legitimacy and authority in legal development.[51] He maps the cross-pollination of international law that happens when international courts cite previous decisions (both their own and those of other courts). Because of the increasing interconnection of legal decisions, he argues that the proliferation of international courts and tribunals may not lead to a fragmentation of international law, but rather to a unity that emerges from shared purpose—a phenomenon that Slaughter in a different context has called a community of courts.[52]

As I suggested above, the discussion about the relationship between legitimacy and authority is really a way to talk about the relationship between political legitimacy and legal authority, or the relationship between politics and law. This is an important point to stress because the way that we theorize that relationship lies at the base of how we think about the possibilities and perils of international law. If we think about the relationship between legitimacy and authority in terms of game theory, there are four possible institutional relations to consider. We can have a legal system with low legitimacy and low authority, or a system with high legitimacy and low authority, one with both high legitimacy and high authority, and finally a system with low legitimacy and high authority. The four quadrants of Figure 7.8 map these four possibilities, and also suggest an analytic narrative for the developmental process of postwar international economic law.

We have seen in the history of economic law instances of a system with both low legitimacy and low authority in the economic governance of the interwar years. Shortly after that period came the early

International economic law beyond the state 173

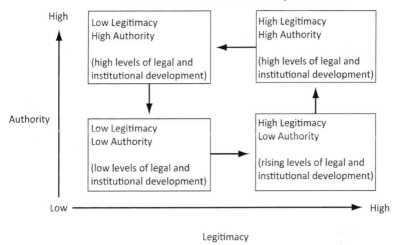

Figure 7.8 Legitimacy and authority in the postwar legal order
Source: Author's own creation.

postwar years in which economic governance under the GATT (and indeed even the early years of the WTO) was typified by high legitimacy and low authority, as Marceau has documented.[53] Members preferred to seek politically legitimate solutions to trading frictions, and sought, as much as possible, to slow the creeping legalization of the trading system. The WTO's legal system has evolved into one with a high degree of political legitimacy and a high degree of legal authority. And finally, we are witnessing the development of a legal system of investment arbitration that increasingly exhibits the traits of a system with high authority and declining levels of legitimacy, a fact concretized by the current search for a process of investment arbitration that is more palatable to governments and publics than investor-state dispute settlement. All four possibilities are on display in the modern system of international economic law.

What then is the functional relationship between legitimacy and authority? Is it reasonable to think of one as prior to the other? We have seen that it is possible to develop a legal system with high legitimacy and low authority, and also possible to maintain a system with low legitimacy and high authority—at least in the medium term. Looking at our historical case—the development of the GATT (and the postwar order in general)—political legitimacy and legal authority are required at the creation of a new legal order, but legitimacy is more important for the development of a system where there is no

174　*International economic law beyond the state*

overarching legal authority. In a modern democratic and industrialized state, legitimacy may derive from authority and vice-versa; but in our postwar international context, authority has tended to derive from legitimacy. Therefore, if we were to choose the more desirable attribute for a legal system, it would be to have surplus of legitimacy.

With the creation of the WTO, we saw that it is possible to increase the legitimacy and authority of a legal system. Once a court enjoys both, its decisions must be authoritative to maintain its legitimacy, and yet the court must be mindful of the source of its legitimacy in order to maintain high levels of authority. There is always the danger that either through exogenous shock or the perverse outcomes of authoritative decision-making, a court may lose legitimacy. Furthermore, once an international court enjoys both high legitimacy and high authority, these attributes are linked in a fragile equilibrium in which changes to one (whether rising or falling) are likely to negatively affect the other.

The interplay between legitimacy and authority are represented as four quadrants on a two-dimensional graph of legitimacy and authority (Figure 7.8). When read beginning in the bottom left quadrant and moving counter-clockwise from low legitimacy/low authority, we can see that when legitimacy rises, authority may rise as well. When legal authority rises, legitimacy may rise or fall, depending on a number of external factors. When legitimacy decreases, authority may be undermined, or at least there is the danger of that. When authority falls, so may legitimacy. So once legitimacy and authority are no longer in equilibrium, in only one instance (an increase in legitimacy), do we see an unequivocal positive outcome for law.

I am positing a logical (but also functional and normative) interaction between legitimacy and authority in which changes in legal authority are correlated with changes in political legitimacy. Even so, this is only one of a range of reasonable interaction patterns that are possible. This pattern, in which authority is predicated upon legitimacy, happens to be the one that has shaped the postwar order. However, we could imagine other logical patterns of relationship in which legitimacy is predicated upon authority; for example, imperial forms of international control from the ancient world, or other coercive forms of interstate relations, where authority tends to create legitimacy rather than the other way around.

Moments of rapid development in international law

For better or for worse, when courts use their own discretion to refine rules based upon prior decisions, they create standards of behavior that

International economic law beyond the state 175

affect the actions of states in the international system. Whether this is really a form of law-making is a matter of semantics and perspective in equal measure. Regardless, the WTO has been a major step forward from ad hoc political solution-seeking to creation of an institutional architecture for the rule of law. Furthermore, the use of precedent is a hallmark of a legal system that enjoys high levels of legitimacy and authority, a balance that remains incredibly delicate for international law. Even so, the speed at which the WTO has accomplished the development of a system of precedent needs to be recognized and problematized beyond the dyad of legitimacy/authority, if only because precedent increases the authority of law through an internal dynamic rather than through multilateral or political means.

With the Grotian moment, Scharf provides a useful way to think about these moments of rapid development, as well a way to consider the future challenges to the international economic legal order.[54] The term was first coined by Richard Falk in the mid-1980s to describe a moment in which "a fundamental change in the existing international system happens."[55] The concept is used to denote changes in the way that law is practiced, or in the way that legal concepts are applied. It may also suggest changes in the structure of the legal system itself. In fact, two of Scharf's main examples, the Peace of Westphalia and the establishment of the United Nations Charter, happened in transformative moments in world history.[56]

Scharf defines the Grotian moment as "a paradigm-shifting development in which new rules and doctrines of customary international law emerge with unusual rapidity and acceptance."[57] The Grotian moment in social scientific terms is something of a Kuhnian paradigm shift, with an added institutional/legal dimension. This means that such a moment does not change everything. It does not stand the concept of law on its head. Rather it hastens the development of law through a paradigmatic shift in perspective that sanctifies current changes. As such, the Grotian moment is "a concept that rationalizes accelerated formation of ... rules."[58] Scharf argues that such great leaps forward are required if international law is to keep pace with economic, political and technological developments that continuously reshape the global order.

The term has been applied broadly in recent years. It has been used to describe aspects of international criminal law post-Nuremberg as well as fundamental changes to the theory of the state wrought by the forces of globalization.[59] It has also been applied to other more specific moments of change within particular branches of international law, such as UN agreements on the weaponization of space in the 1960s,

176 *International economic law beyond the state*

NATO intervention in Serbia in the late 1990s that birthed the Responsibility to Protect, and the terrorist attacks on the East Coast of the United States in 2001.[60] In some ways the Grotian moment is a soft concept that brings us full circle from our earlier discussion of punctuated legal development at the WTO. We may think of the Grotian moment is a useful metaphor for what social scientists have referred to as punctuated equilibrium, shifting institutional momentum, institutional trajectories and even tipping points.

Parry attempts to situate the larger Grotian tradition in international law, examining its antecedents in not only the work of Hugo Grotius himself, but also the 20th-century legal theory of Hersch Lauterpacht and Mary Ellen O'Connell, and the political theory of Martin Wight and Hedley Bull.[61] In this context, the Grotian tradition is frequently defined as a liberal interpretation of the international legal system in which a community of states operates under a system of binding rules. The Grotian tradition is often posed as standing in contravention to a realist understanding of international law such as that of Goldsmith and Posner.[62] In earlier years of the 20th century it was similarly defined against political idealism, broadly defined. In this way, Grotius became identified with a skeptical, tough-minded, equity-oriented brand of institutional liberalism.

Legal theorists such as Hersh Lauterpacht have argued that Grotian tradition is central to international law and as a result, a moral project. Important moments in international law became identified with the thought of Hugo Grotius, not because of any work that he himself did that points directly to a global liberal legal order, but because his work has been defined by 20th-century historians and international relations theorists as belonging to a middle path in international relations between Machiavellian realism and Kantian idealism. Martin Wight argued that "Grotius stood for a rationalist, reformist approach" to understanding the place of rules in relation to international order.[63] Hedley Bull, the founder of English Realism and strong proponent of a view of international order premised upon a community of states, was a proponent of Wight's interpretation, although both scholars recognized that Grotius must be understood in his historic and intellectual context. Following Hobsbawm's dictum that traditions that claim to be old are usually of relatively recent origin, Parry suggests that the Grotian tradition is something of a modern invention.[64] Yet as an invented tradition, it plays a role in developing and maintaining the ideological cohesion of liberalism.

Kingsbury also sounds a cautionary note, arguing that the use of Grotius three centuries later frequently leads to a convoluted approach

International economic law beyond the state   177

to cause and effect in which social scientists and legal scholars read the concerns of the present into the past, something that historians wish to avoid because it places the thought of historical figures into a context that they never imagined. As a result, one must always, "distinguish sharply between the writings of Grotius and the tenets of a Grotian tradition."[65] While the work of Grotius is indeed formative in the sense that his approach to thinking about international rules diverged (sometimes sharply) from the political wisdom of his time, one must really squint to read Grotius as broadly as most modern scholarship attempts to do. And so, the Grotian tradition remains a grand ideological narrative about how the international system works.[66] In that tradition the Grotian moment is a point at which the ideational approaches and technocratic norms that underpin a liberal international order are reinforced by political success or through a developmental process that broadens or deepens the web of law.

The problem with imagining the present to be a turning point in history is that one is always reading the past in terms of its inevitable influence on the present. In the most basic sense, this is true. Everything in the past has led inevitably to the present. However, correlation is not causation, and in the larger context, the only way to know whether this point is a truly significant moment is to read it from a vantage point in the future. To put it simply, if one reads history as an extension of present concerns into the past—that is, history as an object lesson for the present—one can read the present in the terms of a causative culmination of events, and therefore as extraordinary.[67] However, if one reads history as an extension of the past into the present, with an understanding that the relationship between chronology and causation is subtle, and not always straightforward, the issue of momentous achievement becomes more complicated.

Fernand Braudel referred to this broad and deep web of causation as the longue durée, in which most of the events in the past and present are not a beginning nor an end in themselves.[68] Figure 7.9 is designed to be read both as a history of the present (if read right to left) as well as a study in the development of economic law in which the future is uncertain (read left to right). The study of momentous event is not logically fallacious or foolhardy per se, but we need to be cautious about reading present concerns into the past, as Kingsbury points out. And we ought to be able to admit that when we read significant moments of international legal development as a history of the present, we begin with the idea of a Grotian moment and move back through time, mapping the events that led inevitably to this point.

178 *International economic law beyond the state*

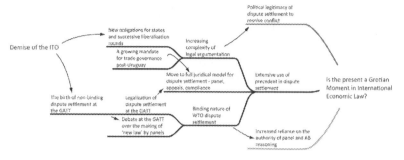

Figure 7.9 A Grotian moment in IEL?
Source: Author's own creation.

When the figure is scanned left to right, it reads as a history of legal development. We begin with the demise of the International Trade Organization. Following the right-pointing arrows, we arrive in the present, where the trading system exhibits high levels of political legitimacy, judicial authority and extensive use of precedent. Reading this narrative as an historical study in institutional development suggests that the question of whether this growing system of precedent is indeed a developmental moment, remains open. We must wait to see what the future has in store. It might be that we will look back upon this moment as the culmination of almost a century's effort to create an effective rule of economic law, or it may be that what appears to be clear legal progress now, will be undone by economic shock, geopolitical instability, or another form of unforeseen catastrophe.

The fact that events in the present appear less momentous when considered as part of a web of causation does not deny the analytic usefulness of the concept of the Grotian moment. Of course, in a strictly linear sense, it means that we cannot know if we are experiencing a transformative moment until we can view it from the vantage point of the future. But in a broader sense, we can, as Scharf and others have done, identify a pattern of development that suggests large implications in the future. Perhaps it is best to think about the Grotian moment in the context of my previous analysis of shifting equilibria along a trajectory of institutional development. Not all inflection points along the historical institutional path are of equal importance. There are some that stand out by virtue of their place as cumulating effects of previous causes. Scholars may venture an opinion on which of those points in the present are likely to have significant ramifications on future legal development, barring any unforeseen complication.

International economic law beyond the state 179

I choose to read the Grotian moment as an era of rapid development in which the way that we practice, organize, or orient ourselves towards the law changes in such a way as to make law more important to politics, governance and institutional organization. We might refer to these as major inflection points that shift or accelerate the logic of development along an institution's trajectory. Read in this light, I think a reasonable argument can be made for the accumulation of precedent at the WTO as a Grotian moment that concretizes and furthers a judicialization process that began more than 50 years ago. It seems a reasonable prediction (although we can't know with entire certainty), that all things being equal, and barring a major catastrophe, the development of a precedential system will continue to accelerate the judicialization of the WTO's dispute settlement system and deepen the web of international economic law.

Conclusion

This chapter has attempted to examine the empirical evidence of the use of precedent at the WTO and place it in the context of both the academic literature around the use of precedent in international law, as well as the literature on the implications of the deepening of law through developmental institutional processes. The first section explored the literature relating to the use of precedent in the international economic legal system. We discussed the growth of that legal system, the challenges around the use of precedent, and then I suggested that scholars are divided on the general usefulness of current ways of considering precedent in the terrain of investment law. I also showed that despite that ambiguity, we are starting to see empirical evaluations of precedent in investment arbitration. Then I moved to the literature on the use of precedent at the WTO, a practice deeply rooted in both the long history of dispute settlement at the GATT as well as the WTO's newer juridical system. At the GATT and subsequently at the WTO, the use of precedent filled a gap between treaty and the changing contours of the global economy. And in both institutions a precedential system evolved with far-reaching implications.

The second section turned to an empirical snapshot of the use of precedent at the WTO. Like in previous chapters, I built a time-sequence study of institutional and legal development that shows a trend towards an intensification of the juridical elements that have proven to be the most successful aspects of the WTO Agreement. The final section turned to the implications of precedent for both our scholarly understanding of economic law as well as for its role in shaping the global regulatory environment. As Sterio so aptly puts it,

180 *International economic law beyond the state*

"from a simple set of tools governing inter-state relations, international law has transformed itself into a global set of norms, rules and regulations, governing most aspects of state existence."[69] While I would quibble with the idea that international law itself accomplished all this, the breadth of the development is incredible, and indeed legal actors have been one of the main engines of transformation.

We discussed an emerging literature that considers the prospects of law-making on the part of international organizations, and I suggested that precedent ought to be considered one of the most prominent and potentially transformative modes of IO law-making. We then moved to a discussion of the relationship between legitimacy and authority in the analysis of the place of precedent in modern institutions for economic governance. I argued that in the postwar order, legitimacy has been an intellectual and normative basis for the development of legal authority. I then suggested that once a legal institution enjoys high levels of both legitimacy and authority, maintaining both requires that they be considered by institutional actors as being in counterbalancing equilibrium. We finally turned to the question of how to think about moments of change that forward the developmental trajectory of law. The Grotian moment, despite its potential for misuse, may be an apt description of the punctuated, or shifting, equilibrium that has typified institutional and legal development in the trade regime.

Future research ought to continue the theoretical and empirical work of this chapter, as well as the analytical propositions forwarded by Pelc, Pauwelyn and others who seek to determine the ways that states use precedent. New research will continue to examine its place in strategies for legal success and the implications of its use not only for winning cases, but for greater success in global markets. We are already at a place where trade litigation and the precedents created are becoming part of a savvy government's strategy for shaping competitive advantage, much as large corporations seek to use the law to shape national regulatory environments today.

Notes

1 Raj Bhala, "The Myth About Stare Decisis and International Trade Law (Part One of a Trilogy)," *American University International Law Review* 14, no. 4 (1999): 845–956.
2 John H. Jackson, *Sovereignty, the WTO and Changing Fundamentals of International Law* (Cambridge: Cambridge University Press, 2006).
3 Krzysztof J. Pelc, "The Politics of Precedent in International Law: A Social Network Application," *American Political Science Review* 108, no. 3 (2014): 547–564.

International economic law beyond the state 181

4 Joost Pauwelyn, "Minority Rules: Precedent and Participation before the WTO Appellate Body," in *Establishing Judicial Authority in International Economic Law*, ed. Joanna Jemielniak, Laura Nielsen and Henrik Palmer Olsen (Cambridge: Cambridge University Press, 2016); Alec Stone Sweet and Florian Grisel, *The Evolution of International Arbitration: Judicialization, Governance, Legitimacy* (Oxford: Oxford University Press, 2017).

5 Jack L. Goldsmith and Eric A. Posner, *The Limits of International Law* (New York: Oxford University Press, 2005).

6 Karen J. Alter, *The New Terrain of International Law: Courts, Politics, Rights* (Princeton, N.J.: Princeton University Press, 2014), 14.

7 Alter, *The New Terrain of International Law*, 20.

8 Alter, *The New Terrain of International Law*, 23.

9 Armin Von Bogdandy and Ingo Venzke, "The Spell of Precedents: Lawmaking by International Courts and Tribunals," in *The Oxford Handbook of International Adjudication*, ed. Cesare Romano, Karen J. Alter, and Yuval Shany (Oxford: Oxford University Press, 2014), 504.

10 Bogdandy and Venzke, "The Spell of Precedents," 505.

11 Bogdandy and Venzke, "The Spell of Precedents," 509.

12 Bogdandy and Venzke, "The Spell of Precedents," 520.

13 Harlan Grant Cohen, "International Precedent and the Practice of International Law," in *Negotiating State and Non-State Law: The Challenge of Global and Local Legal Pluralism*, ed. Michael A. Helfand (Cambridge: Cambridge University Press, 2015), 174.

14 Cohen, "International Precedent and the Practice of International Law," 175.

15 Sungjoon Cho, "Precedent as a Social Phenomenon: System, Language and Symbol," Chicago-Kent Research Paper Series, https://ssrn.com/abstract=2791744.

16 Tai-Heng Cheng, "Precedent and Control in Investment Treaty Arbitration," *Fordham International Law Journal* 30 (2007): 1014.

17 Gabrielle Kaufmann-Kohler, "Arbitral Precedent: Dream, Necessity, or Excuse?," *Arbitration International* 23, no. 3 (2007): 357–378.

18 Susan D. Franck, "The Legitimacy Crisis in Investment Treaty Arbitration: Privatizing Public International Law through Inconsistent Decisions," *Fordham Law Review* 73 (2005): 1582.

19 Irene M. Ten Cate, "The Costs of Consistency: Precedent in Investment Treaty Arbitration," *Columbia Journal of Transnational Law* 51, no. 2 (2013): 420.

20 Stone Sweet and Grisel, *The Evolution of International Arbitration*.

21 Jackson, *Sovereignty, the WTO and Changing Fundamentals of International Law*, 175.

22 See p. 39 of the legal text of GATT 1947 at www.wto.org/english/docs_e/legal_e/gatt47_e.pdf.

23 Bogdandy and Venzke, "The Spell of Precedents," 520.

24 Jackson, *Sovereignty, the WTO and Changing Fundamentals of International Law*, 177.

25 See pp. 17–18 of the legal text of the agreement at www.wto.org/english/docs_e/legal_e/04-wto.pdf.

26 *Japan—Taxes on Alcoholic Beverages*, Report of the Appellate Body WT/DS11/AB/R, paras 107–108, 4 October 1996.

182 *International economic law beyond the state*

27 Bhala, "The Myth About Stare Decisis and International Trade Law (Part One of a Trilogy)."

28 *United States—Sunset Reviews of Anti-Dumping Measures on Oil Country Tubular Goods from Argentina*, Report of the Appellate Body WT/DS268/AB/R, para. 188, 29 November 2004.

29 Felix David, *The Role of Precedent in the WTO—New Horizons?* (Maastricht: University of Maastricht, 2009), https://ssrn.com/abstract=1666169.

30 *United States—Final Antidumping Measures on Stainless Steel From Mexico*, Report of the Appellate Body WT/DS344/AB/R, para. 160, 30 April 2008.

31 Don (Dong Hyun) Song, *The Case against Judicialization of the WTO Dispute Settlement System* (Chicago, Ill.University of Chicago, 2015), http://chicagounbound.uchicago.edu.

32 Pelc, "The Politics of Precedent in International Law."

33 Krzysztof J. Pelc, "The Welfare Implications of Precedent in International Law," in *Establishing Judicial Authority in International Economic Law*, ed. Joanna Jemielniak, Laura Nielsen and Henrik Palmer Olsen (Cambridge: Cambridge University Press, 2016).

34 Pauwelyn, "Minority Rules."

35 Giorgio Sacerdoti, "The Future of the WTO Dispute Settlement System: Consolidating a Success Story," in *Future of the Global Trade Order*, ed. Carlos A. Primo Braga and Bernard Hoekman (Fiesole, Italy: European University Institute, 2016), 46.

36 Joost Pauwelyn, *Conflict of Norms in Public International Law: How WTO Law Relates to Other Rules of International Law* (Cambridge: Cambridge University Press, 2003).

37 Sacerdoti, "The Future of the WTO Dispute Settlement System," 58.

38 Sacerdoti, "The Future of the WTO Dispute Settlement System," 47.

39 The panel report for *US—Textiles Rules of Origin* was handed down in June 2003. India complained that the complexity of American rules of origin legislation for textiles posed a barrier to trade. The European Union had brought two other cases against the United States on the same legislation, both of which were withdrawn after the United States agreed to amend the laws in question. Those amendments did not satisfy India, but the case was ultimately decided in favor of the United States after the panel determined that India was unable to provide evidence of material harm to its textile sector.

40 *United States—Subsidies on Upland Cotton*, Report of the Appellate Body WT/DS267/AB/R, para. 549, 3 March 2005. See also footnote 790.

41 *European Communities—Selected Customs Matters*, Report of the Panel WT/DS315/R, para. 148, 16 June 2006.

42 *China—Measures Related to the Exportation of Rare Earths, Tungsten and Molybdenum*, Report of the Appellate Body WT/DS432/AB/R at footnote 558, 7 August 2014.

43 Oona Hathaway, *Path Dependence in the Law: The Course and Pattern of Legal Change in a Common Law System* (2003). http://digitalcommons.law.yale.edu/lepp_papers/270.

44 Michael J. Gerhardt, "The Limited Path Dependency of Precedent," *Journal of Constitutional Law* 7, no. 4 (2005): 1000.

International economic law beyond the state 183

45 Ian Johnstone, "Law-Making by International Organizations: Perspectives from IL/IR Theory," in *Interdisciplinary Perspectives on International Law and International Relations: The State of the Art*, ed. Jeffrey L. Dunoff and Mark A. Pollack (Cambridge: Cambridge University Press, 2013).
46 Johnstone, "Law-Making by International Organizations," 267–268.
47 Johnstone, "Law-Making by International Organizations," 275.
48 Johnstone, "Law-Making by International Organizations," 278.
49 Francis Fukuyama, *The Origins of Political Order: From Prehuman Times to the French Revolution* (New York: Farrar, Straus, and Giroux, 2011).
50 Joanna Jemielniak, Laura Nielsen, and Henrik Palmer Olsen, "Establishing Judicial Authority in International Economic Law: Introduction," in *Establishing Judicial Authority in International Economic Law*, ed. Joanna Jemielniak, Laura Nielsen, and Henrik Palmer Olsen (Cambridge: Cambridge University Press, 2016).
51 Nathan Miller, "An International Jurisprudence? The Operation of 'Precedent' across International Tribunals," *Leiden Journal of International Law* 15 (2002): 483–526.
52 Anne-Marie Slaughter, "A Global Community of Courts," *Harvard International Law Journal* 44, no. 1 (2003): 191–219.
53 Gabrielle Marceau, "Introduction and Overview," in *A History of Law and Lawyers in the GATT/WTO: The Development of the Rule of Law in the Multilateral Trading System*, ed. Gabrielle Marceau (Cambridge: Cambridge University Press, 2015).
54 Michael P. Scharf, "Seizing the 'Grotian Moment': Accelerated Formation of Customary International Law in Times of Fundamental Change," *Cornell International Law Journal* 43 (2010): 439–469.
55 Richard A. Falk, Friedrich Kratochwil, and Saul H. Mendlovitz, eds., *International Law: A Contemporary Perspective* (Denver, Colo.: Westview Press, 1985); Milena Sterio, "A Grotian Moment: Changes in the Legal Theory of Statehood," *Denver Journal of International Law and Policy* 39, no. 2 (2011): 211.
56 Scharf, "Seizing the 'Grotian Moment'," 444.
57 Scharf, "Seizing the 'Grotian Moment'," 439.
58 Scharf, "Seizing the 'Grotian Moment'," 467.
59 Sterio, "A Grotian Moment."
60 Scharf, "Seizing the 'Grotian Moment'," 450–451.
61 John T. Parry, "What is the Grotian Tradition in International Law?" *University of Pennsylvania Journal of International Law* 35, no. 2 (2013): 299–377.
62 Jack L. Goldsmith and Eric A. Posner, *The Limits of International Law* (New York: Oxford University Press, 2005).
63 Parry, "What is the Grotian Tradition in International Law?" 301–318.
64 Parry, "What is the Grotian Tradition in International Law?" 366.
65 Benedict Kingsbury, "A Grotian Tradition of Theory and Practice?: Grotius, Law, and Moral Skepticism in the Thought of Hedley Bull," *Queen's Law Reports* 17, no. 3 (1998): 5.
66 Parry, "What is the Grotian Tradition in International Law?" 368.
67 Margaret MacMillan, *The Uses and Abuses of History* (Toronto: Viking Canada, 2008).

184 *International economic law beyond the state*

68 Fernand Braudel, *On History* (Chicago, Ill.: University of Chicago Press, 1980).
69 Sterio, "A Grotian Moment," 236.

8 Conclusion

Political futures and the changing terrain of international economic law

- **The argument so far**
- **Hypothesis 1: Systematized institutional dynamics are driving legal development at the WTO**
- **Hypothesis 2: Regional trade agreements extend the use-value of the WTO's centralized institutional processes**
- **Hypothesis 3: Market-oriented intergovernmental mechanisms may further the development of law even when formal multilateral frames are absent**
- **Hypothesis 4: International judicial processes may create law even though state support for such institutional autonomy is slow to materialize**
- **Legitimacy and public participation**
- **Indirect participation**
- **Conclusion: political futures and research trajectories**
- **Institutional dynamics of legal development**
- **Multi-level processes facilitating legal interconnection**
- **Interaction between governmental and market forces in the development of law**
- **The role of institutional autonomy in the creation of law**
- **Final thoughts**

I began this book by describing contemporary feelings of doom and gloom following a number of coordination failures and economic shocks in the post-Cold War period. That pessimism on the part of politicians and publics misses the mark because by any measure the past few decades have been among the best in human history.[1] Global poverty is down; the Great Recession did not become a Great Depression. Stock markets have begun a robust recovery and transition economies have continued their sometimes arduous and always uncertain developmental processes. Right-wing populism remains a very real fear, but

186   *Conclusion*

it appears that in countries where populists carried the day, they did so due to insecurities unique to their political space, rather than the structural fragility of the global economy itself. It is perhaps not too much to argue that international economic law is one of the main reasons why many countries, both rich and poor, are better places to live.

We must not be too quick to hail the birth of a shiny new future. With the potential failure of the Doha Round of negotiations, the problems encountered by the Trade Facilitation Agreement, the proliferation of regional agreements, and the controversies surrounding investor-state dispute settlement, the study of the politics of international economic law is at a crossroads. Future research is likely to move in a number of directions, meeting the need for better analysis of the policy implications of dispute settlement in the context of trade and investment, the political issues associated with a global shift in treaty negotiating strategies, and, concomitantly, a new set of concerns from civil society about the failure of most recent agreements to deliver the economic dividends promised by governments.

This study has highlighted a significant tension in the politics/law interface. Do political and legal processes take place within the context of the other, or are they processes that can be, in certain circumstances, mutually exclusive? This book has argued for the former, while leaving room for an analysis of the political economy of law that takes place within disciplinary boundaries and as a result may privilege research that highlights either political economy or law. Even so, the basic tension at the heart of 21st-century international relations theory and practice remains—the Westphalian system is both a drag on many forms of growth and development, even as it remains the best source we currently have for international legitimacy and authority. This final chapter explores this paradox as it relates to my larger thesis about the shift to a politics of law at the international level.

The first section recaps the argument so far, paying attention to the way that the case studies highlight the analytical significance of the hypotheses I laid out in the introduction. The second section considers the implications of the growing terrain of law and its analytic significance to scholars and policy-makers, highlighting the basic challenge that arises alongside the growth of law. That challenge remains how to think about the relationship between political legitimacy and legal authority, and how to conceptualize the place of public participation in the sphere of law. As has been the practice so far, I include a brief empirical study that highlights the possibilities and challenges inherent in current approaches to facilitating public participation. The

Conclusion 187

final section speculates about possible future relationships between law and politics, and suggests several trajectories of future research.

The argument so far

In the first chapter I formulated my conceptual base as the shift from politics and law to the politics of law. We may at this point in our discussion suggest that by implication we are also marking a shift from a world of state sovereignty and the rules of the international game, to a world in which delegation of sovereignty coupled with the increasing autonomy of international organizations has created a system in which the rules of the game take on a life of their own. This is perhaps a more controversial claim, but one that nevertheless describes the place of law in international economic relations. We then moved to a discussion of the role of interdisciplinarity in IPE and IEL, and I suggested that scholars are now operating in a new multidisciplinary terrain in which the study of economic law may be considered a policy science. Similarly, a more normative understanding of the place of law in governance may be termed a politics of international economic law. In both cases when we take seriously the possible utility of legal studies for the study of global political economy, a new terrain of research possibility opens before us.

Building upon the insights offered by four multidisciplinary analytic narratives, I developed four hypotheses that offer a basic set of touchstones with which to broaden and deepen analysis of the politics/law interface in the global political economy. First, I hypothesized that systematized institutional dynamics are driving legal development at the WTO. Second, I suggested that regional trade agreements extend the use-value of the WTO's centralized institutional processes, contrary to what many policy analysts have predicted, although they continue to be blunt instruments that may not meet the needs of 21st-century societies. Third, I argued that some market-oriented intergovernmental mechanisms further the development of law even when formal multilateral frames are absent. Finally, I posited that international judicial processes create law through the use of arbitral precedent even though state support for such institutional autonomy is slow to materialize. On their own, none of these arguments is entirely unique. Scholars have moved around and through such ideas for a number of years now. However, I think that the time is right to bring these concepts together. To that end, I explored each of these hypotheses through an inductive process in which I provided empirical studies of a set of politico-legal relations in order to lay the analytic foundation for the future testing of

188   *Conclusion*

theoretical propositions around the development of international economic law.

Hypothesis 1: Systematized institutional dynamics are driving legal development at the WTO

Chapter 4 began by asking how social scientists might think about institutional change in the context of legal development. I paired historical institutional methods with legal insights about the development of the trading system in order to suggest that there are two ways to think about change in the legal environment at the WTO. First, some social scientific theory, most often associated with microeconomics, considers change to be the result of external shock. Second, sociological approaches to thinking about institutional development at the WTO suggest that change comes from internal factors, processes and dynamics that were set into play both before and after 1995.

I argued that both internal and external factors drive legal development and institutional growth. To that end I developed a method with which to track the developmental trajectory of the WTO. I examined key political moments to develop a graphical representation of 29 multilateral junctures at the GATT/WTO over the past 75 years. I included trade rounds and all ministerial meetings since the early 1970s. Then I examined the space between these rounds using the history of legal development inside the GATT/WTO recently produced by Gabrielle Marceau and other sources, such as the excellent description of early legal development produced by Robert Hudec 40 years ago.[2]

I showed that through an alternating process of internal legal development and multilateral political deal-making, the trading system shifted institutional momentum until 1995, when that shifting equilibrium model of development was fully institutionalized through mandated biennial ministerial conferences. Using the shifting equilibria approach, we can bring together the conceptual frames of punctuated equilibrium, historical institutionalism, and legal functionalism to analyze the way that internal and external drivers of change have been harnessed for legal development at the WTO.

The last section answered the question, how do shifting equilibria create the momentum necessary for legal development? I suggested that shifting the locus of political debate creates new opportunities to solve institutional challenges. Further, shifting problem-solving to periodic multilateral review creates broad-based buy-in from many states and helps to maintain legitimacy. The evolving development process enjoys a firmer foundation than it might otherwise enjoy because of

Conclusion 189

these regular and periodic shifts. In this back and forth, politics creates need for law, and law responds by creating the frames necessary for politics to operate more effectively. Of course, I am not the first to identify this institutional strategy. More than a decade ago, Helfer wrote about regime shifting, a process by which states and nongovernmental organizations (NGOs) identify problems with certain international public policies (in his case intellectual property rights) and raise these issues in other governance venues as a way to move problematic issues to new contexts in hopes of a better outcome.[3] The WTO has internalized this strategy of shifting footing, and has used it to great effect.

Hypothesis 2: Regional trade agreements extend the use-value of the WTO's centralized institutional processes

Chapter 5 problematized the fact that even as the WTO's governance capacity is increasing, regional agreements have proliferated. How can we understand this proliferation both in terms of its effects on the WTO as well as its place in the larger system of international economic law? This question is usually posed in two ways in the literature. Legal scholars tend to wonder if proliferation raises the possibility of creating silos of law, in which experts operate in a rarefied atmosphere. Political scientists and economists worry that proliferation will undermine the WTO, drawing away resources and undermining its legitimacy with leading traders such as the United States and EU. I linked both questions to an overarching reason why RTAs have been so interesting for both epistemic communities, and that is because by mimicking the WTO, they appear to be competitors and rivals for legitimacy, authority, and influence.

This literature on proliferation focuses on the how and why of RTAs. How have political, social, and institutional forces made possible the economic integration of different countries with different cultures and levels of development? Why are RTAs an attractive option? This massive body of literature explores five major themes, which I called the five I's of regional agreement proliferation. The first is the role that incentives, such as the gains from trade and the potential for economic development, may play in driving regionalization. Second, we may ask about the role of domestic interests in advocating for expansion opportunities. Third, political economists tend to discuss the role of ideas in the growth of free trade. Examples include the ideas of the Manchester School and its drive to end Great Britain's corn laws and ideas about the importance of economic integration for stability which

190 *Conclusion*

helped to create the European Union. Fourth, economists often question what role income levels play in RTA development. Large economies are usually highly developed industrial countries that have intensive trade patterns and make more use of trade governance mechanisms. Finally, a number of scholars have raised the issue of institutional investment, a relatively new set of hypotheses that examine the way that countries that sign at least one trade agreement, tend to sign more. They may view RTAs to be a form of reinvestment, or it might be that the WTO reduces the opportunity costs of regionalization.

But there are two problems that scholars have been unable to anticipate. The first is that proliferation has not been an entirely rational process. Agreements often overlap with others as well as with WTO governance. Further, agreements tend to be implemented when they are still substantively incomplete. Second, how to understand the relationship between RTAs and the WTO? Are these regimes designed with interaction in mind? If so, why the institutional duplication? We may turn to the literature on legal fragmentation, which suggests that the fear of disintegration through too much law is not really an issue. Further, most legal regimes play nicely together, and where they do not, they often have dispute settlement mechanisms to clarify issues.

We then turned to a study of one particular aspect of WTO governance as it relates to RTAs—dispute settlement. We began with discussion of the legal text that established the WTO's exclusive jurisdiction over dispute settlement for covered agreements. I showed that the legal literature has argued against the prospect of regional mechanisms replacing the WTO. For an RTA's dispute settlement mechanism to replace the WTO's system for covered agreements, all signatories to the agreement would have to specifically relinquish their rights at the WTO. This stickiness of exclusive jurisdiction accounts for much of current dispute settlement patterns that favor the WTO. I then reviewed two recent empirical studies that I conducted into how RTA DSMs interact with the WTO.

When RTA dispute provisions are analyzed for dispute settlement exclusions and special provisions, the most common exclusions are clauses that are already covered by the WTO's exclusive jurisdiction. Provisions covering the environment, labor standards, subsidies and government procurement are also common. Most of these areas (except for subsidies) are not yet covered by the WTO. States tend to exclude from dispute settlement those aspects of RTAs already covered by the WTO, as well as those provisions that are not yet covered by the WTO, but may be in the future. In the first instance, there is no need to duplicate efforts. In the second case, there is no need to bind states

Conclusion 191

when they do not yet know the extent of possible multilateral discipline. Either way, states defer to the WTO in the extent of dispute settlement coverage or lack thereof.

When it comes to special provisions for dispute settlement, the most common cover services and investment, with carve-outs for ISDS and a little less generally, for telecom services, financial services, and the movement of people for commerce. In the case of ISDS, the reasons for a special set of provisions are obvious—this is a form of court system that allows individuals and firms, rather than states, to sue other governments. In the case of the rest of the provisions, they modify current dispute rules in small ways to account for special circumstances (to give border officials latitude to stop individuals from entering the country when they have cause, for example).

The third section attempted to answer the question of "why RTAs?," using the insights gained from our empirical study of regional dispute settlement provisions. I suggested two main ways to proceed. The first is the reinsurance hypothesis, which rests upon the twin assumptions that multilateralism is fragile and that trade protectionism is always more politically popular than openness. As a result, states reinsure WTO disciplines at the regional level. There are three reasons why states may wish to reinsure through RTAs. First, regional DSMs are a way to show confidence in the agreement by blessing it with the endowments of the WTO. Second, they are a reasonable way to govern dispute settlement in areas that exceed the governance parameters of the WTO, such as investor-state dispute settlement. Third, full-blooded RTAs reflect the commitment of trade partners to the impartial resolution of trade irritants. Interestingly, the clear majority of RTAs without a dispute settlement mechanism tend to be signed among the former Soviet states, where promises of diplomatic resolution of irritants project an authoritarian shadow.

Second, I discussed the institutional investment hypothesis that argues government must invest in collaborative market regulation endeavors in order to reap the full benefits of both multilateral liberalization as well as new business strategies such as global value chains. To this end, researchers have wondered if the numbers demonstrate that RTAs build on existing liberalization progress at the WTO. For example, on tariff liberalization, we would expect to see regional progress (lower tariffs) in places where multilateral attempts to lower tariffs have faltered. However, we see no evidence that trade partners, unable to lower tariffs more at the WTO, turn to regional solutions. In areas where countries have chosen higher MFN tariffs, they do not tend to grant regional preferences. So RTAs are at best complements to

192 *Conclusion*

WTO disciplines, rather than substitutes– at least when it comes to tariffs. RTAs do, however, play a role in developing areas of liberalization where the Doha Round has faltered, but even here commitments are often incomplete.

What then is the use-value of RTAs in 21st-century business environments? Here the literature confirms the original hypothesis. Blanchard has shown that states tend to invest in RTAs with countries where their firms have vested interests.[4] The presence of RTAs often signals the existence of established corporate ties. A further inducement to RTA development is the existence of the WTO itself, which reduces the opportunity costs of regional institutional development because its own contours provide a solid template for RTA development. Further, in the cases of tariff reduction and the governance of contentious issues, the WTO has already made significant progress, leading the parties of RTAs to believe that in the shade of the WTO, their arrangements stand a better chance of success.

Finally, the stakes of failure are higher in the Doha Round than in regional arrangements, making failure at the regional level less of a concern. In short, without movement on the Doha Round, any movement at the regional level is a win. RTAs are then, in practical terms, a low-cost, low-risk, potentially high-return form of market governance. Even so, they remain a blunt instrument in the context of global value chains that now require more sector-specific governance mechanisms. RTAs build upon existing mechanisms at the WTO, and they may extend their use value in certain ways. But RTAs are a decidedly 20th-century approach to 21st-century business challenges, and as such their days may be numbered, at least in their current form.

Hypothesis 3: Market-oriented intergovernmental mechanisms may further the development of law even when formal multilateral frames are absent

Chapter 6 extended our discussion of multilateral centralization into the realm of international investment agreements. Some legal scholars have suggested that the growth of IIAs over the past 20 years adds up to a *de facto* multilateralization of investment law from below. I suggested that in the absence of collective intentionality, any discussion of multilateralization is something of a dead letter. However, the web of IIAs is indeed an important phenomenon in which legal development is proceeding outside traditional multilateral frames. The process is not driven by politics, but by economics. Further, it is limited in its ability to evolve beyond a web of bilateral deals by the problem of social cost.

Conclusion   193

Coase has persuasively argued that the transaction costs associated with shifts in regulation are costly because change always has costs beyond the immediate corrective.

The first section examined the history of IIAs, paying particular attention to literature that tracks the developmental trajectory of investment law. IIAs proliferate exponentially after 1990. Over 2,600 were in force by the end of 2016. Scholars have long speculated about the necessity of a multilateral mechanism to organize and legitimize this legal network. In 2009 Schill proposed that convergence of standards of protection, treaty language, and dispute mechanisms in IIAs created an emerging multilateral order for investment protection. This is an interesting argument that the centralization of law may emerge spontaneously from many sources—in essence a form of multilateralization from below.

I responded by suggesting that legal convergence is a significant step towards broadening and deepening IEL, but we have a more useful frame with which to think about the organization that occurs when many makers of a product offer it to those who wish to accept it—that of the economy. The multilateralization thesis is a bit forced because the organization of IIAs takes place in the absence of collective intentionality. Ruggie has suggested that the political will embodying multilateralism may be initially negotiated bilaterally, such as in the early GATT rounds, but it must take place in a larger context of collective commitment to generalize the benefits of political agency. Without intentionality, we cannot discuss legal convergence as a multilateral project.

The second section turned to a time-series empirical study of the emergence of key IIA clauses since 1959. The multilateralization thesis assumes a convergence of form and function, as well as an intensification of treaty signing. My brief study of the language used in IIAs suggests that while we do indeed see an intensification of treaty development, the inclusion of important clauses in these treaties remains relatively stable over time. Clauses relating to standards of treatment and dispute settlement, for example, may have proliferated with IIA signing but they have always been a fixture of IIAs.

In fact, the patterns of inclusion of these clauses look very similar to the pattern of treaty proliferation—basically we see more of these clauses because we have more agreements. It is only when we look at legal language affirming state regulatory space that we see convergence towards a model that includes clauses relating to public health, the environment, and the protection of labor standards. So, in practical terms, we do not see a major pattern that suggests the development of a model; rather we see a weak pattern of convergence through

194   *Conclusion*

amplification and a stronger pattern of growth of secondary rules for the protection of national sovereignty.

In the last section I made a three-part argument for a politics of IEL that benefits from the economics of law literature. First, I briefly discussed the relationship between rational choice methods and legal scholarship. Then I turned to the "market for law" literature that suggests the relationship between law-makers and law-takers resembles a marketplace governed by supply and demand. This is an important point because it is frequently asserted that states are the only sources of law at the international level. This research shows that there may be other sources as well, including markets (and the interests of firms, passed through the procedural filter of the state) and international organizations themselves. Finally, I asked about the prospects for multilateral regulation in a global market for law. Economic theory suggests a trade-off between the relative inefficiency of the current governance model and the potential cost of adopting another regulatory system.

Coase argued that with imperfect competition (i.e. economic activity in the real world) came unequal private and public costs associated with social protection. These costs are never zero, and sometimes they are very expensive for both market actors and governments. The costs of addressing social externalities require states to take into account the transaction costs associated with moving from bilateralism to multilateralism. Further, they must consider those costs in terms of their totality, rather than the specific marginal transaction costs in the here and now. This means that states need to consider costs in terms of not only the expenditure of political capital, but also in terms of sovereignty tradeoffs over the coming decades. Ultimately, the current system remains in place because treaty-making states consider the costs of change to be too high at this point in time. They prefer the status quo to the potential efficiency (and possible equity) gains of a multilateral model—at least for now.

It is not surprising then that early discussions around the creation of a multilateral dispute settlement mechanism for investment law are taking place between Canada and the EU. These states depend upon stable investment frames and understand the importance of continued legitimacy for the long-term viability of the system of bilateral treaties. Interestingly, it was also Canada and the EU who originally argued for the creation of a formal institutional system for trade during the Uruguay Round in the late 1980s. We might think of this proposed multilateral investment court as a half-measure that moves towards a multilateral solution while attempting to avoid the higher costs associated with a full-scale multilateralization of investment law. Both

Canada and certain member states in the EU see relative gains in equity and the increased legitimacy of a multilateral mechanism to be in their long-term better interests. They stand to lose a lot if the erosion of legitimacy leaves them with less protection for corporate investment. Given the totality of costs associated with change, they are willing to invest in the future.

Hypothesis 4: International judicial processes may create law even though state support for such institutional autonomy is slow to materialize

The final case study continued our study of the increasingly central role played by law in international economic relations. At the WTO, the use of precedent is a primary indicator of the growing authority of international economic law. Precedent does not operate in the same way at the international level as it does at the level of the state, but both systems share the same basic principle that judicial practice creates a body of legal decision that must be consulted when judges and lawyers examine new cases. The question of precedent in IEL has been minimized for many years because the political legitimacy of the systems for trade and investment regulation required that diplomats stress the practical, multilateral nature of regulation rather than the rise of binding international law. But it has become increasingly apparent that precedent is necessary for the interpretation of law around trade and investment.

The first section reviewed literature on precedent in IEL and then I followed with an empirical discussion of the use of precedent in investment and trade regulation. Finally, I discussed the implications of precedent for how we think about international judicial authority and the changing nature of economic law. The new design of international courts emphasizes compulsory jurisdiction and makes it harder for states to block cases they want to avoid. In this context precedent creates a number of challenges and opportunities. It creates expectations that are both the result of the signed treaty as well as unforeseen consequences of it, and precedent may increase the unknown implications of international law. Even so, precedent is unavoidable because courts dealing with a quickly expanding case-load need an authoritative guide with which to create reference points for deciding cases. Ultimately, the question of precedent is much more than a question of appropriate judicial role. It is more a question about how to translate legal logic and culture into the international context—how to create an international rule of law.

196 *Conclusion*

Precedent in investment arbitration offers a way to increase the legal authority of arbitral decisions because investment arbitration documents are increasingly finding their way into the public sphere, and inconsistent decisions undercut the legitimacy of the system. Some scholars have disagreed with this assessment. Ten Cate, for example, believes that arbitrators ought to place more weight on contextual legitimacy of decisions rather than imposing a precedential system that may narrow the vision of adjudicators, and create a form of tunnel vision in which congruence with previous cases matters more than the ability of arbitrators to make the best decisions for disputing parties.[5] Even so, the use of precedent is rapidly rising. Stone Sweet and Grisel have shown that 97 percent of all precedent citation has taken place since 2000.[6]

At the WTO, discussions around the use of precedent and the practice of citing cases are much older. They date back to the early 1960s when GATT began to develop a systematic practice of case citation. Importantly, the GATT did not formally limit the impact of precedent on trade law, causing some analysts to speculate about its outsize impact on the future of trade regulation. However, the WTO charter dealt with the looming problem of a strong precedent system in an institution that was, at least in formal terms, dedicated to political solutions to trade frictions. The Charter empowers the Ministerial Conference with a 75 percent vote to adopt official interpretations of WTO agreements. In this way it reserves the right to definitive legal interpretation for the membership at large. Yet within this frame a softer precedential system flourishes. Pelc shows that states are drawn to the logic of precedent and use it strategically to shape the competitive environment of the global economy.[7] The fact that they continue to invest in precedent while decrying the potential for judicial activism suggests something about the fraught place of precedent in a system in which final authority for the execution of law lies with the subjects of that law—states.

Turning to the empirical study of the use of precedent at the WTO, I asked four questions. First, how many GATT and WTO cases are subsequently cited as precedent? Second, do the number of cases cited increase over time? Third, which cases are cited the most, and are there certain very authoritative cases? Finally, do some WTO members rely on precedent in litigation more than others? I showed that citation, as a legal practice, is on the rise at the WTO. Furthermore, we see a trend towards citing fewer GATT decisions and more WTO cases. I also showed that certain prominent early cases are cited heavily, suggesting a certain path dependence in WTO judicial citation, similar to what

Conclusion 197

legal scholars have noted in domestic courts. Finally, I showed that when we break down citation by member, the United States and EU are not substantially different from all other members when it comes to citing cases in their arguments. We see a fairly uniform increase in precedent citation across the board, suggesting that the use of precedent may be a good indicator in the future of legal expertise among the membership. At the very least, it suggests that most members that engage in dispute settlement use law firms that believe strongly in the use of precedent.

Next, we turned to the implications of precedent. Here I asked three questions. First, what is precedent's law-making potential at the international level? Second, what role do political legitimacy and legal authority play in accelerating or undercutting this process? Finally, is this recent era of intensive legal development a Grotian moment? Precedent springs from a delegation of state authority. Delegating authority in the international context is often a somewhat unintended, but entirely foreseeable outcome of the growth of international legal mandates and capacities. Yet it creates challenges because as the autonomy of international organizations grows, so does the democratic deficit. This is why governments that increasingly rely upon semi-autonomous international organizations may simultaneously (and publicly), withhold support for that autonomy in symbolic ways.

Any discussion of the relationship between legitimacy and authority is really a way to discuss the relationship between political legitimacy and legal authority, or the relationship between politics and law. I took a simple game theoretic approach to mapping the functional relational possibilities between legitimacy and authority. With the creation of the WTO we saw that it was possible to increase both the legitimacy and the authority of international economic law. But once a court system enjoys both, its decisions must be authoritative in order to maintain legitimacy, and yet the court must also be mindful of the source(s) of that legitimacy in order to maintain its authority.

I represented possible relational positions between legitimacy and authority in four quadrants on a two-dimensional game board. I posited a logical and functional set of interactions between legitimacy and authority in order to show that, at least in our postwar context, levels of legal authority are frequently correlated with changes in political legitimacy. However, we could imagine other contexts in which legitimacy follows authority. The main issue here is that while the courts of international economic law enjoy high legitimacy and high levels of legal authority in the present, we are seeing storm clouds on the horizon in the form of civil society concerns about ISDS and populist

198   *Conclusion*

right-wing anger about the place of WTO dispute settlement in national policy-making. A court system that loses its sources of political legitimacy is in danger of instability and a corresponding decline in its legal authority.

Then we moved to a discussion of how to think about the previous two decades of rapid legal development. I applied the concept of the Grotian moment to consider changes in the way that law is practiced (or the shift in the way that law or legal ideas are applied). As a concept, the Grotian moment has enjoyed something of a renaissance in legal studies and has been applied across a wide array of international legal endeavor. I have engaged with this concept while being mindful of its limitations. It is intellectually sloppy to imagine that the present is momentous because it is a culmination of the past. I have suggested that if we are to take the Grotian moment as an analytic tool, we must not read history as an extension of present concerns into the past. Rather, we must begin with history that takes the past on its own merits. We need to understand that momentous change in the present may be significant when considered from a vantage point in the future, or it may not. Even so, the Grotian moment is important because it highlights the way that moments of legal development can have tremendous impact both in qualitative and quantitative terms, on the development of law.

If we were to sum up these case studies with a single sentence, we might say that the depth and reach of international law is vast, and growing exponentially; nobody yet knows the extent of its impact upon the state. Perhaps the most learned response to that assessment could be, why bother with sovereignty at all? Why not just acknowledge that the increasingly porous divide between the national and the international means that there is a functional argument for the expansion of the unaccountable authority of international law, even to the extent that it overrides state sovereignty in certain cases—because it gets things done that states cannot do on their own.

Sovereignty is always somewhat arbitrary because it represents a space, place, institution or person that has been invested with authority. Of course, it further suggests that the things we value for their social, organizational, philosophic, or legal functions may be invested with an authority that conveys their importance, and that concomitantly, we may decide, through any manner of mechanism, to withdraw the imprimatur of sovereignty. In the Westphalian context the highest form of authority is that of the sovereign state, and when states are said to give up some sovereignty to gain something else (market access, the collective good of regulation), we assume that sovereignty has been

Conclusion 199

delegated to another state, another institution, or at the very least into a larger collective intention. In this way it is reasonable to speak of the sovereign authority of international law, or the sovereignty of rules, when these rules represent the collective intention of member states.

Further, sovereignty has a value to governments and citizens that goes far beyond its functional place in the delegation of legal authority, if only because states view their delegation of sovereign authority as both a transaction and an investment. Somewhat counterintuitively, sovereignty matters more than ever in a world of expanding international law because legal authority rests upon a base of political legitimacy that requires that international organizations steer a careful course between a practical need for institutional autonomy and a respect for the embodied sovereignty of citizens delegated to them for that purpose.

Walker problematizes the question of sovereignty alongside pre-modern conceptions of authority, both rooted in philosophical and historical dimensions of hierarchy as well as spatial dimensions of place and the wider world.[8] In one way, sovereignty is about inside versus outside, place versus other places, the particular versus the universal. But the idea of sovereign authority also suggests multiple ways to think about sovereignty—as a state practice, as a way to, in Walker's conception, authorize authority, or in my own words, to legitimize authority. The legitimation of authority raises the question again of the relationship between political legitimacy and legal authority, which I will discuss in greater detail below.

Legitimacy and public participation

In Chapter 3 I argued that in the multidisciplinary world of international economic law scholarship, there are two emerging schools of thought that treat the theory and method of global governance quite differently. These schools of thought diverge in their ontological assumptions about the basis of political agency at the international level; they also diverge in their ways of knowing, rooted as they are in quantitative and qualitative epistemologies (if we permit an over-simplification). I also suggested that they are nevertheless linked to each other through shared history and the sharing of certain modes of investigation. Deductive and inductive methods, and the creation and testing of hypothesis, are two sides of the same coin of discovery.

There is another way that hypothesis-testing and hypothesis-offering research converges in our study of the politics of law. In the policy science approach I described, the main challenge to deeper integration and the growth of law is twofold. On one hand, in structural terms it is

200 *Conclusion*

a lack of sovereign authority on the part of international institutions. On the other, it is a democratic deficit, which is defined as the attenuation of political legitimacy beyond the state. The unstated assumption is that legitimacy flows from democratic participation, and sovereign delegation strains the authority of international law, which exists at a remove from citizenship. At its most simple, we can call this the problem of systemic anarchy and the democratic deficit.

In the legal realist, or politics of IEL approach, the main challenge in structural terms is the piecemeal and unfinished nature of international community, which remains incomplete for reasons having to do with the history of human development. In political terms the main challenge is the lack of international (or global) consensus on the normative foundations of order—a point frequently phrased in terms of global equity and social justice. At the most simple we can call this the problem of community and an equitable basis for future development.

In practical terms then, we have come full circle. The two sides of our coin view the structural challenge to the future development of international law to be problems related to a lack of autonomous authority beyond the state and the corresponding unfinished nature of global community. They understand the political challenges to be about democratic attenuation and a corresponding lack of a fair (legitimate) basis for development. The structural problem is one of authority and the political and procedural problem is one of legitimacy. And I would argue that the basic (and very practical) question that lies at the base of these overlapping concerns, is how to create law from the bottom up, when the dominant approach to law-giving (especially between states or across jurisdictional boundaries) in human history has been the top-down legitimization of law through the authority of the conqueror.

This basic problem of how to grow law up from the soil of the state cannot be resolved for largely historical reasons having to do with the persistence of the Westphalian system and the historic inequalities brought about by war, conquest and empire. In both these cases only time will sort out the complexities. Either because (from the policy science perspective) technological and organizational advances will make the Westphalian order obsolete, or because (from the politics of law perspective) the slow growth of global justice will incrementally account for past atrocity. In either case, a lack of a global authority beyond the state is a problem that cannot be resolved by effective public policy on its own.

Therefore, both policy scientists and legal realists make normative appeals to the cultivation of international political legitimacy, either in

Conclusion 201

terms of institutional processes, in the case of the policy science approach, or in terms of institutional outcomes, in the politics of law approach. And so behind (and perhaps prior to) the problem of authority is the problem of legitimacy. In both multidisciplinary approaches, the problem of legitimacy is one that may begin to be addressed through wise policy. Interestingly, the problem of legitimacy is tackled, at least in part, in both approaches by increasing public participation in processes of global governance. In policy science more public participation decreases the democratic deficit. In the politics of international economic law, more public participation increases the chance of more equitable outcomes by increasing the number of stakeholders around the table.

Sitting the public at a table that has been set for states is a challenge, but increasing legitimacy to increase authority is a much smaller challenge compared to the alternative, which is the imposition of authority with which to legitimize legal developmental efforts. There are at least three ways to think about public participation in the processes of IEL. First, groups and individuals may participate in direct ways, either by gaining standing in intergovernmental organizations, or by gaining standing in juridical processes. This incorporation of non-state actors is not without precedent. One need only point to ISDS processes for a ready example of such inclusion. However, we might also argue that the inclusion of non-state voices has a way of amplifying the voices of the wealthiest states, which tend to host well-informed and well-funded NGOs and think tanks. Direct inclusion of non-state participants may undermine the legitimacy of trade multilateralism in which the voices of small economies have only recently begun to carry weight.

Non-state actors may also participate in intergovernmental processes indirectly. At the WTO, for example, NGOs, business groups, academics and other members of the interested public may submit amicus curiae briefs to dispute settlement panels. We will discuss this form of participation in more detail below. Finally, the public can participate in legal process in attenuated ways, which is usually limited to observation. In the world of investment regulation, there is very little opportunity for attenuated participation. Few processes are open to the public and even arbitral decisions may be sealed at the discretion of disputing parties. However, in trade multilateralism there is more transparency. Some dispute panels have recently been opened to public observation. Likewise, the WTO contains several transparency-enhancing mechanisms such as the Trade Policy Review Mechanism and the Public Forum. Further, the WTO, like other intergovernmental organizations, participates in exercises to increase transparency through access to

202 *Conclusion*

information that involves cooperating on cross-sector studies, offering its reports and analysis for free, offering all dispute settlement reports online, and inviting criticism and analysis by sponsoring outlets for academic discourse.

Indirect participation

I have discussed the limits of public participation in international economic law. Direct participation is a non-starter in systems where only states have legal standing, such as at the WTO. There are similar limits to participation on the other side of the glass. Observation is never a satisfactory form of participation, even though the act of observing likely intervenes in the processes being observed in many small ways. Indirect participation has become the preferred mode of intervention, used by a number of NGOs and business interests in both investment and trade disputes. Fach Gomez shows how the use of amicus curiae briefs, which have a history in English common law and have been used in American courts for many years, have made their way into international law. They are used not only in investment and trade tribunals, but also in the International Criminal Court, the International Criminal Tribunal for the former Yugoslavia, and others.[9] She suggests that they are a good start towards protecting the public interest in these courts through limited rights of participation.

There are some basic challenges with the use of amicus briefs in economic law. For example, at least in the realms of trade and investment, courts do not have to accept them. De Brabandere reports that, in investment regulation, the ICSID in 2006 allowed the use of amicus briefs, but limited their use by requiring the tribunal to consider whether the amicus had significant interest in the case before allowing a brief.[10] In the WTO, the Appellate Body maintains a discretionary right to accept or reject amicus briefs as it sees fit. In both jurisdictions, submitting an amicus brief is not a guarantee that it will be considered. As Steger has stated, "[t]he rights of participation in the WTO dispute settlement system belong exclusively to the states [that are] Members of the WTO." As a result, she suggests that the issue of accepting amicus briefs is not about participation, but rather it relates to the duty of panels to "assess the matters before them."[11]

However, Steger is not dodging the question. Rather she is directing us back to the original intent of amicus briefs, which were designed to offer the court advice (evidence or contextual facts) that it could not get from the litigating parties.[12] If amicus briefs maintain their proper role, serving in an advisory capacity at the pleasure of the court, then

Conclusion 203

there is no real question of whether we are seeing a creeping right of participation on the part of non-state groups. Furthermore, this limited role is fair, despite the limitations it imposes upon participation because it would be unjust if parties with no obligations under an agreement had the right to enforce obligation of other parties to the agreement.[13] Steger's reasoning clarifies much about the amicus system that troubles small economies. Even so, it bears repeating that advising the court is a form of participation, although perhaps not a form that requires a reconsideration of the role of non-state actors in the state-to-state dispute settlement system.

While legal scholars like Steger aim to consider amicus briefs in their proper procedural role, others hope that they may become a sort of surrogate for nongovernmental participation in dispute settlement. Hernandez-Lopez is optimistic that the inclusion of amicus briefs is a road to NGO participation at the WTO.[14] They enshrine, at an international level, the prospect of nongovernmental concerns being heard. This is an idea that is not alien to the EU and United States, which already have certain mechanisms in place for citizen participation. But for those states that do not have such mechanisms, the freedom of panels to consider amicus briefs offers a way to put public concerns in front of WTO panelists.

Crema analyzes the rules around amicus briefs across trade and investment law to ascertain their suitability for public participation. He shows that in balance, the system is not yet fully "public, effective, and transparent."[15] Similarly, Schadendorf notes that the jurisprudence on when to permit amicus briefs in investment proceedings is inconsistent. Some tribunals recognize the need to consider public interest and human rights concerns when deciding cases, but "whether they are taken into account is hard to measure."[16] De Brabandere agrees, echoing Steger's position when he concludes that "participation as *amicus curiae* is not tantamount to participating *as a party in the proceedings*" (original emphasis).[17] Furthermore, a limited degree of access is unlikely to develop into a formal standing as a participant.

It is generally understood that the use of amicus briefs is on the rise in investment arbitration but most of the evidence for their increasing prominence is circumstantial.[18] Legal scholars rely upon the fact that they see an increasing number of amicus submissions as part of the investment disputes that are made public. This measure coupled with the significant rise in the use of investment tribunals leads scholars to believe that the use of amicus briefs is similarly rising. Yet without the numbers to back up this assertion, we are left to surmise about their use.[19] It appears from scholars' preliminary assessments that the

204 Conclusion

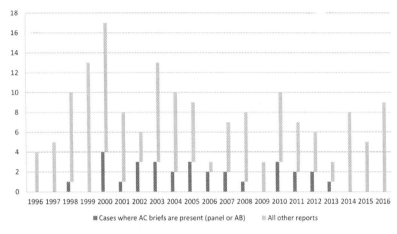

Figure 8.1 Panels with amicus curiae briefs, by year
Source: WTO Dispute Settlement Database.

numbers will be quite a bit larger than we have seen so far at the WTO. Yet despite their increasing use, we remain uncertain about their overall impact on the terrain of investment law.

The same may be said about amicus briefs at the WTO. The uncertain place and limited role of amicus briefs is becoming clear from usage patterns. I examined the panel and Appellate Body reports for every case completed at the WTO. Some panels report the submission of briefs whether they are considered by the panel or not. Others do not, and evidence may exist in the written submissions of the parties, or not at all. In this study, I relied upon the reporting by the panel itself because briefs that are not a part of national consultation processes (which many members do not yet have) are submitted directly to the WTO. Amicus briefs have been filed in 30 cases since 1998, when the practice was allowed.[20] This is not a large number, but it does suggest that the WTO is developing evidentiary rules and a judicial track record for dealing with amicus briefs. Overall, the general trend is to report the submission of the brief to all parties, consider their opinions of the brief, and request that if any parties find it to be useful to their case, they ought to submit it into evidence along with their written submissions. Essentially, the brief ceases to be the work of a separate actor and becomes part of a member's written submission. Figure 8.1 shows the use of amicus briefs sorted by the year of panel report.

The number of amicus briefs suggests a certain lack of enthusiasm on the part of would-be intervenors in WTO cases, which raises at least

Conclusion 205

Table 8.1 The submission of amicus curiae briefs

Dispute	Year	Short title	Panel report	AB report
DS58	1998	US—Shrimp	Yes	Yes
DS122	2000	Thailand—H-Beams	No	Yes
DS135	2000	EC—Asbestos	Yes	Yes
DS138	2000	US—Lead and Bismuth II	Yes	Yes
DS160	2000	US—Section 110(5) Copyright Act	Yes	No
DS212	2002	US—Countervailing Measures on Certain EC Products	No	Yes
DS231	2002	EC—Sardines	No	Yes
DS236	2002	US—Softwood Lumber III	Yes	No
DS141	2003	EC—Bed Linen	Yes	No
DS248	2003	US—Steel Safeguards	No	Yes
DS257	2003	US—Softwood Lumber IV	No	Yes
DS265	2004	EC—Export Subsidies on Sugar	Yes	Yes
DS277	2004	US—Softwood Lumber VI	Yes	No
DS269	2005	EC—Chicken Cuts	No	Yes
DS294	2005	US—Zeroing	Yes	No
DS308	2005	Mexico—Taxes on Soft Drinks	No	Yes
DS291	2006	EC—Approval and Marketing of Biotech Products	Yes	No
DS315	2006	EC—Selected Customs Matters	Yes	No
DS332	2007	Brazil—Retreaded Tyres	No	Yes
DS337	2007	EC—Salmon	Yes	No
DS339	2008	China—Auto Parts	No	Yes
DS316	2010	EC—Large Civil Aircraft	Yes	No
DS367	2010	Australia—Apples	Yes	No
DS371	2010	Thailand—Cigarettes	Yes	No
DS379	2010	US—Anti-Dumping and Countervailing Duties	No	Yes
DS384	2011	US—COOL	Yes	No
DS381	2011	US—Tuna II	Yes	Yes
DS406	2012	US—Clove Cigarettes	No	Yes
DS412	2012	Canada—Renewable Energy	Yes	Yes
DS400	2013	EC—Seal Products	Yes	Yes

Source: WTO Dispute Settlement Database.

206 *Conclusion*

two questions. First, when are amicus briefs filed? Do they come in before the panel, or are they more likely to be filed before appeal and after the panel's initial report has been circulated? Secondly, who submits amicus briefs? We assume that they are a tool for intervention on the part of civil society, but submissions suggest a more nuanced picture. Table 8.1 begins to answer the first question about the timing of amicus briefs. Of the 30 cases where the submission of an amicus curiae brief is reported, we have 19 reports of amicus curiae submissions at the panel stage, and 18 reports of submissions at the appeal stage. To break it down in more linear terms, seven cases report amicus curiae submissions at both the panel and appeals stage, 12 report submissions at only the panel stage, and 11 report submission of an amicus curiae brief at only the appeals stage of dispute settlement.

We have assumed that cases with a significant public interest component tend to attract amicus briefs. However, Table 8.1 suggests that this is not necessarily the case. There are indeed several high-profile cases on this list such as *US—Shrimp*, *EC—Asbestos*, the Canada/US softwood lumber cases and *EC—Seal Products*. But the list also contains cases that are of less interest to civil society such as *US—Zeroing*. If we cannot assume that amicus briefs are the domain of civil society, then who submits amicus briefs? According to WTO filings, briefs are submitted by civil society groups, trade and industry groups, and academics. In one case an amicus brief was submitted by a state member that had failed to reserve its third-party status on the dispute. Civil society did indeed file amicus briefs in a plurality of the 30 cases (NGOs filed amici in 44 percent of cases). However, business groups filed amici in 22 percent of cases, labor groups in another 5 percent of cases, and institutes and think tanks in 12 percent of cases, so the easy assumption that amicus briefs are dominated by civil society is perhaps overstated.[21]

What happens to amicus curiae briefs once they are submitted? The short answer to that question is, not much. If briefs are filed on time, they are circulated to the parties. This means that the parties read and digest the brief, and the panel notes that the parties have been given this opportunity. Sometimes the panel makes a note of its right to take into consideration all materials it deems pertinent. In other cases, the panel notes that should the parties wish the material to be a part of the case, they should incorporate it into their submissions. In almost all cases, the panel takes pains to note that the amicus material was not determinative in its final decision.

Two issues hold amicus briefs back from being more effective. First, there is no legal requirement for the panel to consider them. Second, as

Conclusion 207

a matter of practice, panels tend to disregard these submissions. In most instances the panel and/or AB report states that although the brief was submitted and circulated to the parties, the panel disregarded it when rendering a decision. There is a good reason for this. Panelists likely worry that if they allow a brief from a non-member to influence the outcome of a case, it will undermine the legitimacy of the process with the membership. If this is the case, it raises the question of why industry, civil society, and academic groups bother to submit a brief. Just because panels cannot be seen to be favoring (or even considering) amicus briefs, does not mean that they don't have some bearing on the outcome of the case, even if only in a very limited and tangential way. Furthermore, if they are read and digested by panelists, there is an opportunity to shape state argumentation. Likely, this is the main goal of most amicus briefs—to support state efforts at the WTO.

Even so, amicus briefs are unlikely to become a back door for greater civil society participation in the processes of international economic law. This means that for the foreseeable future, economic law remains the domain of state actors, with a more limited role for firms and other economically interested actors in investment arbitration. There are implications for the future of international economic law because non-state actors are relegated to very small windows of indirect and attenuated forms of participation, raising the concern about the relationship between political legitimacy and legal authority. The future must contain a larger role for non-state actors in global governance if the legal system is to maintain its authority. Even so, it is not clear what role timing and sequencing play in this instance. Must states and international organizations move quickly to create a place for publics, or will nongovernmental actors understand that opening spaces for participation in the processes of economic law takes time? We do not yet know, and importantly, state actors themselves are crossing this river by feeling the stones, to paraphrase Wolfe.[22]

Conclusion: political futures and research trajectories

My argument has emphasized a multidisciplinary method to highlight the many opportunities for fruitful collaboration to be found between political economy and legal studies. To that end, the case studies began with the insights found in legal theory and used these as a springboard for an empirical analysis of legal development that usually developed along the lines of a time-series study or other form of sequential empirical analysis. From there I moved in eclectic directions, suggesting the usefulness of the study for multidisciplinary legal and/or

208 *Conclusion*

political economy work. I attempted to consider the economic dimension of political economy research in at least one study, and highlighted the interplay between historical critical and legal theoretic work in another. In each study, a focus on multidisciplinarity revealed more than it obscured, and offered new ways to think about institutional growth and legal development.

In this final section I will identify at least four trajectories of future research in the politics and policy of international economic law. These trajectories highlight the institutional dynamics of legal development, the multi-level processes facilitating legal interconnection, the interaction between governmental and market forces in the development of international law, and the role of institutional autonomy in the creation of law beyond the state. These themes certainly do not exhaust potential avenues of research, but they do highlight some of the most significant possibilities for contribution to this emerging field, and they suggest the range of potential endeavor, and the great potential for future collaborative work among political economists and legal scholars.

Institutional dynamics of legal development

The first study of shifting equilibria at the GATT/WTO suggests that there is still much work to be done in the empirical evaluation of the previous seven decades of legal development. Historians of political economy and law will have much to say in the coming years about the institutional processes, legal agreements, and multilateral political dynamics that have shaped the regulation of trade and investment. Historians of global governance and international economics are likely to make much of the ways in which institutional dynamics helped or hindered the processes of legal development.

In the second instance, thinking about the timing and sequencing of institutional momentum in the context of legal development opens the possibility of thinking about the close interaction between political and legal processes, which Nourse and Shaffer have called the simultaneity of politics and law.[23] This research also suggests possible reconsiderations of the conceptual relationship between multilateralism and legal development. As I mentioned in Chapter 4, research that problematizes and explains the relationship between consensus building and constitutionalism remains under-developed, as does research that studies the comparative development of different mechanisms of international economic law that have grown in scale and scope of mandate in the postwar period. Up to this point we have focused on economic

Conclusion 209

imperative and political facilitation. Now, we need more scholarly research that examines the increasing importance of legal architecture as a driver of integration.

Multi-level processes facilitating legal interconnection

The analysis of dispute settlement mechanisms in regional trade agreements suggests that legal proliferation has several implications for future research on the linkages between regional and multilateral governance. As I suggested in Chapter 5, there are two things we know: that RTAs are probably an intermediate step in the development of regional mechanisms for the coordination of value chains; and RTAs as they are currently deployed do not necessarily undermine the centrality of the WTO. I also suggested that there is at least one big thing we do not know, and that is what the future holds for regional trade governance. We might see a renewed movement towards plurilateral and megaregional agreements even though these are an uphill climb in the current global political environment. Further, current megaregional projects are beginning to fray around the edges. For example, a Trans-Pacific Partnership that includes the United States is effectively off the field of play, at least during the current presidential administration.

All things being equal, the future of trade governance is likely to be more plurilateral agreements that take advantage of existing WTO architecture, fewer megaregional projects, and very likely fewer regional trade and investment agreements. We may see a more concerted effort toward multilateral agreements in specific issue areas, such as services and investment, but even there the odds are longer in the current political climate. Scholars and policy-makers have begun to consider the web of international economic law in terms of the liabilities, highlighting the political and legal problem of de-integration, or to be syntactically correct, the disintegration of governance institutions. For scholars it seems logical to imagine that the forces of integration may move in more than one direction. Citizens may recall their delegated sovereignty.

Prior to the UK's European Union membership referendum in 2016, we did not have an example of a leading economic power seriously considering the institutional and legal process of de-integration. At this point the possibility of a British exit from the EU, or Brexit, is not so much about the unraveling of economic integration, so much as it is about the UK reconfiguring its relationship to international economic law, moving from a common market to a system in which its

210   *Conclusion*

relationship with international market regulation will look more like that of the United States or Canada. In the future (although this is by no means assured), the UK may have some sort of formal relationship with the EU as well as a better-articulated set of relations at the WTO and through bilateral and regional trade and investment agreements. Leaving the EU is not unthinkable given the challenges it has faced following the financial crisis. The surprise was that the first country to leave was a leading economic power rather than a beleaguered economy such as Greece, or Italy. The politics of IEL are not always rational and the place of global politics in theorizing the authority of economic law, is still uncertain. State authority and state power are still at the heart of any attempt to explain the legitimacy of international economic law.

Interaction between governmental and market forces in the development of law

In Chapter 6 we discussed the web of bilateralism for investment governance and its prospects for evolutionary development towards some form of multilateral institution. I suggested that scholars are divided on whether values or interests play a deciding role in multilateral success. Perhaps in the changing terrain of economic law, governments will consider their values and interests to line up behind some form of multilateralism, if only to combat various forms of creeping protectionism that have been highlighted by recent events in the United Kingdom and United States.

I also suggested that a market for law is one particularly significant way of thinking about the organizing forces behind legal proliferation in the previous 20 years. Our discussion adds a much-needed dimension to the trade multilateralism literature in which one often gets the sense that legal development proceeds in a somewhat straightforward and orderly fashion. The common thread running through the literature seems to be a trajectory of institutional development and a rational commitment on the part of governments to engage legal processes to benefit from economic integration. The world of investment law puts the lie to this easy assumption. IIAs frequently operate in opaque ways and they do not necessarily offer a way forward for those researchers looking for more effective mechanisms of governance.

With the current forces of instability shaking international organizations, from Brexit, to the rise of populist nationalism in the United States, policy-makers have begun to explore ways to shore up the bilateral web of investment agreements. This network is particularly

Conclusion 211

threatened by potential political instability because its judicial system has long been one of the most problematic aspects of governance. Investor-state dispute settlement had the potential to be a novel experiment in allowing non-state actors to participate in international economic law. But by allowing investors to sue states, IIAs open a larger door for predatory interests to prey upon small economies, than they open for nongovernmental organizations to partake in the processes of investment law.

In the current system of investment governance, foreign firms taking aggressive legal positions enjoy a distinct advantage over states. They have access to a larger number of judicial mechanism than domestic firms or their host states because they may sue in both the host jurisdiction as well as through investment agreements.[24] Therefore, discussions around the development of a multilateral dispute settlement mechanism for investment to replace the bilateral network of ISDS and state-to-state mechanisms is long overdue.[25] Its architecture, the political process of development, and its potential deployment in a burgeoning network of IIAs is likely to provide much research potential for scholars of law and political economy for many years to come.

The role of institutional autonomy in the creation of law

In the last case, we considered the prospects of law-making by international organizations, and I suggested that precedent is perhaps the most potentially transformative mode of semi-autonomous lawmaking. I linked our analysis to a discussion of the relationship between legitimacy and authority, arguing that the legal authority of the postwar order is predicated upon its legitimacy in the eyes of voting citizens in leading nations. Furthermore, there is a complex connection between political legitimacy and legal authority; maintaining both increasingly requires a careful consideration of their equilibrium by institutional actors in international courts.

Future research ought to continue the theoretical and empirical work in this vein. More work is needed in the ways that states use international legal precedent. New research will continue to examine the use of both precedent and legal strategy in the development of competitive advantage. Further, we need to link all these issues to the developing politics of an emerging legal environment in financial governance at the International Monetary Fund and the G8/G20. Continuing with these financial considerations, we also need more research into how countries will share the costs of the growing legal system. The research potential of this shift to the politics of law at the global level is

212 *Conclusion*

virtually limitless: climate change regulation; the regulation of trade and investment in energy; fair trade; how to meet the legal needs and competitive interests of emerging powers; and of course, not forgetting the larger theoretical questions of de-integration, and the political importance of democratic legitimacy to legal authority.

Final thoughts

In the introduction to this book I stated two goals. First, I aimed to take the measure of the growing legal realm and place it at the heart of the study of trade and investment. Second, I attempted to show how legal insights broaden and deepen our analysis of global governance. I argued that social scientists, economists and political scientists, in particular, have not integrated legal insight into our way of understanding the world to the degree that we ought. We are living through a major cognitive shift from politics *and* law to the politics *of* law beyond the state. The study of law has become increasingly important, not only as a terrain of competition, but also as a forum for debating global public policy. While the spotlights of protectionism and ethno-nationalism throw into relief the political instabilities that may yet undermine the legal system, they also underscore the importance of law to political order. And in doing so, they spotlight the significance of law to the future study of international political economy.

Notes

1 Kishore Mahbubani and Lawrence H. Summers, "The Fusion of Civilizations," *Foreign Affairs*, 18 April 2016.
2 Gabrielle Marceau, ed., *A History of Law and Lawyers in the GATT/WTO: The Development of the Rule of Law in the Multilateral Trading System* (Cambridge: Cambridge University Press, 2015); Robert Hudec, *The GATT Legal System and World Trade Diplomacy* (New York: Praeger Publishers, 1975).
3 Laurence Helfer, "Regime Shifting: The Trips Agreement and New Dynamics of International Intellectual Property Lawmaking," *Yale Journal of International Law* 29, no. 1 (2004).
4 Emily Blanchard, "A Shifting Mandate: International Ownership, Global Fragmentation, and a Case for Deeper Integration under the WTO," *World Trade Review* 14, no. 1 (2015): 87–99.
5 Irene M. Ten Cate, "The Costs of Consistency: Precedent in Investment Treaty Arbitration," *Columbia Journal of Transnational Law* 51, no. 2 (2013): 418–478.
6 Alec Stone Sweet and Florian Grisel, *The Evolution of International Arbitration: Judicialization, Governance, Legitimacy* (Oxford: Oxford University Press, 2017).

Conclusion 213

7 Krzysztof J. Pelc, "The Welfare Implications of Precedent in International Law," in *Establishing Judicial Authority in International Economic Law,* ed. Joanna Jemielniak, Laura Nielsen and Henrik Palmer Olsen (Cambridge: Cambridge University Press, 2016).

8 R.B.J. Walker, *After the Globe, Before the World* (London: Routledge, 2009).

9 Katia Fach Gomez, "Rethinking the Role of Amicus Curiae in International Investment Arbitration: How to Draw the Line Favorably for the Public Interest," *Fordham International Law Journal* 35 (2012): 521.

10 Eric De Brabandere, "NGOs and the 'Public Interest': The Legality and Rationale of Amicus Curiae Interventions in International Economic and Investment Disputes," *Chicago Journal of International Law* 12, no. 1 (2011): 85–113.

11 Debra P. Steger, "Amicus Curiae: Participant or Friend? The WTO and NAFTA Experience," in *European Integration and International Coordination, Studies in Transnational Economic Law in Honour of Claus-Dieter Ehlermann,* ed. Armin von Bogdandy, Petros C. Mavroidis, and Yves Meny (The Hague: Kluwer Law International, 2002), 420.

12 Steger, "Amicus Curiae: Participant or Friend?," 421.

13 Although a reasonable argument can be made that national citizens are bound by the obligations of trade agreements even though they are represented by their governments at the WTO. Steger, "Amicus Curiae: Participant or Friend?," 446.

14 Ernesto Hernandez-Lopez, "Recent Trends and Perspectives for Non-State Actor Participation in World Trade Organization Disputes," *Journal of World Trade* 35, no. 3 (2001): 469–498.

15 Luigi Crema, "Testing Amici Curiae in International Law: Rules and Practice," *The Italian Yearbook of International Law Online* 22, no. 1 (2013): 123.

16 S. Schadendorf, "Human Rights Arguments in Amicus Curiae Submissions: Analysis of ICSID and NAFTA Investor-State Arbitrations," *Transnational Dispute Management* 10, no. 1 (2013): 23.

17 De Brabandere, "NGOs and the 'Public Interest'," 101.

18 Eugenia Levine, "Amicus Curiae in International Investment Arbitration: The Implications of an Increase in Third-Party Participation," *Berkeley Journal of International Law* 29, no. 1 (2011): 200–224.

19 A. Saravanan and S.R. Subramanian, "The Participation of Amicus Curiae in Investment Treaty Arbitration," *Journal of Civil and Legal Sciences* 5, no. 4 (2016): 1–6.

20 Theresa Squatrito, "Amicus Curiae Briefs in the WTO DSM: Good or Bad News for Non-State Actor Involvement?" *World Trade Review* 17, no. 1 (2018): 1–25.

21 Squatrito, "Amicus Curiae Briefs in the WTO DSM," 8.

22 Robert Wolfe, "Crossing the River by Feeling the Stones: Where the WTO is Going after Seattle, Doha and Cancun," *Review of International Political Economy* 11, no. 3 (August 2004).

23 Victoria Nourse and Gregory C. Shaffer, "Varieties of the New Legal Realism: Can a New World Order Prompt a New Legal Theory?," *Cornell Law Review* 95, no. 61 (2009): 63–136.

214 *Conclusion*

24 Simon Lester, "Does Investor State Dispute Settlement Need Reform?" *Cato Unbound: A Journal of Debate* (2015), www.cato-unbound.org/2015/05/11/simon-lester/does-investor-state-dispute-settlement-need-reform.
25 Susan D. Franck, "The Legitimacy Crisis in Investment Treaty Arbitration: Privatizing Public International Law through Inconsistent Decisions," *Fordham Law Review* 73 (2005): 1521–1625.

Index

Note: Page numbers in *italics* denote references to Figures and page numbers in **bold** denote Tables.

Abbott, Frederick M. 26–7
Aggarwal, Vinod K. 111
Alter, Karen J. 151
American legal realist movement 52
amicus curiae briefs 202–7, *204*, *205*
Appellate Body (AB) 157–8, 170–1, 202
Artiran, Pinar 98
attenuated delegation 170

Baldwin, Richard 112–13
Barthel, Roland 30
Bendersky, Corinne 30
bilateral investment treaties (BITs) 124–5, 126–7, 139–40, 210
Bishop, Matthew Louis 110, 112
Blanchard, Emily 113, 192
Block-Lieb, Susan 45
Bogdandy, Armin Von 152, 156
Braudel, Fernand 177
Bretton Woods institutions 1, 8, 49, 118–19n33
Brexit 209–10
British industrialization 21
Broude, Tomer 7–8, 28–9
Bull, Hedley 176
Busch, Marc L. 7–8, 28–9

Campbell, John L. 24
Canada-United States Free Trade Agreement 92
capital-exporting states 123

Carr, E. H. 25, 54
Cass, Deborah Z. 40
Chaisse, Julien 98
Chakraborty, Debashis 98
Chalamish, Efraim 126–7
Charter of the Economic Rights and Duties of States (CERDS) 124
Cheng, Tai-Heng 153, 154
Cho, Sungjoan 153
Closer Economic Relations Agreement 92
Coase, R.H. 137, 140, 194
Coase Theorem 140
code of Fair Treatment for Foreign Investment 124
Cohen, Benjamin J. 22
Cohen, Harlan Grant 152
commercial arbitration 154
complex interdependence 22–3
compliance 137–8, 159
compulsory jurisdiction 98–9, 150–1
Condliffe, J. B. 91
consensus building 19–20, 32, 84, 208
constitutionalism 40–3, 54, 57, 208
constitutional order 41
constrained openness 44
constructivism 40, 42–3
constructivist political economy, functionalism and 39
consultation mechanism 136
Cooley, Alexander 92–3, 96, 141
Crawford, Jo-Ann 92, 93

216 *Index*

Crema, Luigi 203
critical constitutionalism 54
critical junctures, defined 69–70

Davey, William J. 74
David, Felix 157
Davis, Ross C. 44–5
De Brabandere, Eric 202, 203
de-integration 117
delegated authority 170, 197
democratic deficit 171, 197, 200–1
democratic theory 171
dependency theory 49
Diebold, William 72–3
direct participation in interventions 202
disciplinarity and international economic law 18–21
Disputer Settlement Understanding (DSU) 89
Dispute Settlement Body (DSB) 159
dispute settlement mechanism (DSM) 81, 89, 190, 209
dispute settlements: challenges facing 159–60; convergence in 134–5; development of 156; in regional trade agreements *101*; special provisions for 190–1. *See also* precedent
dispute settlement system 74, 98–100
Doha Round of trade negotiations 1, 70, 75–6, 101, 115, 125, 186, 192
domestic interests 49, 93–4
domestic rationality 51
Drezner, Dan 2
Duina, Francesco 93
Dunoff, Jeffrey L. 20, 97

eclectic theorizing 20
economic integration 93–4
economics, defined 6
embedded liberalism 65–6
Engels, Friedrich 6
equilibria 68, 75 *See also* shifting equilibria
European Communities (EC) 157
European Economic Community (EEC) 91
European Free Trade Agreement (EFTA) 91

European Union (EU) 74, 92, 182n39, 189–90, 209–10
Evenett, Simon J. 111
exogenous shock 67, 69
explicit delegation 170
externalism 20

Fabbricotti, Alberta 109
Falk, Richard 175
Fernandez-Stark, Karina 114
Fiorentino, Roberto V. 92, 93
foreign direct investment (FDI) 125
foundational law 42–3
fragmentation. *See* legal fragmentation
Franck, Susan D. 138–9, 154
Franco, Renzo 75
free trade 21, 27–8, 73
Friendship, Commerce and Navigation (FCN) treaties 123–4
Frost, Jetta 30–1
functionalism 37–40, 57, 68–9

G8/G20 1, 211
game theory 172
GATT (General Agreement on Tariffs and Trade): Article XXIV 91; cases cited as precedent 161–4, *164*, 196; dispute settlement 80–1; flexibility of 91; Generalized System of Preferences (GSP) 91–2; as Janus-faced approach to law 11; legal development at 69–70, 84; Most-Favored Nation (MFN) clause 71; multilateral intervention in 70; negotiating basis of 71; nonviolation, nullification and impairment clause 65; purpose of 72; services trade deals 125; shifting equilibria 65–9; strategic treaty interpretation 156. *See also* Uruguay Round
Generalized System of Preferences (GSP) 91–2
generic multilateral order 126
Gereffi, Gary 114
Gerhardt, Michael J. 166
Germain, Randall 25
Gersick, Connie J. G. 66–7
Gill, Stephen 54

Index 217

global commercial regulation 141
global governance 8, 37–40, 55, 65
global investment regulation 143
global marketplace 137–41
global order 32, 40–1
global political economy. *See* international political economy (IPE)
global social compact 9
Goldsmith, Jack L. 47, 54, 176
governance competencies 121
governance institutions, proliferation of 97
government procurement provisions 104
Grisel, Florian 154–5, 196
Grotian moment 175–9, *178*, 180, 198
Grotius, Hugo 176
Guzman, Andrew 48, 137–8

Hall, Peter A. 67
Halliday, Terence C. 45
Hannah, Erin 55
Hart, H. L. A. 11
Hathaway, Oona A. 68, 166
Hegemonic Stability Theory 145n40
hegemonic stability theory 22, 49
Helfer, Lawrence 82–3, 189
Henckels, Caroline 99
Hernandez-Lopez, Ernesto 203
Howse, Robert 65, 121
hub-and-spoke model 130
Hudec, Robert 80
Humphrey, John 114

ideas, as driver for economic integration 94
imperfect competition 140, 194
implied delegation 170
incentives for regionalization 93
incomplete contracting theory 92–3, 96
indirect expropriation 134
indirect participation in interventions 202–7
individualism, methodological 48
indivisibility, as a social construction 130
insitutional investment hypothesis 112–15, 191

institutional autonomy 211–12
institutional causality 68
institutional change 66–7
institutional development 76–8, 85n15
institutional investment hypothesis 95, 116
institutionalism 39, 42, 51, 67
institutional liberalism 176
institutional multilateralism 131 *See also* multilateralism
institutional political economy, functionalism and 39
integration-creates-opportunity-and-growth hypothesis 93
intellectual property rights 104
intellectual property rights governance 82
interdisciplinarity: defined 19, 31; and international economic law 19; in international political economy 21–5, 26–9
interests 93–4
internalism 20
international adjudication 152
International Centre for the Settlement of Investment Disputes (ICSID) 124
International Chamber of Commerce 124
International Court of Justice 155
international courts 150–2, 172
international economic law (IEL): characteristics of 26; defined 7–8; disciplinarity and 18–21; fragmentation of 118–19n33; growth of 41–2; interdisciplinarity in 21–5; international political economy and *46*; legal realist approach to 57–8; multidisciplinarity and 46–7; new legal realism and 53; as policy science 26, 47–51, 57; politics shaping evolution of 28–9; precedent in 195; public participation in 201; rational choice approach to 54–5; referring to trade law 7; regulation of 8; transformative power of 12
international investment agreements (IIAs): clauses relating to

218 *Index*

standards of treatment 134, *134*, 193–4; dispute settlement clauses *135*; as example of multilateralism 122; legal language affirming state regulatory space *135*; Mapping Project 133; multilateral centralization of 192; proliferation of 123–9, *133*, 193

international investment law 128–9, 138–9 *See also* investment law

international law (IL): enforcement mechanism 137; functional development of 38; growth of 3; international relations and 20–1; normative equivalence in 96; political economic approach 109–10; political elements of 28; positivist approaches to 47; rapid development in 174–9; rational choice explanation of 137–8; rationality of 48. *See also* law

International Law Association 124

International Monetary Fund 39, 211

international political economy (IPE): defined 6–7; international economic law and *46*; multi-disciplinary approach to 32; neoliberal IPE 24; political realism 25; politics/law interface in 187; sociologists approach to 24

international regulation 38, 41, 171

international relations (IR) 20–1

international society 9

International Telegraph Union 132

International Trade Organization (ITO) 71–3, 178

international trading order 42

interpersonal assumptions in multi-disciplinary groups 30–1

interventions, indirect participation in 202–7

investment agreements 144n17

investment arbitration 153–5, 196, 203

investment law 123–8, 137–9, 153–4, 172, 192–5, 203–4, 210–11 *See also* international investment law

investment protection 123

investment treat arbitration 128

investment treaties 136

investor-state dispute settlements (ISDS) 90, 134, 191

Irwin, Douglas A. 71

isomorphic development 69

Jackson, John H. 8, 156

Jemielniak, Joanna 172

Johnstone, Ian 170–1

Jones, Benjamin F. 30

Jones, Kent 75

Jupille, Joseph 51, 141

juridical mechanisms 116

jurisdictional competition 138–9

Kairys, David 44

Kaufmann-Kohler, Gabrielle 154

Kennedy, David 28

Keohane, Robert O. 22–3

Kindleberger, Charles P. 21–2, 94

Kingsbury, Benedict 176–7

Kirshner, Jonathan 23

Klassen, Jerome 94

knowledge creation, barriers to 30

Koskenniemi, Martti 8, 28, 96

Krasner, Stephen D. 10

Lake, David 6, 49–51

Lang, Andrew T. F. 27–8

Lauterpacht, Hersch 176

law: defined 9, 11; intangible elements of 27; as means for social progress and reform 2–3; in political science 20; politics of 8–10; purpose of 9; role in states and market 6–7; as rules 10–11. *See also* international law (IL)

League of Nations 4

Leal-Arcas, Rafael 126

legal argumentation 44

legal authority 172–4

legal convergence: creating multilateral community 127–8; multilateralization and 129–37, 193; without multilateral coordination 143

legal decision-making 134–5

legal density 38

legal development: at GATT/WTO 69–70; institutional dynamics of 208–9

Index 219

legal fragmentation 89, 95–8, 111, 118–19n33
legal functionalism. *See* functionalism
legal interconnection 209–10
legal language 132–3
legal legitimacy, precedent and 149
legal order, political foundations of 45
legal precedent. *See* precedent
legal realism 47, 51–6, 58, 200
legitimacy and authority 172–4, *173*, 180, 197–8
Lenin, Vladimir 43
Levinthal, Daniel A. 67
Lim, C. L. 118–19n33
Limao, Nuno 112
limited path dependency 166

Manchester School 21–2, 189–90
Marceau, Gabrielle 11, 68, 98, 99, 173, 188
market for law 14, 123, 137, 139, 143, 194, 210
market-oriented intergovernmental mechanisms 192–5
Marquis, Christopher 67
Marx, Karl 6
material interests, OEP focus on 50
Mattli, Walter 51, 141
Mavroidis, Petros C. 71
McGinn, Kathleen 30
McGinnis, John O. 40, 94
Mercurio, Bryan 118–19n33
methodological pluralism 55–6
MFN tariffs 112–13, 191
Miles, Kate 123, 125
Miller, Nathan 172
Monnet, Jean 94
Most-Favored Nation (MFN) clause 71, 112–13
most-favored status 130
Movsesian, Mark L. 40, 94
Muchlinski, Peter 139–40
multidisciplinarity 19, 29–33
multilateral agreements 125–6
multilateral economic governance institutions 126–7
multilateral institutionalism 136
multilateral intervention 70

multilateralism: American commitment to 131–2; anatomy of 132; defined 129; as example of bilateral negotiations 130–1; goal of 138; international investment agreements as 122; legal approach to 42; reinsurance hypothesis and 110; success of 131
multilateralization of investment law 126, 136, 192–3
multilateral trade governance 73–4
Muzaka, Valbona 110, 112

national treatment (NT) 134
neoliberal IPE 24
new formalism 52
new IPE 24–5
new legal realism. *See* legal realism
nongovernmental organizations (NGOs) 189, 201
non-violation, nullification and impairment clause of GATT 65
normative communitarianism 56
normative individualism 48–9
normative realism 8
normative space 20
norm diffusion 40
North American Free Trade Agreement (NAFTA) 91–2
Nourse, Victoria 53, 208
Nye, Joseph S. 22–3

O'Connell, Mary Ellen 176
O'Hara O'Connor, Erin A. 138–9
Ohlin, Jens David 48
Oliver, Michael J. 24–5
Open Economy Politics (OEP) 23
open economy politics (OEP) 49–50
Organisation for Economic Co-operation and Development (OECD) 113–14
organized hypocrisy 10
Osterloh, Margarit 30–1
Ostry, Sylvia 55, 80

Parry, John T. 176
path dependence 67, 68, 69–70, 160, 166
Paulus, Andreas L. 41
Pauwelyn, Joost 41, 158

220 *Index*

Pelc, Krzysztof J. 158, 196
Petersmann, Ernst-Ulrich 42, 81
Pierson, Paul 68, 85n15
Polanyi, Karl 12
political backsliding 158
political development 65
political economy 6, 22
political legitimacy 172–4
political realism 4–5, 25
political science: defined 6; inter-
    disciplinarity dialogue in 21–2; law
    in 20
politics/law divide 3–5, 7–8, 186
politics of international economic law
    (PIEL) 54, 55–6
politics of law 8–10, 187, 199–200
Pollack, Mark A. 20
Porges, Amelia 7–8, 28–9
positivism 20, 47
Posner, Eric A. 47, 54, 176
post-Cold War democratization pro-
    cesses 125
post-colonial states, gaining control
    over natural resources 123
postwar legal order *173*
precedent: articulation of law beyond
    the state 150–3; cases cited as 161,
    161, *167*, *168*, 196; defined 151;
    dispute settlement creating 149;
    implications of 197; international
    law-making 152; in investment
    arbitration 153–5; law-making
    potential of 169–71; in law-making
    process 152; legal legitimacy and
    149; as primary indicator to grow-
    ing authority 195; professional
    practice and 152–3; reliance on
    155–6, 166–8; at the World Trade
    Organization 149–50, 155–9, 196–7
preferential trade agreements (PTAs)
    94–5, 112–13
primary rules 11
private law 26
professionalization and judicializa-
    tion 152–3
proliferation 89, 95–6, 97, 189
protectionism 111
PTA tariffs 112–13
public international law 26, 44, 47–8,
    129

public participation, legitimacy and
    199–202
punctuated equilibrium 64,
    66–7
punctuation points 69

rapid development in international
    law 174–9
rational choice theory 54–5, 67,
    137–8, 158, 171
rationalism 53
realism. *See* legal realism
reciprocity 138
regime interaction 97, 118n30
regimes 131
regime shifting 82–3
regime theory 5
regional dispute settlement systems
    98–100
regional integration 92, 95
regional trade agreements (RTAs):
    development of 114–15; develop-
    ment trends 100–9, *102*; dispute
    settlement arrangements 100, *101*,
    190; dispute settlement exclusions
    104, 190; excluded clauses *104*,
    106–8; extending use-value
    189–92; governments vested inter-
    ests in 111; legal clauses of 102–5,
    103; proliferation of 89; reinsur-
    ance hypothesis 110–12; special
    provisions in 105–10, *105*, **106–8**,
    190–1; as stumbling blocks
    112–13; supporting ISDS 90; value
    chains and 113–14; World Trade
    Organization and 96, 99–100
regulation. *See* global commercial
    regulation
reinsurance hypothesis 110–12, 116,
    191
retaliation mechanisms 138
Ribstein, Larry 138
Rochester, J. Martin 9
Roe, Mark J. 67
Ruggie, John Gerard 126, 129–30,
    131, 136–7
rule of law 42, 81, 195
rules, law as 10–11
rules-based system for trade
    79–80

Index 221

Sacerdoti, Giorgio 159
Schadendorf, S. 203
Scharf, Michael P. 175
Schill, Stephan 127, 130, 131, 145n26, 193
Scott, James 55
secondary rules 11
Seghezza, Elena 112–13
Seidl, Roman 30
services trade deals 76, 125
Shaffer, Gregory C. 52, 53, 208
shifting equilibria: facilitating legal development 84; at GATT/WTO 65–9, 208–9; implications of 64; institutional development and 70, 188–9; path dependent development and 68; resolving institutional challenges 82; in world trading system 70. *See also* equilibria
simultaneity of politics and law 84, 208
Slaughter, Anne-Marie 5
Snidal, Duncan 26–7, 51, 141
social behavior 67, 69
social cost 122–3, 137–41, 143, 192–3
social scientific theory 188
socio-legal theory 43–5, 57
sovereign rules 10–13
sovereignty 10, 198–9
space between, the 76–82
spirit of the law 20 *See also* law
spontaneity principle 52–3
Spruyt, Hendrik 92–3, 96, 141
stare decisis principle 149, 151, 155
state-to-state dispute settlements 134
Steger, Debra P. 202
Sterio, Milena 179–80
Stone, Randall W. 83, 141
Stone Sweet, Alec 154–5, 196
Strange, Susan 25
structural power 25
Sturgeon, Timothy 114
Sykes, Alan O. 71
systematized institutional dynamics 188–9

tariffs 112–13, 191
technocratic development 65
Ten Cate, Irene M. 154, 196

Thelan, Kathleen 85n15
Tilcsik, Andras 67
Trachtman, Joel 26, 38, 41–2, 48–9, 109–10
trade, history of 91–3
Trade Act of 1974 80
trade agreements, national employment policies and 97
trade governance 73–4, 116–17, 209
trade law 7
trade liberalization 95
trade multilateralism. *See* multilateralism
Trade Policy Review Mechanism 201–2
Trade-Related Aspects of Intellectual Property Rights (TRIPS) 82
trading system 27–8, *70*, 79–80
transnationalization process 94
Trans-Pacific Partnership (TPP) 92, 209
treaty proliferation 14, 133–4, 193–4
Trommer, Silke 55
Truman, Harry S. 72, 73

United Nations 124
United Nations Conference on Trade and Development (UNCTAD) 122
Uruguay Round 71, 74, 79, 101, 111, 194
Uzzi, Brian 30

value-chain governance 113–14, 116
van Aaken, Anne 109–10
Vandevelde, Kenneth J. 123
Venzke, Ingo 31, 152, 156

Walker, R.B.J. 199
Wallerstein, Immanuel 24
Wang, Chen-Yu 28
Westphalian system 4, 10, 186, 198, 200
Wight, Martin 176
Williams, Peter 79
world order 22–3, 43
World Trade Organization (WTO): amicus briefs at 204–6, *205*; Appellate Body (AB) 157–8, 170–1, 202; bilateral negotiations at 83; cases cited as precedent 161, *161*,

222 *Index*

162, 163; centralized institutional processes 189–92; challenges to 84; constitutional role in global economic legal order 40–1; creation of 11, 81, 156; dispute settlement training module 98–9; exclusive jurisdiction 98–100; governance competencies 121; impact on regional trade agreements 99–100; interstate coordination in 83; legal development at 69–70, 84, 188–9; legal environment change at 63–4; as Madisonian constitution for world trade 40, 94; mapping case citations at 159–61; multilateral intervention in 70; multilateral liberalization process 75–6; in post-Uruguay Round era 92; precedent at 149–50, 155–9, 196–7; problems facing 75; public international law and 44; purpose of 74–5; shifting equilibria 65–9; state litigation strategies at 171; substantive decisions and future agenda **77–8**; transparency in 201–2

Wuchty, Stefan 30

Yang, Songling 99
Yearwood, Ronnie R. F. 44–5
Young, Margaret A. 97